Enduring Polygamy

The Politics of Marriage and Gender:
Global Issues in Local Contexts

Series Editor: Péter Berta

The Politics of Marriage and Gender: Global Issues in Local Context series from Rutgers University Press fills a gap in research by examining the politics of marriage and related practices, ideologies, and interpretations, and addresses the key question of how the politics of marriage has affected social, cultural, and political processes, relations, and boundaries. The series looks at the complex relationships between the politics of marriage and gender, ethnic, national, religious, racial, and class identities, and analyzes how these relationships contribute to the development and management of social and political differences, inequalities, and conflicts.

For a list of all the titles in the series, please see the last page of the book.

Enduring Polygamy

Plural Marriage and Social Change in an African Metropolis

BRUCE WHITEHOUSE

RUTGERS UNIVERSITY PRESS

NEW BRUNSWICK, CAMDEN, AND NEWARK, NEW JERSEY

LONDON AND OXFORD

Rutgers University Press is a department of Rutgers, The State University of New Jersey, one of the leading public research universities in the nation. By publishing worldwide, it furthers the University's mission of dedication to excellence in teaching, scholarship, research, and clinical care.

LIBRARY OF CONGRESS CATALOGING-IN-PUBLICATION DATA

Names: Whitehouse, Bruce, 1971- author.
Title: Enduring polygamy: plural marriage and social change in an African metropolis / Bruce Whitehouse.
Description: New Brunswick: Rutgers University, 2023. | Series: Politics of marriage and gender: global issues in local contexts | Includes bibliographical references and index.
Identifiers: LCCN 2022030610 | ISBN 9781978831131 (paperback) | ISBN 9781978831148 (hardback) | ISBN 9781978831155 (epub) | ISBN 9781978831162 (pdf)
Subjects: LCSH: Polygyny—Mali—Bamako. | Marriage—Mali—Bamako. | Social change—Mali—Bamako. | Women—Mali—Bamako—Social conditions— 21st century. | Bamako (Mali)—Social conditions—21st century.
Classification: LCC HQ696.3.Z9 B35 2023 | DDC 306.84/23096623—dc23/eng /20220628
LC record available at https://lccn.loc.gov/2022030610

A British Cataloging-in-Publication record for this book is available from the British Library.

All figures are by the author unless otherwise indicated.

References to internet websites (URLs) were accurate at the time of writing. Neither the author nor Rutgers University Press is responsible for URLs that may have expired or changed since the manuscript was prepared.

♾ The paper used in this publication meets the requirements of the American National Standard for Information Sciences—Permanence of Paper for Printed Library Materials, ANSI Z39.48-1992.

rutgersuniversitypress.org

For Rokia and Zachary

FIGURE 0.1 *Les Dimanches à Bamako* by Rokia Whitehouse (2021).

CONTENTS

LIST OF ILLUSTRATIONS

Figures

Tables

SERIES FOREWORD

The politics of marriage (and divorce) is an often-used strategic tool in various social, cultural, economic, and political identity projects as well as in symbolic conflicts between ethnic, national, or religious communities. Despite having multiple strategic applicabilities, pervasiveness in everyday life, and huge significance in performing and managing identities, the politics of marriage is surprisingly underrepresented both in the international book publishing market and the social sciences.

The Politics of Marriage and Gender: Global Issues in Local Contexts is a series from Rutgers University Press examining the politics of marriage as a phenomenon embedded into and intensely interacting with much broader social, cultural, economic, and political processes and practices such as globalization; transnationalization; international migration; human trafficking; vertical social mobility; the creation of symbolic boundaries between ethnic populations, nations, religious denominations, or classes; family formation; or struggles for women's and children's rights. The series primarily aims to analyze practices, ideologies, and interpretations related to the politics of marriage, and to outline the dynamics and diversity of relatedness—interplay and interdependence, for instance—between the politics of marriage and the broader processes and practices mentioned above. In other words, most books in the series devote special attention to how the politics of marriage and these processes and practices mutually shape and explain each other.

The series concentrates on, among other things, the complex relationships between the politics of marriage and gender, ethnic, national, religious, racial, and class identities globally, and examines how these relationships contribute to the development and management of social, cultural, and political differences, inequalities, and conflicts.

The series seeks to publish single-authored books and edited volumes that develop a gap-filling and thought-provoking critical perspective, that are well-balanced between a high degree of theoretical sophistication and empirical richness, and that cross or rethink disciplinary, methodological, or theoretical boundaries. The thematic scope of the series is intentionally left broad to encourage creative submissions that fit within the perspectives outlined above.

Among the potential topics closely connected with the problem sensitivity of the series are "honor"-based violence; arranged (forced, child, etc.) marriage; transnational marriage markets, migration, and brokerage; intersections of marriage and religion/class/race; the politics of agency and power within marriage; reconfiguration of family: same-sex marriage/unions; the politics of love, intimacy, and desire; marriage and multicultural families; the (religious, legal, etc.) politics of divorce; the causes, forms, and consequences of polygamy in contemporary societies; sport marriage; refusing marriage; and so forth.

Enduring Polygamy: Plural Marriage and Social Change in an African Metropolis offers a comprehensive and well-balanced overview of why and how polygamy—specifically, polygyny—matters in the contexts of a fast-changing African metropolis (Bamako) and of a globalized state surrounding the metropolis (Mali). Through an analysis of the complex and often context-specific factors contributing to the flourishing of polygamy as well as the social, cultural, economic, and political consequences of this practice, the chapters attempt to de-stigmatize and de-exoticize polygamy, which is often portrayed both in scientific and media discourses as a tribalized and ethnicized or racialized practice. *Enduring Polygamy* contributes to the existing literature in at least two ways. First, by highlighting male discourses, ideologies, and interpretations about gender and polygamy, it offers a more gender-sensitive and gender-balanced picture of the phenomenon. Second, the ethnographic research on which the monograph is based was carried out in and focuses on a social setting where polygamy is not a marginalized and strange phenomenon but a mainstream cultural institution in family formation and intimacy—it is both a product and a producer of post-colonial urban existence in contemporary Mali.

Péter Berta
University College London
School of Slavonic and
East European Studies
Budapest Business School,
Department of Communication

Enduring Polygamy

Introduction

It's Complicated: Polygamy and the Marriage System in Bamako, Mali

Oumar and Sira were a couple, probably my favorite couple in Bamako. They were in their thirties, a few years older than I, when I first got to know them. After I got married in 2002, my wife Oumou and I would visit them whenever we were in Mali's booming capital city. Oumar and Sira seemed to have a very modern marriage. After growing up in different parts of the country, they had met in Bamako and married for love—something many Malians could not do but increasingly desired. Rather than working in the civil service, as members of Bamako's elite had done throughout the twentieth century, both were in the private sector, Sira as a manager in the Mali office of a global NGO (nongovernmental organization) and Oumar as an architect.

The pair lived with their four children in a two-story house Oumar had designed in the city's Faladié neighborhood, south of the Niger River. Their family household, however, had accommodations for extended kin; directly across the narrow, sandy street from their front door, Oumar's parents occupied a house he had built for them. This arrangement seemed like a happy medium between a Western nuclear family and an African extended family, with two nominally separate units that frequently intertwined.

 . I always enjoyed visiting with Oumar and Sira, conversing with them in French or in Manding. As I chatted with her one afternoon in 2008, Sira dropped a bombshell: Oumar was planning to take another wife. I later learned that his relationship with this other woman, a twenty-something named Korotimi, had been a long-standing open secret. She lived in a different neighborhood and had met neither Sira nor her children, then between the ages of ten and eighteen. Sira was pondering how to thwart Oumar's plans and suspected her mother-in-law across the street of manipulating him into remarrying.

In 2010, on my next visit, I noticed the Faladié house was not being kept up: broken light fixtures needed replacing and cracks were visible in the plaster ceiling. Having celebrated his second marriage the year before, Oumar was spending half his nights with Korotimi across town, where he was renting a house for her. He volunteered nothing about her when I saw him, and I did not feel comfortable asking about it. (One of my weaknesses, as an ethnographer and as a friend, is a reluctance to broach sensitive subjects. I blame my Yankee upbringing.) Sira, for her part, confided she felt deeply betrayed by her husband's actions. Not only had she never met her co-wife, she also refused even to utter Korotimi's name. She said there was no emotion left in her relationship with Oumar. "For me, it's as though he's not even there," she stated with some bemusement—"as though we never had children together." She hoped to leave him, but was biding her time until she could move into a house of her own. Even if their marriage endured, I realized, I could no longer think of Oumar and Sira as a couple. Their situation had become more complex.

The following year, shortly after I had begun a ten-month research stint in Bamako, Oumar stopped by the house Oumou and I were renting to chat. He seemed weary and distracted, talking at length about aging and about a friend recently dead from a heart attack. Oumar feared meeting the same end; he was working too much, he said, and was under too much pressure at home. If he had known what a burden his double-marriage, double-household arrangement would become, he admitted, he never would have entered into it. The only people who had tried to dissuade him from marrying again were Sira and her family, but he had ignored them. Oumar struggled to live a life divided between two houses. Whichever item of clothing he needed always seemed to be somewhere else. He had trouble finding his papers for work and keeping up with demands on his time and resources. The good news, I learned, was that he was getting along better with Sira, who had established cordial relations with Korotimi.

When Oumou and I called on them in 2019, Sira was still living in the two-story house in Faladié. Oumar had significantly spruced up the place and even had built a spacious new sitting room in the courtyard. He continued dividing his time between his two wives but no longer looked overwhelmed by this arrangement; in fact, I observed during a relaxed afternoon chatting and listening to music in the new room, he seemed at peace with it. As for Sira, she had dropped her plans to move out and reconciled herself to Oumar's polygamous marriage. She and Korotimi even were paying each other social visits. By then in their fifties, Sira and Oumar had found solace in Islam, Mali's dominant religion, reading the Qur'an (which, even as lifelong Muslims, they had seldom read before) together regularly. They were preparing for their eldest daughter's wedding, and Oumar now had two young children, an infant and a toddler, with Korotimi. Polygamy had put a tremendous strain on Sira, Korotimi, Oumar, and their children, but they were adjusting to it.

Bamako is full of tales about polygamous marriage, some harrowing, some heartwarming, many ambivalent, all of them complicated. The city lies in the

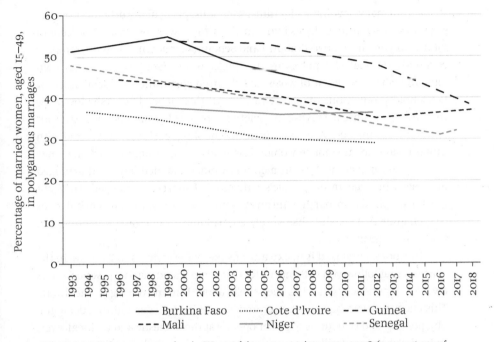

FIGURE I.1 Polygamy rates in six West African countries, 1993–2018 (percentage of currently married women who were in polygamous marriages when surveyed).

Source: Demographic and Health Surveys.

heart of a region—West Africa, and particularly the western Sahel—with the world's highest rates of polygamy. In 2018, 24.6 percent of Bamako wives shared their husbands with at least one co-wife, as Sira did. In rural Mali, that rate hovered near 50 percent (DHS 2019). Rates in other West African countries ranged between 20 and 45 percent.

The story of Oumar, Sira, and Korotimi is one of many I have heard or witnessed in Bamako over the years. By the time Sira informed me of Oumar's intent to remarry in 2008, I had already decided to study urban marriage. As my research proceeded, I chose to make polygamy my central focus, the lens through which to examine a host of topics, from kinship and social structure to male-female relations and gender oppression. This book concentrates specifically on *polygyny*, the form of plural marriage in which a man is married to multiple wives. But since polyandry, in which a woman is married to multiple husbands, is absent in Mali and rare worldwide, and since Malians widely use the French word *polygamie* to designate the marriage of one man to multiple women, throughout this book I use "polygamy" rather than "polygyny." (For variety's sake, I also use the terms "polygamous marriage" and "plural marriage.")

Rates of plural marriage have declined slowly throughout Africa, even in the western region, where they have been highest (see figure I.1). This gradual slide stems from many ongoing social transformations, particularly urbanization; the share of sub-Saharan Africans living in cities and towns rose from 15 percent in 1960 to 41 percent in 2020 (Tabutin and Schoumaker 2020). There is a stronger economic rationale for polygamy in villages where families grow their own food and where the labor of wives and children constitutes a crucial asset for household production, than in cities where their labor is overshadowed by their living expenses. As African societies urbanized, economic incentives for polygamy diminished. Access to modern schooling, positively correlated with urban residence, also made women less likely to enter polygamous marriage (Bledsoe 1990). And as African men and women married later and arranged marriages became rarer, people's valuation of marriage changed; they put greater emphasis on partner intimacy and less on traditional marital roles (see chapter 1). This shift has surely contributed to polygamy's decline, but also to its reinvention.

This book's first goal is to explain why polygamy endures in Bamako. In the chapters that follow, you will encounter this complicated marital practice as city dwellers experienced it and as they spoke about it to me during my fieldwork. This encounter can help you better understand how gender, culture, demography, politics, and structures of power operate at the domestic and national levels in Mali. Polygamy's resilience over time becomes clearer when we view it within its full social and cultural context.

But first, we need to consider polygamy's problematic image in the present day, as well as its significance in human history and society.

What Kind of Problem Is Polygamy?

Polygamous marriage is routinely presented, particularly by Western scholars and commentators, as a social problem. Journalists and social scientists often have framed polygamy as a tyrannical practice that oppresses women, harms children, and renders whole societies prone to conflict. Some Malians also discuss polygamy in these terms. A former head of Mali's Ministry for the Promotion of Women, Children, and the Family has described polygamy as "one of the evils that corrupt our society" (Traoré 2016, 5).

Polygamy's critics have associated it with many terrible things over the years. In the United States during the late nineteenth century, opponents of Mormonism used fears of polygamy to stoke a moral panic against the faith, portraying Mormons as violent and undemocratic (Song 2016). Nativist politicians in twenty-first-century France blamed urban unrest on Muslim immigrants' polygamous family structure (Selby 2014). Westerners have long used polygamy as an index of African backwardness, of what separates "us" from "them" (Taiwo 2010; Willey 2016). It has served as a rhetorical cudgel with which to assail members of those groups we have considered insufficiently civilized, advanced, or modern.

This history of associating plural marriage with barbarism makes polygamy a potentially risky subject for any Westerner to analyze. It is difficult, if not impossible, to discuss it without falling into the traps laid by this problematic history.

A few Western scholars, including political scientist Ronald Den Otter (2015) and sociologist Lori Beaman (2014 and 2016), have positioned themselves as advocates of the right to polygamous marriage. On the African continent, case studies have found polygamy better adapted than monogamy to settings ranging from Acholi villages in northern Uganda (Amone 2019) to apartheid-era South African townships (Anderson 2000) to rural Côte d'Ivoire (Clignet 1970) to urban Nigeria (Sudarkasa 1973). Some scholars have represented polygamy as a solution to Western social ills, alleviating problems of family disruption (Kilbride 1994), while Afrocentric and African feminist analyses (e.g., Cook 2007, Dixon-Spear 2009, Nnaemeka 1997) have cast polygamy as an alternative to Eurocentric monogamy. Their research rejects the notion that polygamy can be equated only with women's suffering and oppression.

But experts in many fields have taken explicit stands against plural marriage.[1] Legal scholar John Mubangizi (2016) and economist Michèle Tertilt (2005 and 2006) have called for its abolition, as have political scientist Rose McDermott and colleagues in their book *The Evils of Polygyny: Evidence of its Harm to Women, Men, and Society.* "One of the most parsimonious reasons for poor state outcomes, low rates of economic development, and horrific human security," concludes their analysis of survey data from six countries, is "the prevalence of polygyny and the negative consequences that flow from it" (McDermott et al. 2018, 98). Such analyses cast polygamy as a problem demanding a solution—in this case, abolition. Many human rights and women's rights activists have labeled polygamy as a "harmful cultural practice."

One of the most common traps is inappropriate comparison. As Den Otter (2015) observed, critics tend to compare the worst kinds of polygamy to the most idealized kinds of monogamy. Judging polygamy based on forced and child marriage is like judging monogamous marriage based on cases of wife beating; such comparisons only distort how we view plural marriage and the people practicing it. I tend to agree with anthropologist Niara Sudarkasa that "no institution has been more maligned by observers of African societies" than polygamy (1982, 142).

I have not always had an open mind about plural marriage; in fact, it has taken me years to abandon many of my ethnocentric judgments of the practice. Before going to Mali as a Peace Corps Volunteer and integrating into a polygamous household in the late 1990s, I viewed polygamous marriage as an outdated practice headed for extinction. While getting to know people in polygamous marriages helped me develop a more informed perspective, I seldom questioned discourses framing polygamy primarily as a social problem. My own marriage has always been monogamous and will remain so (my wife Oumou, who hails from Mali, has always agreed with me on this point). With respect to polygamy as an institution, however, I have come to appreciate that I cannot adequately understand it while still harboring ethnocentric judgments about it.

The field of anthropology promotes an analytical approach characterized by cultural relativism, the imperative to understand a different culture on its own terms rather than judge it according to one's own cultural standards.[2] Cultural relativism requires putting unfamiliar beliefs and practices into the appropriate context to view them the way cultural insiders do. Such a stance has its limitations, as we will see. But applying cultural relativism to the study of polygamy has given me new insights into the practice.

After cultural relativism, another central (but less acknowledged) anthropological orientation is egalitarianism. Insofar as we oppose the subordination of various categories of people, including women, in social hierarchies, anthropologists tend to be egalitarians. We often internalize this ethos during our training. Like many of my peers in the discipline, I support gender equality.

Studying polygamy puts these two fundamental stances, cultural relativism and egalitarianism, squarely into tension. In the following chapters, I attempt to harness rather than resolve this tension through an analysis of polygamous marriage that is open-minded yet unflinching. A relativistic stance helps me evade the traps set by my own culture's long association of polygamy with barbarism; my anthropological duty here is to portray marriage in general, and polygamy in particular, from the perspectives of Bamako residents themselves. At the same time, an egalitarian ethos alerts me to instances of abuse and injustice. I take seriously the many criticisms levied, especially by Bamako residents, against gender oppression within marriage, and I pay close attention to gendered power disparities at multiple levels of society. The concept of agency, the capacity to exercise autonomy through meaningful choices, will be helpful as we seek to understand these inequalities. I consider who has power over their marriage choices, who does not, and what this imbalance illuminates about larger social structures in Mali.

In these pages, I frame polygamy neither as a problem demanding a solution nor as the solution to a problem, nor as an issue demanding a moral stand. This book does not advocate "saving" Bamako's women from polygamy (cf. Abu-Lughod 2002); it does not argue that polygamy is a Good Thing or a Bad Thing. It tries to approach polygamous marriage on its own terms, as an institution and a set of practices deeply embedded in social structures and everyday lives. It describes and analyzes polygamous marriage in one cultural context and time, showing how Bamako residents experienced it in the early twenty-first century. After reading this book, you may find yourself able to make better judgments about polygamy in this context (and possibly others), or you may decide to refrain from judgment.

Cultural relativism is neither the position that right and wrong do not exist (that is called "moral relativism") nor a politically correct fear of offending people of other cultures. It is the recognition that 1) communities of human beings use many different standards to determine what is right or desirable and what is not; and 2) these standards vary between and sometimes even within communities. There is, for example, no universal definition of a good marriage. As anthropologist Paul Bohannan and historian Philip Curtin (1971, 104–105) once wrote about African marital standards: "It is possible . . . to create a deeply intense relationship between husband and wife that probably most men cannot enter into with two women at once. If the intense and unique quality in that relationship is what is most highly valued, then polygyny must be opposed. But if something else—say security of position and many children—is most highly valued, polygyny is not a contradiction."

This raises a crucial question for our analysis of polygamy: What do people in Bamako value in marriage? Is it a deeply intense, emotionally fulfilling relationship exclusive to intimate partners? Is it a socially validated, secure position within a household that enables men and women to act as respected members of society? Is it having and providing for dependents, particularly offspring? Is it a close-knit network of supportive kin and in-laws? Bamako residents desire all these benefits but seldom in equal measure. What one thinks about polygamy depends largely on what one values most in marriage.

Because its study is fraught with perils, both practical and ethical, polygamy constitutes a serious problem to me as a white, male American anthropologist. Some scholars avoid the topic in their writings so as not to reinforce prevailing ethnocentric discourses about peoples whom Westerners deem "the Other." Others believe white Westerners cannot write about polygamy among Africans, or even about Africans in general, without propping up those discourses and the global power hierarchies underlying them.

Anthropology, however, has a long tradition of fostering cross-cultural understanding through the conscientious exploration of cultural difference, and as a cultural anthropologist, I have chosen to examine polygamy in one specific setting by balancing objectivity with relativism. Relativism is an arduous path toward understanding, but it can be traveled by anyone willing to put their biases aside. You can begin by suspending both your impulse to moral judgment and your certainty in your own position regarding polygamy, if only for as long as you read this book.

In the chapters to follow, I contest ethnocentric representations of polygamy and challenge the assumption that polygamy is a root cause of women's oppression—whether in Bamako or elsewhere in Africa and the Muslim world. Many critiques of this form of marriage are legitimate. My argument in this book, however, is that polygamy is not the real issue when it comes to the oppression of women. Rather, studying polygamy demonstrates that women's oppression stems from multiple factors, including pressure to marry, the prevalence of patriarchy and gerontocracy, a marriage market that favors men, and a legal system that protects men's prerogatives. Legally abolishing polygamy would, therefore, fail to improve women's lives in communities like Bamako, where it is well established. To understand why, in this book, we will come to grips with structures of power—not least among them the institution of marriage itself.

Polygamy as a Human Institution

Forms of polygamy have likely always existed among humans and continue to exist in the modern world. "In Mali there's polygamy that's official, but in Europe there's unofficial polygamy," the late Fatoumata Siré Diakité, a prominent Malian women's rights activist, told me in 2012. "In Europe a man is officially married to one woman but he has several mistresses," she continued, "so polygamy is everywhere, officially or otherwise." As Diakité suggested, even formally monogamous Western cultures have hidden forms of polygamy. A sociologist studying offshore wealth managers found billionaires' plans bequeathing wealth to mistresses and secret children "so common as to have become something of a cliché in the offshore world" (Harrington 2016, 125). But while those forms of non-monogamy carry social stigma, this book examines polygamous marriage in a setting where it is a mainstream, legitimized practice.

Scholars disagree over whether humans are "hard-wired" for polygamy. Evolutionary biologist David Barash (2016, 4) has found humans "biologically predisposed," though not predestined, to polygamy, but added that since monogamy can confer evolutionary benefits, human biology "does not foreclose" it (2016, 136). To anthropologist Agustín Fuentes, monogamy is merely one of many human sexual and marital possibilities, a social construct rather than a biological phenomenon: "We can be monogamous, but our bodies and minds are not specifically designed for it" (2012, 205).

People often characterize a particular behavior pattern—like monogamy or polygamy—as "unnatural" if it does not suit their view of human nature. But anthropologists know that, given the vast range of human cultural variation, "natural" and "unnatural" are misleading labels; humanity's most striking feature is its plasticity. To most anthropologists who study marriage, neither polygamy nor monogamy is better adapted to human nature than the other, and humanity is neither essentially monogamous nor essentially polygamous. Each option is available; which one prevails in a given human population depends less on genetic predispositions than on cultural and environmental factors.

Across the expanse of human history, polygamous marriage is not the exception to some universal marital rule; it *is* the rule. Nearly 84 percent of recorded societies have been documented as "socially polygynous," meaning that, at some point, men in those societies could legitimately marry multiple wives (Ember, Ember, and Low 2007). Native North America was polygamous prior to European settlers' arrival, and even within European Christendom, polygamy was not always rejected.[3] In the long view, strictly monogamous societies are outliers.

Nevertheless, Westerners still tend to think of polygamy (as I once did) as dying out. In the early 1960s, as African states emerged from decades of European colonial rule, distinguished American sociologist William Goode predicted that polygamous marriage on the continent "will, without question, eventually almost completely disappear as a pattern of behavior" (1963, 188); "The new legal codes are gradually moving toward its abolition, women will avoid it where they can, and men will not generally be able to afford it." Many scholars believed that under conditions of urbanization, formal schooling, and modern cash economies, polygamy "tends to become an economic liability [and] gradually ceases to be a common practice and a cultural ideal" (Hillman 1970, 63). Prominent strains of Western thought, including Marxism and modernization theory, saw polygamy as a passing stage of social evolution in "primitive" societies, one that would inevitably give way to exclusive monogamy.

But let's check any evolutionist assumptions at the door. Plural marriage continues to be practiced across a wide swath of humanity, from Southeast Asia (Bao 2006; Koktvedgaard Zeitzen 2018; Nurmila 2009) to North America (Bennion 2016; Song 2016).[4] Like others who have studied polygamy in the modern era (e.g., Dorjahn 1959; Orubuloye, Caldwell, and Caldwell 1991), I do not expect it to go away.

By adapting to the demands of urban life, polygamy has remained an important institution in twenty-first-century West Africa. In Bamako, as mentioned, about one in four wives was in a polygamous marriage. Roughly half of adults, moreover, experienced a polygamous union at some point in their married lives (Antoine 2006; Antoine and Marcoux 2014; Miseli 1998). Most such unions (nearly 88 percent) were "low-order." Like Oumar's family, they consisted of a husband and two wives, while higher-order polygamy (involving a husband with three or four wives) was rare (DHS 2019).

Every polygamous marriage begins monogamously, and most ultimately revert to monogamy. A long-term marriage study in one Malian village showed that 80 percent of senior men's polygamous marriages turned monogamous, whether upon a wife's death or at the time of divorce (Hertrich 2006). Many Bamako marital careers, likewise, alternated between polygamous and monogamous phases. Where every monogamous marriage is potentially polygamous, polygamist husbands are not necessarily different from monogamous husbands in anything except the number of wives they have at a specific moment in time—namely, whenever a surveyor categorizes their marriage as polygamous or monogamous. We must, therefore, avoid thinking of polygamy as an individual-level variable (Clignet 1970; Ezeh 1997); it describes marriages, not persons, and it is rarely a permanent marital state. This fact has helped people adapt plural marriage to the conditions they inhabit.

Why Polygamy?

To fulfill this book's first goal of explaining why polygamy has endured in Bamako, I will consider the factors that could lead a man to have multiple wives simultaneously, or a woman to marry an already married man. Scholars have long debated polygamy's root causes, but with plural marriage as a historical norm, it is monogamy, not polygamy, that is the anomaly. Others can speculate about why monogamy became the exclusive marital form in so many human societies around the globe,[5] but my task is to explain polygamy's resilience in one particular urban community during the 2010s. Theories and hypotheses originating in multiple scholarly disciplines have tried to explain polygamy. Not all are relevant to this study; theories linking polygamy to systems of agricultural production (e.g., Boserup 1970; Goody 1973), for example, fail to explain it in urban settings (such as Bamako), where it lacks a clear economic rationale. I will concentrate, instead, on three broad categories of explanation that will illuminate the marriage practices explored in these chapters.

Many biologists, evolutionary psychologists, and economists have seen polygamy (specifically polygyny) as reflecting men's varying degrees of evolutionary fitness—essentially, that plural marriage is a function of male inequality. This argument assumes that the biologically "fittest" males are the most attractive marriage partners, and that females enter polygamy by choosing the most desirable husbands, many of whom already have other wives. Some scholars have borrowed from naturalists' polygyny threshold model, which presumes a "difference in resources between two competing males—one a bachelor and the other already mated—to make it worthwhile for a female to choose the latter" (Barash 2016, 86). Applied to human marriage, this model has ascribed polygamous outcomes to the choices women make as they consider the resources offered by potential husbands. To celebrated economist Gary Becker (1974), polygamy was the consequence of a sexual selection process in which the wealthiest men attract more wives (see also Grossbard 1980). The explanation that polygamy stems from women's choices to maximize their marital utility by marrying successful polygamous men is known as the "consumption hypothesis" (Ickowitz and Mohanty 2015) in reference to such marriages' presumed material benefits.

Other scholars have hypothesized that wives in polygamous marriages pool their domestic labor more efficiently than wives in monogamous marriages. A woman sharing her husband with a co-wife also might share household chores like cooking and childcare with her. A cooperative distribution of tasks can benefit the entire polygamous household, particularly the wives. Researchers have identified such advantages to polygamous organization in Bamako (Marcoux 1997) and other African cities (Anderson 2000; Steady 1987). These explanations reflect the "labor-sharing hypothesis" (Ickowitz and Mohanty 2015).

The final category considers structures of power that disadvantage women. Anthropologists often have linked polygamy to male competition for prestige (Bao 2006; Bao and Jankowiak 2008). Feminist economists have challenged assumptions by Becker and others that polygamous marriage is generally advantageous for women by pointing to gendered hierarchies restricting women's agency and limiting their marital choices (Bergmann 1995; see also Grossbard 2016). The "oppression hypothesis" contends that polygamous marriage stems primarily from women's lack of agency (Ickowitz and Mohanty 2015).

We will see that plural marriage's persistence in Bamako cannot be reduced to a single factor or theory. Unlike scholars trained to value parsimonious or "elegant" solutions, anthropologists tend to be skeptical of simple models meant to account for human behavior. Rather than trace human action to one root cause, or even a few root causes, we are trained to seek complex explanations. Simplistic models are inadequate if we want to understand both how polygamy endures and how it impacts people's everyday lives.

Accordingly, another core anthropological approach is holism—analyzing a given practice within its full cultural, social, material, and political context. In this book, a holistic approach means not looking at polygamy in isolation, even for analytical purposes. As Jacqueline Solway observed in Botswana, "The occurrence of polygyny is not an independent variable, ebbing and flowing with changing fashion; instead, polygyny is an integral social institution which must be understood in the context of the larger social system" (1990, 48). This book's holistic approach situates polygamy within the framework of Bamako's marriage system, demonstrating this practice's complexity.

What Is a Marriage System?

What I call a "marriage system" has gone by other names, including "nuptiality regime" (Lesthaeghe, Kaufmann, and Meekers 1989) and "matrimonial system" (Hertrich 2006; Pison 1986).[6] People marry for many reasons: to strengthen their social networks; to forge a political or business alliance; to attain adult status; to gain a sexual partner; to satisfy a religious duty; to improve their material circumstances; to legitimize existing offspring; to produce new offspring; to establish an intimate emotional relationship; to obtain legal benefits; to get their parents off their backs, among many purposes and intentions. These reasons are neither universal nor equally weighted everywhere. A society's marriage system can inspire, channel, magnify, reward, or frustrate its members' reasons for marrying.

A marriage system consists of the cultural practices, social norms, formal and informal institutions, and power relations that shape the formation and experience of marriage in a society. Demographic characteristics, including birth rates, population growth rates, the average age at first marriage, and the relative distributions of ages and sexes within the population, comprise one important component of the system. Rules and norms regarding spousal selection, roles within marriage, and relations between in-laws comprise another. Also in the mix are the kinship structures determining who is considered a relative, where and with whom spouses will dwell after marriage, and how family wealth is transmitted across generations. Among the questions to which a marriage system provides answers are these (a far from exhaustive list):

- Are people expected to marry from a young age? Do females marry significantly younger than males? What barriers and incentives do they face to marriage? Under which circumstances may someone legitimately remain single? May individuals freely opt out of marriage?
- Which criteria are used to select a spouse? Whose input goes into the selection? When individuals' proposed spouse is selected for them, do they have the right to refuse the match? Which social categories will a person be encouraged or warned not to marry into?
- What is owed to a new spouse's kin? Is a bridewealth or dowry payment required to make a marriage legitimate in the eyes of the community? If so, what rules govern such payments?
- How will sexual relations be governed within marriage? Is extramarital sex strictly prohibited or tolerated for husbands, wives, or both?
- What are the rights and obligations within marriage? How do men's marital roles differ from women's?
- What is the place of childbearing within marriage? How many children are spouses expected to have? Who is recognized as the children's most important kin, and what role will they play in the children's upbringing? What happens if a couple cannot conceive a child?
- Under which circumstances is divorce possible, and how does the process of divorce occur?

And, of course,

- Can a person be married to more than one spouse simultaneously?

Answers to some of these questions may be codified in state laws and regulations or left to religious doctrine, local custom, or family precedent. Others may be matters of personal choice. Yet few of these questions in any society are left entirely to autonomous individuals. Theories about marriage often assume that such decisions are made by two persons (or more, in the case of polygamy) based on their individual endowments and preferences. This assumption, foundational to celebrated analyses of polygamy in the fields of evolutionary psychology and economics, defies actual practice.

For Bamako residents, choices about marriage—everything from when and whom to marry to whether a union would be polygamous or monogamous—have been not necessarily for them alone to make, nor even for couples to decide together. Marriage was never about the individual; in many cases, we will see, *marriage was not even about the couple* but, instead, reflected the prerogatives of kin groups. To illustrate: Malians defined marriage as exclusively heterosexual; people who engaged in homosexual relations in private were expected to submit to prevailing norms of heterosexual marriage in public (Broqua 2009). As marriage is always more than an aggregation of personal choices, we must analyze individual marital decisions within the structures of power that shape them.

To comprehend why polygamy endures in Bamako, we must consider the norms, laws, and hierarchies constituting Bamako's marriage system. This book's chapters will examine the system's elements and their role in maintaining modern polygamy. Each chapter will consider how this marriage system affects women's options. This leads into the book's second goal: to shed light on the relationship between polygamy and gender oppression. We must understand the agency (that is, the capacity to exercise autonomy by making meaningful choices) and the power (the ability to influence others) that men and women command in their own lives and relative to one another. Polygamous marriage, I will argue, is better grasped as an expression of women's lack of agency in particular domains than as a specific *cause* of women's oppression. Women's marital options are determined especially by their bargaining power—meaning, in this case, their ability to negotiate the conditions of marriage both before and after their entry into marriage. In this book's final chapters, I will show how women's limited bargaining power makes polygamy a frequent outcome within Bamako's marriage system.

First, however, we will acquaint ourselves with the city in which this marriage system operates.

All Roads Lead to Bamako

Westerners thinking of Africa probably don't picture Bamako, which seldom appears in images showcasing African culture. Carol Beckwith and Angela Fisher's *African Ceremonies* (1999), two hefty volumes of gorgeous photography, focuses on the rituals of rural communities, including some in Mali. They show headdress-wearing Dogon dancers in cliffside villages of the country's central Mopti region. They also show members of the Bwa people, from the Mali/Burkina Faso border zone, in full-body costumes at masked rituals. Bamako residents (known in French as "*Bamakois*," or "*Bamakoises*" for females) certainly attend their share of weddings and funerals. Yet they are absent from *African Ceremonies*, perhaps because buyers of such books don't see cities as the "real Africa."

Upon Mali's independence from France in 1960, Bamako was a colonial town with fewer than 130,000 residents; fifty years later, it had 2 million. (Had New York City grown at the same rate from 1960, it would have had over 100 million

inhabitants by 2010.) In two generations, Bamakois saw their community transformed from a sleepy administrative town to sprawling metropolis—growth that
fit into the wider pattern of sub-Saharan Africa's unprecedented demographic
expansion (Guengant 2017). Bamako's annual population growth rate of between
4 and 6 percent made it, by one estimate, Africa's fastest-growing urban area.[7] By
2019, the city was home to nearly 3 million people, more than one in ten Malians
(INSTAT 2019). Its population has been projected to reach 23 million and to over-
take several major world cities, including Los Angeles, Rio de Janeiro, Mexico
City, and Beijing, by century's end (Hoornweg and Pope 2017). While other Malian
cities and towns also have grown rapidly, none approached the runaway growth
of Bamako, which was an order of magnitude larger than Mali's next-largest city.

Most of this growth has been "natural" (i.e., driven by births among existing residents), a fact with major implications for marriage and polygamy (see
chapter 5). The rest of this growth stemmed from migrants to the city; at the last
census, 43 percent of its residents were born in other parts of Mali (Mesple-Somps
et al. 2014). As birth rates remained high and child mortality fell throughout the
late twentieth and early twenty-first centuries, Mali's rural population also grew,
but demographic and climate-induced stresses on agriculture pushed more and
more villagers off their farms and pasturelands and into the city (Toulmin 2020).
Since the 2010s, these economic migrants have been joined by streams of "internally displaced persons" fleeing political violence in central and northern Mali.

Some migration into Bamako was circular. By the early 2000s, girls from
rural Mali were spending considerable time in the city as domestic workers.
Unmarried and mostly unschooled, they came to save up money and expand
their horizons before returning home to marry; a year of cooking and cleaning
for Bamakois families became a rite of passage for young village women. (Interestingly enough, this circular migration was pioneered by girls from Dogon and
Bwa communities, those same photogenic settings of the "real Africa.") After
leaving Bamako, they brought back to their villages not only their earnings but
also new urban outlooks, especially about marriage and the types of relationships they aspired to. They stressed romantic attachment and other modern values (Engebretsen et al. 2020; Hertrich and Lesclingand 2012 and 2013; Kassogué
2014; Lesclingand and Hertrich 2017; Sauvain-Dugerdil 2013; Toulmin 2020).
These circular migrants helped extend Bamako's cultural influence deep into
the Malian countryside.

To anyone living in or even occasionally visiting Mali in the early twenty-
first century, signs of burgeoning growth were everywhere. Malian telephone
numbers, which expanded from five to six digits only in the 1990s, had eight
digits by 2010. New vehicle license plates added a digit during the 2010s to accommodate more cars and trucks on the road. Adjacent city neighborhoods came
to feel distant because of the increasingly congested streets between them. But
the clearest sign of growth came from new residential areas sprouting up on

FIGURE I.2 Houses under construction in Heremakono, on Bamako's southern outskirts (2011).

Bamako's outskirts. Most of this growth was horizontal; where crops and fruit trees had recently grown, one- and two-story concrete-block homes were going up on seemingly every plot of land out to the horizon. Most were occupied well before completion, often by poor rural transplants (Marie 2011). On the city's fringes, where annual population growth could reach 17 percent, land speculation was rampant (Bertrand 2021; Bourdarias 1999; Neimark, Toulmin, and Batterbury 2018). Public infrastructure lagged behind these peripheral neighborhoods' expansion; streets and power lines were constantly extended to meet rising customer demand, and many inhabitants purchased jugs of water from peddlers or drew it from wells because municipal pipes had not yet reached their homes (see figure I.2).

In Bamako's densely populated central districts, much growth was vertical, as landlords and homeowners added stories to their properties to accommodate more residents and businesses (Bertrand 2021). Sidewalks and other public spaces were clogged with street vendors plying their wares. Municipal authorities periodically deployed police to chase them out; vendors returned soon after the cops departed.

By the early twenty-first century, the city seemed saturated. The average Bamako household, at 9.4 people, was 16 percent larger than the national average (Mesple-Somps et al. 2014). "For a long time, Bamako was the city where, for example, a young person from the bush, during the dry season, could come and work at some kind of job, have some cash for his family and go back," said Alimatou, a journalist I interviewed in 2011. "This ended years ago. Now the people who come here don't leave. Before, people came to relatives who could receive them.

Now, even for students who come for secondary school or university, there's nobody who can take them in because there's too many of them!" Rapid urbanization was placing considerable economic strain on the city and its residents.

The Political Economy of Malian Urban Life and Marriage

Even as Bamako's population increased by over 350 percent between 1976 and 2009 (Mesple-Somps et al. 2014), its economy stagnated. Mali was relatively poor at independence in 1960, but lackluster economic growth, persistent youth unemployment,[8] inflation, cyclical drought, and fiscal austerity in the 1980s depressed already low urban living standards. Currency devaluations in 1984 and 1994 made urban life significantly more expensive (Bertrand 2013; Marcoux and Piché 1998), and the cost of living continued to skyrocket during the 2010s. These changes diminished economic opportunity, delaying young people's entry into employment and marriage (Bagayogo and Coulibaly 2014; Bleck and Lodermeier 2020). Youth in cities throughout the region experienced similar difficulties transitioning to adulthood (Calvès 2016; Dery and Bawa 2019; Hannaford 2017; Masquelier 2005).

This period had its bright spots. School enrollment soared: while 45 percent of Bamakois in 1998 had attended school, that number climbed to 60 percent in 2009 (Mesple-Somps et al. 2014). Bamako residents' literacy rate rose from under 45 percent in 2001 to nearly 60 percent in 2016 (INSTAT 2017). Market-friendly reforms facilitated access to communications technology and media. In the 1990s, the Malian state telephone monopoly's landlines were prohibitively expensive and unreliable; one might need to repeat-dial a number dozens of times to place a single domestic long-distance call. After the turn of the century, as the phone company was privatized, along with many other state-owned businesses, the arrival of cellular service brought telecommunications to the fingertips of almost every adult Bamakois. By 2018, nine of ten adults in the city had mobile phones; their use constituted households' sixth-largest expense, after food, housing, fuel, clothing, and electricity (DHS 2019; INSTAT 2018). More than 70 percent of city households had internet access (often slow and erratic through smartphones), and more than 83 percent owned televisions (INSTAT 2019).

As Mali was unevenly integrated into the global economy, its government underwent a parallel liberalization process. Under President Modibo Keita (in power from 1960 to 1968), Mali's one-party state was socialist and heavily interventionist; after Keita was toppled in a coup led by an army officer named Moussa Traoré (in power from 1968 to 1991), the state was authoritarian and military-run. In 1991, after a coup toppled Traoré, Mali began a transition to political pluralism; a constitutional referendum and parliamentary and presidential elections followed in 1992. The national government decentralized some authority to local elected officials. Privately owned newspapers, radio broadcasters, and television stations flourished in Mali's formerly state-controlled media sector. New spaces for political expression and debate emerged as Malians adapted from *waajibifanga*—literally "rule by obligation" (i.e., authoritarian rule)—to *jemufanga*, "rule by voice," or democracy (de Jorio 1997).

Despite this apparent progress, Malians were frustrated with their country's direction in the early twenty-first century. Participation in elections was weak, with turnout never surpassing 40 percent of eligible voters. The quality of public services suffered. Public schools that had seen huge influxes of new students during the 1990s remained too poorly staffed and resourced to instruct their students adequately, when they weren't shuttered by teacher- and student-led strikes (Bleck 2015). And with urban costs of living still rising and the political elite hoarding the benefits of economic liberalization, people in positions of public trust—from civil servants to elected officials—were increasingly suspected of corruption. According to one cynical refrain among Malians who remembered the days of socialist and military rule, "Under Modibo Keita, people were too ashamed to steal; under Moussa Traoré, people were too afraid to steal. Now people are neither ashamed nor afraid."

This refrain fit into a public discourse of moral critique and despair frequently heard in Bamako throughout the 2010s. Many residents complained that marriage was becoming meaningless, corrupted by materialism and hypocrisy. More generally, though, they felt that society had lost its bearings, that nothing was sacred anymore, and that everything was for sale. It was increasingly difficult to tell sincere from dishonest people, authentic goods from counterfeit, reliable information from falsehoods. Amid rampant materialism and deceit in everyday life, who could be trusted in marital relations or matters of state? Through bribery or connections, one could procure everything from property deeds to diplomas to drivers' licenses without any valid claim to them. (A martial arts instructor I knew even suspected that unqualified students had paid bribes for their black belts—but, he insisted, this never happened in his dojo.) Old behavioral codes had fallen away, and nobody knew what would replace them. Many Malians equated liberalization with disorder, irresponsibility, and the breakdown of authority from the household to the community and the national level (Schulz 2021).

What I initially had perceived as a crisis inhibiting many young people's passage to independent adulthood was clearly affecting society more broadly. In postcolonial Mali, politics (in Manding, *politiki*) was widely associated with fraud and regarded as "the inverse of religion" (Bleck 2015, 136). Some Malians, seeing their society as inherently undisciplined, openly longed for the days of authoritarian rule. "We need a dictatorship," a young man told me one evening in March 2012. A few weeks later, after two decades of elections and pluralism, it felt as though history had been wrenched into reverse when another military coup toppled a president near the end of his term. As many Malians welcomed

the putsch, the rest of the world realized that Mali's supposedly democratic institutions were badly broken.

In this environment of uncertainty and economic hardship, some Bamakois
viewed the age-old practice of polygamous marriage as ill-advised. Ali, a thirty-
nine-year-old husband interviewed in 2012, said:

> Sure, our religion allows us to take [additional wives], our culture allows it,
> but on the other hand, our means are too limited. A high-level civil ser-
> vant can't rent a house for 75,000 francs [about US$150] per month when
> his salary is only 120,000 francs [about US$240]. He's supporting two
> wives, in two different houses—he's paying rent, groceries and expenses
> for both. No, this guy's a thief, do we even need to say that he's a thief?

Despite many economic shocks to Bamako's marriage system (Marcoux 1997;
Marcoux and Piché 1998), polygamy rates remained relatively high throughout
this period. As I will show, the institution of polygamy proved resilient even in
the face of sweeping social change and economic hardship. To ask why polygamy endures is to ponder the reasons for this resilience.

Afropolitan Cultural Dynamics

Three main currents of cultural influence shaped life in modern Bamako. One
is the Mande people,[9] an ethno-linguistic identity category that includes
Bamanan (also known as Bambara), Maninka, and other ethnic groups long present in Bamako and elsewhere in the region. They spoke Manding, the city's
lingua franca and the mother tongue of more than three-quarters of its residents
(RGPH 2011). Bamakois of all backgrounds embraced Manding; it was the medium
of transactions in the market, sermons in the mosque, and pop songs on the
radio. Mande social structure differentiated community members according to
their ancestral origins as noble, casted, or descended from people subjugated
within local systems of slavery.[10] This classification continued to influence relationships, especially marriage, in the twenty-first century. While the noble/slave
distinction no longer mattered to many Bamakois, other distinctions remained
important: since caste groups—*jeli* or "griots" (oral historians, musicians, and
praise singers), *numu* (blacksmiths), and *garanke* (leatherworkers)—were endog-
amous, caste people could marry only other caste people (Schulz 1999). Society
also was knit together by a system of joking and ritual insults known as *senen-
kunya*, facilitating social interaction across distinctions of caste and ethnicity
(Douyon 2006). This system was widely traced to the Mali Empire, which ruled
over much of the region from the thirteenth to the seventeenth centuries and
after which the Republic of Mali was named.

The second cultural current is Islam, present in the western Sahel for nearly
a thousand years. If Islam in the region was limited mainly to merchants and

political elites in the early 1900s, by the end of the century more than 90 percent of Malians identified as Muslim (Soares 1999). Islam in the region became known for its firm separation between religion and politics and for its tolerance toward unbelievers (Launay 1990). In twenty-first-century Bamako, Muslims adopted various interpretations of their religion, from Sufism to Salafism, from the orthodox and puritanical to the syncretic and mystical (Soares 2006).

The third cultural current is Western modernity, in the form of French-inspired rationalism, science, schooling, government, and consumerism. Over more than six decades, French colonial rule transformed Malian life. It laid the foundations of the modern Malian state characterized by secularism, bureaucracy, and highly centralized political authority. It constructed a legal framework inspired by Enlightenment ideals (see chapter 6). It crafted a system of public schools based on a standard curriculum and competitive exams. It also reorganized economic production and intensified Mali's integration into the global capitalist system, setting the stage for a twenty-first-century national economy dependent on exporting raw materials—notably cotton and gold—and importing manufactured goods, just like under colonialism.

To live in postcolonial Bamako was to draw from and navigate between all three of these cultural currents. Each current was associated with a distinct language: Mande with Manding, the primary language of daily life; Islam with Arabic, the language of Muslim worship and scholarship; and Western modernity with French, the language of government offices, schools, and some media. Each current claimed a different writing system: the N'ko script (see description below) for Mande, the Arabic script for Islam, and the Latin script for Western modernity. And each current measured time differently: a Mande solar calendar numbered the years from the founding of the Mali Empire, the Islamic lunar calendar numbered the years of the Hijri era, and the solar Gregorian calendar numbered the years of the Common Era.[11] All three currents were associated with particular methods of celebrating marriage and ordering the most highly valued qualities within marriage (see chapter 6).

Labeling a practice as "traditional" in Bamako had little to do with its cultural authenticity or traceability through history, particularly since most Bamakois' ancestors had likely not observed it themselves. Rather, something became "traditional" in large part because people understood it *in contrast to* cultural practices associated with Islam or Western modernity. For example, the Manding writing system known as N'ko, written from right to left, was developed in the mid-twentieth century but came to be seen as an authentically Mande counterpart and competitor to the Arabic and French writing systems with which Manding speakers were already familiar (Donaldson 2019).

During my fieldwork, there were advocates of each of Bamako's three main cultural currents who encouraged their fellow Bamakois to value that current over the others. Boosters of Mande culture included public intellectuals, often adepts of N'ko writing and sometimes using the French title *traditionaliste*, who urged their compatriots to get back to their Mande roots. Islam's exponents included imams and Islamic scholars who implored Muslims to adhere more rigorously to their religion. Exponents of Western modernity included university professors and policy experts preaching liberal Enlightenment values. Members of all three groups made their case on TV, radio, and social media.

Despite cultural purists' efforts to brighten the boundaries between them, these currents usually blended together seamlessly in everyday life. Each current was associated with distinctive styles of apparel, for instance, but Bamakoises switched between styles depending on the occasion, or assembled outfits combining elements of all three (e.g., an African wax-print ensemble worn with a hijab and high heels) rather than always dressing in a single style. The high-quality damask cloth known as *bazin riche*, the mainstay of Bamakois' "traditional" finery, came from industrial looms in Europe. Linguistically, codeswitching was the rule, and French words found their way into the Manding spoken even by people who had never studied French; meanwhile, many words understood to be Manding (like the words for *book*, *obligation*, or *Monday*) derived originally from Arabic. Popular music embraced hybridity. Consider General Ballody, a young man known for rapping in Manding about Islam; his renown came from blurring the boundaries between these cultural currents.[12] Bamako's youth-driven cultural mélange was a form of Afropolitanism, "a diverse configuration of existential projects in a world embedded in and emergent from an increasingly urban and extroverted Africa" (Skinner 2015, 182).

While Bamako's Afropolitan confluence of culture was often, as with popular music, a space of great dynamism and innovation, it also could be fraught with risk and controversy—especially concerning gender norms. Unlike many Muslim-majority societies, twenty-first-century Bamako was not typically a place of strict gender segregation; males and females casually shared space on public transportation, in classrooms and offices, and in residential courtyards. Yet gender ideologies inspired by Mande culture and Islam, both stressing complementarity between male and female, did not always coexist harmoniously with Western Enlightenment-inspired ideologies stressing gender equality. Frictions between these ideologies made the overt renegotiation of gender roles tricky. If cosmopolitanism in music was largely unquestioned, cosmopolitanism in marriage and gender roles was another story. Part of this book's aim is to explore such frictions and how their impact influenced polygamous practices and the institution of marriage in Bamako.

Among the Bamakois: A Note on Research Methods

Malik was a forty-five-year-old Bamakois. In a land where many were illiterate and where poverty was rife, he was among the fortunate few with a modern education and an office job. He drove a car to work and watched news broadcasts from France via satellite. He used Gmail, Skype, and WhatsApp daily. His favorite book was Dale Carnegie's *How to Win Friends and Influence People*. He also had two wives, and his articulate views challenged my assumptions about polygamy.

Malik was part of a sample of Bamako husbands and wives interviewed for this research between March and June of 2012. Two Malian research assistants recruited them according to various criteria (sex, age, educational attainment, and type of marriage) and conducted structured interviews with them in French or Manding according to the interviewee's choice. While our aim was to recruit fifty wives and fifty husbands, due to some missing early responses we had to interview fifty-eight husbands to get a full set. We selected participants to reflect the city's diversity: the sample included people of various ethnic, socioeconomic, and educational backgrounds, hailing from almost every neighborhood. Because sample members were not randomly selected, their views do not necessarily represent those of the city's general population, and in two specific ways, our sample is *not* an accurate reflection of the wider community. We inadvertently overrepresented better-educated males (those with secondary education or higher), and we deliberately overrepresented people in polygamous marriages (half the interviewees of each sex were married polygamously). With respect to the latter, our aim was not to compare polygamists with monogamists, but to ensure that our interview sample included sufficient perspectives from people in polygamous unions. I refer to these interviewees collectively throughout this book as "our interview sample"—it was very much a team effort.

I never met Malik, nor any of the 107 other participants in our interview sample. I know them solely from their interview transcripts. Only Noumouké, my male research assistant, met with Malik and interviewed him for over an hour. I can, therefore, offer no ethnographic description of Malik—what he wore, his demeanor or facial expressions. I chose *not* to participate in these interviews because an interviewer's identity can significantly shape interviewees' responses, particularly concerning sensitive subjects. In Benin, Douglas Falen (2011)—a white American anthropologist—found that female interviewees expressed support for polygamy far more often when asked by a local woman (forty-four of sixty-four cases) than when asked by him (just one of twenty-seven cases). Studying male attitudes about marriage in Senegal, Véronique Gilbert (2018)—a white Canadian anthropologist—found that men cited very different justifications for polygamy to her male Senegalese assistant than they did to her. By hiring Noumouké to canvass husbands and hiring Nana, a Malian woman, to canvass wives, I hoped to minimize this "interviewer bias." In the following chapters, I regularly quote interview sample participants, identifying each with a single pseudonym followed by a parenthetical reference specifying gender (M for male, F for female), age, occupation, and number of wives/co-wives at the time of their interview; for example: "Malik (M, 45, office worker, two wives)." You need not remember which interviewee said what, but you can use the pseudonyms if you choose to identify patterns in given interviewees' responses.

Alongside the interview sample, this book relies on fifty semi-structured interviews I conducted in French and Manding during three separate field-work stays in Bamako (July–August 2010, August 2011–June 2012, and December 2019–January 2020). Most of these interviewees were "key informants,"such as scholars, journalists, radio hosts, imams, bloggers, Catholic priests, women's rights activists, *jeliw* (members of the griot caste), judges, marriage brokers, parliamentarians, and ritual specialists known as marabouts (see chapter 3). I identify most of them by single-name pseudonyms, and the rest—those like Fatoumata Siré Diakité, who asked me to do so—by their full names. These key informant interviews helped me discern broad patterns over time regarding marriage and gender.

Another tool I relied on was focus group discussions. Another pair of research assistants and I conducted twenty-four of these discussions with small groups (six to twelve people) in a dozen neighborhoods throughout the city between July 2010 and June 2012. Most of these groups were single-sex and incorporated people of similar marital status and educational backgrounds, though we also conducted two mixed-sex discussions. We guided each group through a series of questions about contemporary marriage in Bamako. Most discussions were in Manding; a few were in French. Early discussions helped refine our questions for subsequent groups and for our interview sample. Some anonymous focus group participants are quoted in this book.

Between interviewees and focus group participants, my research team and I canvassed more than 300 Bamakois between 2010 and 2020. Such structured interactions are most valuable when contextualized through participant observation, allowing deep engagement with a community and facilitating a holistic ethnographic perspective. Participant observation is especially productive when fieldwork extends or recurs over a long period. My visits to Oumar and Sira in Faladié, spanning more than a decade, for example, helped me appreciate how plural marriage may change over the life course. Had I known them only for a year, I would have come away with a narrower view of their relationship and its complexities.

Finally, I collected municipal marriage records from one Bamako administrative division,[13] forming a sample of 1,020 civil marriages established between 1991 and 2016. By cross-checking my ethnographic evidence against these marriage records and existing demographic surveys, I charted continuities and changes in the city's marriage system.[14]

How Not to Read This Book

Before wrapping up this introduction, let's consider some pitfalls to avoid in the coming chapters. Particularly for those new to the ethnographic genre, it is easy to make certain logical mistakes when reading about other cultures. I highlight four common types of error here.

Inappropriate comparisons. Comparisons between cultures can hinder a relativistic perspective. We should seek to understand Bamako's marriage system on its own terms, and use caution in comparing it to drastically different marriage systems. While I will draw your attention—especially using chapter epigraphs and endnotes—to parallels between marriage in Bamako and marriage elsewhere, my aim in presenting each topic is to enable you to view these topics from a perspective approaching that of Bamakois themselves. With cultural relativism as my guiding approach, I have tried to refrain from the invidious comparisons made by too many Western analyses of polygamous societies. Cultural anthropologists do not understand a community by enumerating what it lacks or how it falls short of some global standard; we understand it by trying to view it through the eyes of its inhabitants.

Evolutionist parallels. I occasionally will highlight similarities between the marriage practices of different times and places. Women's average age at first marriage in early twenty-first-century Bamako, for example, was similar to that of nineteenth-century Britain. Yet such parallels do not put Bamako two centuries behind Britain on some shared developmental path, nor are they evidence that Bamako's path leads inexorably to polygamy's demise. While historical processes often follow patterns, societies follow divergent trajectories.

The assumption that polygamy is everywhere the same. Scholarly claims about polygamy in one setting routinely cite evidence from studies of polygamy conducted in wildly dissimilar settings, apparently under the belief that these disparate sources describe the same phenomenon. Too many assume that polygamous household organization in Cairo is no different from polygamous household organization in Kuala Lumpur or Salt Lake City. But because there is "no single, monolithic polygamy" (Pearsall 2022, 3), my findings on polygamy in Bamako will not necessarily illuminate polygamous practices in South Africa, Bangladesh, or the United States. Some aspects of Bamako's marriage system might fit other cultural and geographic contexts, while others are place-specific. When citing scholarly evidence in the chapters ahead, therefore, I draw mainly on research conducted in Mali and neighboring countries (particularly Burkina Faso, Côte d'Ivoire, The Gambia, Guinea, Niger, Nigeria, Senegal, and Sierra Leone). I use supporting evidence from outside this region sparingly, marking many of these citations with "cf." (meaning "compare"). Once again, my approach privileges the representation of Bamako's marriage system in its own context over comparisons between different cultures and marriage systems.

The assumption that ethnographic observations convey a culture's timeless essence. Since at least the late twentieth century, anthropologists have recognized cultures as dynamic systems continually reshaped by changes in politics, technology, environment, and many other domains. While we know that our observations at any point in time are mere snapshots of communities in constant flux, we often couch our writing in "the ethnographic present," described as "the practice of giving accounts of other cultures and societies in the present tense" (Fabian 2014, 80). For example, an ethnographer might write that "Marriage is universal in Mali," and we might understand this to describe *all* time, not just the time in which the observation occurred. As a literary convention, the ethnographic present gives the illusion of permanence to ethnographers' descriptions. But although marriage has long been universal in Mali and generally remained so during the ten years bounding my field research, that universality has begun to weaken in Bamako (see chapter 1 and conclusion). To dispel the illusion of timelessness in this book, I have phrased my observations and analysis in the past tense, reserving the present tense for generalizations I deem eternally valid (such as "culture is never static") and for the ethnographic interludes between chapters. Frequent temporal markers situate Bamako "in the 2010s" or "in the early twenty-first century" because culture is dynamic, even in settings more often associated with the hidebound perpetuation of custom.

This book guides you through Bamako's marriage system, with each chapter focusing on a different aspect. Chapter 1 demonstrates the universality of marriage in Bamako and describes spouses' roles and responsibilities within marriage. Chapter 2 shows how social structures and norms influenced the formation of polygamous unions. Chapter 3 looks at the shifting shape and internal dynamics of polygamous households. Chapter 4 analyzes the cultural and religious discourses and ideologies pertaining to polygamy, particularly the intersections of gender and power. Chapter 5 shows how the demography of the city's "marriage market" shaped people's real and perceived options both prior to and during marriage, and conditioned women's agency and marital bargaining power regarding monogamy. Chapter 6 traces the effects of Bamako's multilayered legal environment on marital formation and conduct, particularly with respect to men's initiatives to take additional wives and women's ability to resist those initiatives. The concluding chapter considers social changes afoot that could significantly increase women's agency and bargaining power in the future.

An approach of cultural relativism informs this book's first goal: to show how polygamy endured in Bamako by helping you understand marriage and polygamy as Bamakois themselves understood it. An egalitarian ethos informs the book's second goal: to illuminate the relationship between polygamy and women's agency. As we will see, that relationship is more nuanced than many of polygamy's critics have made it out to be.

INTERLUDE ONE

The Midnight Callers.

"When a father speaks, the child cannot answer back."

Mid-March 2012: I am invited to the studio of a private Bamako radio station to attend the live broadcast of a popular evening phone-in show about family and relationships. In the studio, I find a panel of four people: Tonton (the host) plus three commentators, each explicitly representing a particular point of view. Youma offers advice from a woman's perspective; another woman, Khadidja, speaks from an Islamic perspective; and a man named Tiekoro, a specialist in the N'ko writing system, covers a "traditional" perspective. All are in their thirties except Tiekoro, who looks older. True to his role as a guardian of tradition, Tiekoro habitually corrects his fellow panelists whenever they, like most Bamakois, slip French words into their spoken Manding during the show. If you want to say "research," he tells them, don't say *recherche*, say *ɲinini*. For "since," don't say *depuis*, say *kabini*. Excepting Khadidja's occasional quotations from the Qur'an in Arabic, conversation is entirely in Manding. As I settle into the studio, the panelists are absorbed in their preparations and I am able to sit and observe silently.

The panel's first case for discussion concerns a young male professional who recently returned to Bamako after three years of study in Canada. He wrote to Tonton explaining that his father wants him to marry a cousin (his uncle's daughter), whom the young man dislikes. He has his eye on another young woman whose virginity he already took. But his father won't listen; for him, it is about repaying a debt of gratitude to his brother, in whose house the young man was raised along-side the girl in question. Their shared upbringing makes the young man especially uncomfortable with the match, which seems like incest to him. His siblings all were allowed to marry whomever they chose, and he considers it unfair that he should be denied that right. His uncle has offered a brand-new villa for him to move into when he marries his cousin. But facing the young man's resistance, his father has begun to threaten him with supernatural sanctions (curses and sorcery) if he won't toe the line. The young man doesn't doubt that his father is capable of delivering on these threats.

As Tonton sees it, the young man has no choice but to give in. Local wisdom holds that only the elderly can recognize a good potential wife, so it is in the young man's interest to go along with his father's plan. Khadidja, while finding the father's mentality rather outdated, doesn't disagree, and adds that a good Muslim should respect his father. To Youma, the problem is that the young man has not given fair consideration to his cousin because he is too attached to his girlfriend. Tiekoro, the traditionalist, is categorical that the son must obey his father: "When a father speaks, the child cannot answer back," he says. The panel is united in advising the young man to submit to his father's plan for him.

The next caller is a 24-year-old female caller who married a man through a private Islamic ceremony and has two children with him. Now that he has married another woman via a civil ceremony (see chapter 7), the caller worries that her union is on shaky ground. She wants her husband to bring her to the municipal office and formalize their marriage. Khadidja tells her that nothing can take her status as first wife away, even if she never gets a marriage certificate; a religious wedding is socially recognized in Mali, and the fact that she has children by this man establishes her seniority. The panelists suggest that the woman enlist the help of her husband's kin to convince him to grant her a civil wedding.

Another woman phones and says she is engaged to be married, having already borne two children to her fiancé. She wants to know if her children are illegitimate. The panelists ask for details: When was the engagement formalized? Was bride-wealth paid before the children were born? It was, the caller says, leading Khadidja to say that both children are perfectly legitimate in the eyes of Islamic law.

Tiekoro adds that the children are legitimate also from the standpoint of local custom. The panel is once again agreed.

The last case concerns a female caller whose husband came home several months ago to find the couple's live-in domestic worker cleaning the bathroom attached to the couple's bedroom. To some Bamakois, at least, the household head's bedroom—and, by extension, any *ensuite* bath—is sacrosanct, off-limits to anyone except the husband and his wife or wives. The husband in question is so angry with his wife for allowing this breach of protocol that he is refusing to speak to her, has banned her from his bed, and has rebuffed attempts at reconciliation, even from his own mother. The studio panelists are divided. Tonton and Tiekoro sympathize with the husband (Tiekoro opines that the latter probably already had warned his wife against allowing such intrusions), but Khadidja and Youma repeat an expression, *Woro tan t'an kɛ jɔn ye*; that is, "ten kola nuts [symbolizing marriage] do not make slaves of us." They are making a larger argument about women's rights and responsibilities within marriage, and this time the panel cannot reach a consensus.

Later, Khadidja lists for me the husband's likely objections to the worker's presence in his bedroom. First, she could try to steal something; second, she should stay away to avoid tempting him sexually; third, a malefactor could have induced her, a poorly paid servant, to plant an amulet or some kind of substance intended to harm the husband or his wife. These all are valid concerns, Khadidja says, adding that many Malian men share a preoccupation with their private space. But she thinks this husband must be unusually stubborn and worries he might even divorce his wife if his family cannot persuade him to forgive her.

It is well past midnight when the two-hour show ends. Tonton offers to drive Khadidja, Youma, and me home; Tiekoro goes home alone. As we cross the bridge across the Niger River, I ask why nobody spoke up for the young man who hoped to avoid marrying his cousin. "Things are complicated here," Tonton tells me, uncertain whether an outsider like me can understand the power of tradition and elders over Mali's younger generation. In his view, Malian society took a wrong turn at independence when its ruling elite chose to follow the individualistic norms of Western modernity, granting everyone the freedom to follow their own path. This choice has led, Tonton says, to men and women's unwillingness to tolerate suffering in their relationships; to short-lived marriages; to generalized dishonesty; to the collapse of all values; and to the universalization of selfishness. Tonton claims that any woman tired of her husband can now go to a judge and falsely claim to be the victim of abuse, and the judge will side with her either because he is corrupt or because he wants to seduce her. Youma speaks up to say she knows of one such case. Before dropping me off, Tonton confides that he must be very careful to avoid saying anything on air that might not sit well with prominent listeners.

Back home, questions haunt me. Do all the panelists filter their advice to avoid scandalizing the powers that be? Can there be no middle ground between tyranny and anarchy? And has patriarchal authority in Bamako really gone kaput? Surely, I think, many listeners take comfort in hearing radio personalities say that sons should obey their fathers. Maybe this message gives them the sense that despite the disruptions to urban life and families, some things haven't changed.

What do these callers' stories and the hosts' responses tell us about what marriage in Bamako looks like today?

1

"Marriage Is an Obligation"

The Marital Life Course

Without thinking highly of men or matrimony, marriage . . . was the only honorable provision for well-educated young women of small fortune, and however uncertain of giving happiness, must be their pleasantest preservative from want.

–Jane Austen, *Pride and Prejudice* (England, 1813)

"You Need a Husband!"

"I'm single, and I'm 33 years old, and it's a disaster," Halima said wearily, provoking sympathetic laughter from a girlfriend seated nearby. Wearing Western clothes (neither conservative nor risqué) and a simple straightened hairstyle, Halima projected an image of professionalism and distinction. Though her demeanor was quite serious, her blunt manner of airing the delicate matter of her unmarried status was humorously transgressive. The only one of her parents' children yet to marry, Halima had studied abroad, earned a graduate degree, and landed a respectable job with a Bamako-based NGO at the time of our 2012 interview. Yet nothing removed the stigma of being single, especially in her own family's eyes. "When I achieve something professionally or in my education," she told me, "I bring the news to my relatives and they say 'Fine, that's good. But . . . a husband, that's what we're waiting for. Do what you like for everything else, but you need a husband!'"

The pity and concern from people outside her family was no better, Halima quickly added. "On religious holidays when they come to pay their respects, as soon as they find out you're an unmarried lady of a certain age, they gather around you to offer condolences as if you were sick! They say *Allah ka cɛko nɔgɔya* [may God help you to find a husband]. But you want to say, 'God is making it harder!'" Halima, nevertheless, held out hope for marriage on her own terms. "I don't hide my refusal to sacrifice my own career or be submissive like a baby," she told me. "From the first meeting [with a man] I talk about my intentions, how I think, and perhaps it's a bit too free for them."

This chapter begins with Halima's story and her refusal to compromise her personal and career aspirations for the sake of marriage, not because this was common in Bamako but because it was highly unusual. Women's median age at first marriage was 19.8 in Bamako, and at 18.0 in Mali, where 95 percent of women were married by the time they turned thirty (DHS 2013 and 2019).

To understand polygamy in this setting, we first must get to know the institution of marriage more broadly. This chapter explores how marriage structured the life course—the sequence of stages comprising a life—as well as how gender norms shaped marriage in Bamako and in Mali. This context will help illuminate the personal encounters with polygamy that we will examine in later chapters.

Gender and Universal Marriage

Around the globe, marriage has been receding rapidly in the twenty-first century. In the United States, the proportion of married adults has fallen since 1970. Marriage rates also dropped in countries as diverse as Russia, Brazil, and Japan; nine of ten Europeans lived in countries where marriage rates had sunk consistently since the 1970s (Cohen 2018a). And while marriage had long been considered universal on the African continent (Tabutin 1988; E. van de Walle 1968), just 27 percent of South African women age fifteen to forty-nine were currently married (Mohlabane, Gumede, and Mokomane 2019). As societies urbanized, many city dwellers either delayed marriage or forged informal unions, forgoing customary, religious, and civil ceremonies (Antoine and Marcoux 2014; Pike, Mojola, and Kabiru 2018).

For most adult Malians, however, while the experience of matrimony had altered significantly, marriage remained mandatory during the 2010s. As Halima's example suggests, it was difficult to remain single and be considered a true adult in Malian society, where respect, social status, and full personhood were contingent upon marriage (Antoine, Djiré, and Nanitelamio 1998; Brand 2001; Schulz 2012a). Living with a partner outside of marriage was exceedingly rare. In 2018, only 0.6 percent of Bamako adults were living in nonmarital cohabiting relationships, according to one survey.[1] For Malians, wrote demographer Véronique Hertrich (2013, 382), getting married was "a valued, essential and uncontested stage in the transition to adulthood." It also was viewed as an Islamic duty, as the Prophet Muhammad reportedly described marriage as "half of religion." Malians also saw marriage as a necessary precondition of motherhood, the other pillar of women's adult status (Brand 2001; Hess, Ross, and Gililland 2018). To be considered a complete person, Bamakoises needed to marry *and* bear children.

Marriage was universal for Bamakois, but it affected men and women differently. On average, men in Bamako entered marriage in their mid- to late twenties, nearly a decade later than women.[2] Women's mean age at first marriage rose gradually for years, partly because they were going to school in greater numbers and staying in school longer (Hertrich 2006). But because urban men's mean age at marriage also rose (Antoine 2006), the gap between men's and women's mean ages at first marriage—sometimes called the "differential marriage age" (Goody 1976, 64)—declined only slightly. Bamako's differential marriage age in the 2018 Demographic & Health Survey was 8.7 years, down from about ten years over the previous decade (DHS 2019). In my sample of 1,020 weddings recorded in one municipal marriage office over a twenty-five-year span, grooms were older than their brides in 95 percent of cases; brides were older than their grooms in only twenty-six cases, and were the same age in another twenty-nine. The sample's 850 first-time grooms were 8.8 years older than their brides, on average, while husbands in our interview sample were 10.5 years older than their first wives. Triangulating between these sources, I approximate Bamako's mean differential marriage age at nine years; this figure features prominently in my discussion of the city's marriage market (see chapter 5).

Husbands have tended to be older than their wives in every society and era, but Mali's nine-year average age gap was well above global norms. At the beginning of the twenty-first century, first-time grooms around the world were 3.5 years older on average than their brides.[3] Assuming that women married to much older men have less power than women married to men of similar age, we might view differential marriage age as a "proxy for female agency" (Carmichael 2011, 3): the narrower the gap, the more agency women have in society. If this interpretation is correct (I will return to it below), the nine-year gap signified Bamako women's relative lack of agency.

Wide age gaps might have been an expression of men's paternalistic views toward women. In rural Mande communities, historically, a husband was expected to "tame" and "educate" his young bride (Luneau 2010), and some husbands dispensed regular beatings intended to "correct" wives' behavior (Burrill 2015; Peterson 2011). Many Malians believed that a woman received two upbringings, first from her parents, then from her husband. In this view, a girl attained full womanhood only once marriage had shaped her character and comportment. When surveyors studying child marriage asked parents in western and northern Mali why they had married off their daughters before the age of eighteen, the most common justification was *"Pour mieux éduquer la fille"*—to better bring up/educate the girl (WILDAF 2018, 49). This marital regime rested on a power hierarchy maintained partly through gender-based violence, but more through gendered norms and economic imperatives.

Some Bamakoises expressed a preference for older husbands. Mamou (F, 31, secretary, one co-wife), a wife in our interview sample, reported having broken up with a boyfriend prior to marriage because they were the same age. "In my understanding of things, the man must be older than the woman," she said. At the time of her interview, Mamou was in her second marriage, to a man fifteen years her senior whom she called "Papa." Like many wives in Bamako, she observed a prohibition on calling her husband by his first name; husbands had no reciprocal prohibition.[4]

The high differential marriage age was not due primarily to individual or cultural preferences, however. "I think it's economic," one woman in a focus group responded when asked why men married so much later than women in Bamako. "It takes time to save up the money to get married and start a family. So it's always later that men get married, and then they always take someone much younger than they are, whereas a woman wants to get married right away, and there's nobody her age who's ready."

Indeed, evidence suggests that Bamako men's later entry into marriage stemmed from their delayed entry into economic activity (Antoine and Djiré 1998; Hertrich 2006; Hertrich 2013). Young men wishing to marry could seldom do so amid the economic constraints of urban life (described in this book's introduction).[5] High unemployment and soaring costs associated with the transition to married life obliged many Bamako men to remain single into their thirties.

Chief among these costs were housing, wedding-related expenses, and bridewealth—that is, payments by the groom or his family to the bride or her family prior to marriage. Such payments were required under both Mande and Islamic custom. While Malian law capped bridewealth payments at 10,000 francs (about US$20), grooms in twenty-first-century Bamako frequently paid 500,000 francs (US$1,000) or more, well over Mali's per capita annual income.[6] Men spent years saving to meet these costs and establish households. As for romance, young urbanites certainly dated and fell in love, but this activity often was unrelated to their marriage plans (Doquet 2014; cf. Hannaford 2017). A young woman might have a passionate romantic relationship with a young man while fully expecting to have to marry someone else—namely, an older, more economically established man with whom her bond might revolve less around emotional intimacy than the everyday requirements of childrearing, managing a household, and caring for his parents. "I know young women who had their own boyfriends, they'd studied together and loved each other and everything, but at a certain moment, the guys wanted more social stability before committing themselves, so the women married the first men who proposed to them," said Penda, a female journalist in her twenties whom I interviewed in 2010.

Unlike males, most females in Bamako married while still in their teens. Social expectations and economic imperatives made it difficult for young women to delay marriage, and female interviewees reported that their greatest fear before marrying was failing to find a husband. For some Bamakoises I met, especially later in the decade, the deadline to move out was in their mid- or even late twenties.[7] Fatou, another educated, cosmopolitan professional like Halima, was at age twenty-eight grappling with her unmarried status when I spoke to her in 2012. As she put it to me:

It's hard to find a man you love and who has the financial means, all of that together—it's difficult. And women don't give themselves time to look; by a certain age, if they don't find one, they stick to somebody. . . . At a certain age, 22, 23, 24, 25, girls still dream of a prince charming. But from age 25, they wake up one morning and say, "My God, I'm 25!" And they start to go over the list of suitors they'd rejected.

Other women, especially those who had grown up in poor households, felt the deadline looming even earlier in their lives. A wife named Sadjo (F, 22, market vendor, no co-wife) opined that "from age 15, a girl no longer has the right to stay with her parents."

Malian families tend to be patrilineal (meaning that kinship is traced and property inherited through the father's line) and patrilocal (meaning that brides move in with their husband's families upon marriage).[8] A daughter in this context is regarded as a temporary member of her parents' household, since she will depart after marriage (Ba Konaré 1993). Halima explained why families pressured their daughters to marry and leave their natal homes:

In your parents' home you're seen as the one who will leave someday. . . . Economically, a woman cannot remain with her father; when the sons marry, their wives move in with them, so there's less and less space for her. She needs to go somewhere else. Culturally, even when she has a degree and she works, she cannot get her own place and live alone; that's really something else. So the first place she finds to settle down, she'll take it.

Here, Halima pinpointed a gender norm she knew from personal experience: women, even educated ones who provided for themselves economically, were virtually unable to live independently of husbands, fathers, or other male kin. The obstacles to women living on their own were largely cultural, not legal, and stemmed from narrow collective definitions of women's place in society. "So long as she is unmarried, she exists only as her father's daughter, thus as a child," Bamako resident, novelist, and essayist Moussa Konaté put it (2010, 54). "From the moment she marries, she is placed under the authority of another man, her husband." There was almost no space in which she could live respectably by herself.[9] A married woman like Sira, considering whether to divorce her husband (see this book's introduction), had to take this fact into account. Single women in Bamako were, in the words of anthropologist Saskia Brand (2001, 125), a "subversive category: they undermine the rules of the game." Halima described matters more starkly: "An unmarried woman is like a pestilence in society."

Furu ye waajibi ye, says a Manding proverb: "Marriage is an obligation." To become complete adults, young people simply had to marry. But while marriage was universal, its place in the life course was different for males and females.

A young man could delay his entry to marriage as he worked to establish himself and accumulate resources. Unlike daughters, sons often could expect a place in their parental home until and often after marriage. "In general, the family doesn't really want their son to marry a woman and move out, live in a different house," said Fily, an unmarried thirty-year-old male civil servant whom I interviewed in 2011. "They prefer that the child stay at home, to help his mother out." And after exiting a marriage, a man might remain single for years, even indefinitely but a woman usually had to stay married until she died, except for brief interludes. Since many Bamakoises perceived a shortage of eligible men (see chapter 5), they feared being labeled as too discriminating toward suitors. Some simply succumbed to pressure, finding it easier to settle for unappealing husbands than to remain single.

A woman like Fatou or Halima who held out past the age of twenty-five for an ideal suitor faced diminishing prospects. With enough money, she might find a mate needier than she. She might, like the Senegalese women studied by Kringelbach (2016a), "marry out" with a foreign, often Western, husband. She might become a wealthy man's second, third, or fourth wife (cf. LeBlanc 2007). Otherwise, she might conceive a child with a boyfriend in hope of marrying him later—a risky strategy, but four of the fifty wives in our interview sample nonetheless volunteered that they had followed this path.[10] Along with remaining single, these were a young woman's options. The strictures of universal marriage pressed more lightly on Bamako's men, who could take more time to answer its call. The pressure on women to marry, and to marry young, frequently led them into polygamous marriages they would not otherwise have considered.

The "I Love You" Era: Companionate Marriage and Its Discontents

Malians' marriages once were arranged mostly between extended families or clans. Such unions cemented bonds between kin groups, made or maintained political alliances, elevated a family's social standing, or redistributed productive and reproductive resources both between and within communities and households (B. Camara 2011; Hertrich 2007; Meillassoux 1981; Schulz 2012a)—all functions familiar to readers of nineteenth-century English novelists like Jane Austen and to followers of the British royal family.

In many Mande villages, even into the twenty-first century, elders would arrange a *balima furu* (kin marriage) between two junior relatives, preferably paternal cross cousins. Two families seeking brides for their sons might exchange daughters in a *falen* or sister exchange marriage (Burrill 2015; I. Camara 2002; Grosz-Ngaté 1988). The reciprocity of such marriages eliminated the need for bridewealth payments between families.

Some unions were forced. In the southern Wasulu area in the 1800s, a girl refusing to marry the man chosen for her could be tied by the neck and beaten by her father, while a young man unwilling to accept his arranged marriage might flee his village (Peterson 2011). Still, in the 2010s, some Malian parents (mostly in rural areas) betrothed their children before they were old enough to walk, and a teen's consent was by no means sought, let alone required, for a union to be finalized. Many families regarded a romantic bond between partners with suspicion. Ibrahima Camara, professor of educational sciences, described how marriages were established in Mali's southern Wasulu area in the late twentieth century:

> Matters of sentiment must be attended to, but they are not at the heart of the process. Marriage is an institution which cannot be left to the vagaries of impulse, however noble they may be. . . . Many parents continue to intimidate their daughters into accepting the boys they propose. The child "belongs" to the group [i.e., the father's patrilineage], which is concerned primarily with perpetuating itself: all desire for autonomy in such a central domain can only be viewed as unnatural and dangerous. (2002, 210)

Solo, an unmarried man in his twenties, explained to me in 2012 how the process of arranging a marriage might begin in Bamako.

> Suppose I'm the head of a family and I see that my son is reaching the age to marry. I start visiting families, looking for one that raises their children right. I see a girl there and try to find out if I might have her for my son. But I won't make the initial approach—generally I'll send an emissary, a *jeli*[11] who will ask if the girl is available and say that so-and-so wants her [to marry] his son. That's the first contact. And the girl's family won't agree until they've been satisfied on a few points. Did the young man in question have a good upbringing? What does he do for work? What's his religion? After all this, they put their two children in contact. If they like each other or think it can work out, that's when things get going.

While arranged marriages remained common in rural Mali in the twenty-first century (see, e.g., Diarra 2018; Kassogué 2014; Toulmin 2020), young Malian urbanites preferred to choose their own spouses, whether for monogamous or polygamous marriages (Brand 2001; Castro 2012; Doquet 2014; Sølbeck 2010; Whitehouse 2016). Rather than let parents make the match for them, they wanted to initiate their own matchmaking process, following criteria of mutual romantic attraction and affection, before presenting their desired mate for parental approval. "People used to marry much more for family, people insisted much more on family relations, and they searched for a mate within a family that got along well with their family, or a family they knew well," Nanténé, a twenty-five-year-old unmarried female interviewee explained in 2012. "But today it's very individual: the man meets the woman at work, or on Facebook—in ways unimaginable 30 years ago."

Male elders, who previously controlled the marriage process for the young men and women in their charge and who now sensed their power slipping away, complained that *du fanga tiyenna*—or, as memorably translated by anthropologist Dorothea Schulz (2012b, 48), "patriarchal authority has gone kaput."[12] Fathers could compel sons to enter arranged marriages (see Interlude 1), but such cases were exceptional in twenty-first-century Bamako. By the last decades of the twentieth century, as their elders' power declined, young people increasingly claimed the right to find their own spouses, and some Bamakois referred to their times as *n b'i fɛ tile*—the era of "I love you" (Miseli 1998, 33).

Romantic love is a nearly universal, cross-cultural, and timeless phenomenon (Jankowiak and Fischer 1992); people falling in love in modern Mali experienced nothing new by doing so. Two romantic ideals were relatively novel (i.e., only a few generations old), though contested: 1) the notion that a romantic bond constituted a necessary, even sufficient, justification for marriage; and 2) the notion that young people were best positioned to make decisions about something as crucial as their own marriage partners.[13] Through consumption of global media (notably Hollywood films and Latin American *telenovelas* dubbed into French), a generation of Malian youth became steeped in these twin notions, leading to enormous shifts in romantic and marital expectations (Brand 2001; Doquet 2014; Schulz 2007; Sølbeck 2010).

The "I love you" era brought sexual complications and risks. Where Mande families once demanded that brides marrying into their households be virgins (Brett-Smith 2014; I. Camara 2002; Golaszewski 2020), having intercourse before marriage became the norm for Bamakois of both sexes and was no longer stigmatized in most families (A. Diallo 2004). In a study asking urban Malian females to identify their primary motivation for their first sexual encounter, 65 percent of respondents named "love" (Gueye, Castle, and Konaté 2001). While seldom openly discussed, premarital sex was commonplace, and parents bemoaned their inability to monitor and control their children's sexuality. Median age at first sexual activity in Bamako was about seventeen for women and twenty for men (DHS 2013 and 2019), and many Bamakois had come to regard sex as "not only normal, but an essential part of any fulfilled relationship" (Boileau et al. 2008, 178).

An unmarried male focus group participant explained his views on premarital sex: "Love doesn't just mean sex, but if I have a girlfriend and refuse to make love to her, she'll say 'I must be dating a woman!' So to show her that I'm a man, I take action. And I don't think it's a sin." Even conservative Muslim men and women in our interview sample described premarital sex as normal and unavoidable—provided that it led to marriage. Young urban Malians increasingly used modern contraception to control their fertility (Coulibaly 2014) and learned about sex from online pornography produced in the United States or Europe; girls expected greater "reciprocity of pleasure" in their sexual relations (Doquet 2014, 408).

Opportunities for love and sex before marriage were more plentiful in the 2010s in part because Bamakois were marrying later. Thanks to longer schooling, delayed entry into employment, and changing social norms, most young Bamakois were experiencing a stage of youth marked by continued economic dependence but heightened social autonomy extending several years from the end of childhood/schooling until the onset of marriage (Sauvain-Dugerdil and Ritschard 2009; Schulz 2012a). This stage lasted longer for males than for females due to the differential marriage age. Such a life stage would have been unthinkable to many elders, who had transitioned directly from childhood to marriage and adulthood.

Based on the above synopsis, Bamako's "I love you" era might seem like a familiar modernization tale: rather than remain bound by the retrograde demands of kin, young people followed their hearts (to use a well-worn romantic phrase) toward more enlightened gender roles and individual romantic fulfillment in marriage. In short, one might conclude that Bamakois were becoming more modern by embracing companionate marriage, "a marital ideal in which emotional closeness is understood to be both one of the primary measures of success in marriage and a central practice through which the relationship is constituted and reinforced" (Wardlow and Hirsch 2006, 4). This ideal entails some core assumptions: that one deserves happiness in marriage, that one must choose one's spouse, and that one's spousal relationship should take priority over relationships with kin (including parents).

The apparent global trend toward companionate marriage is a compelling but oversimplified story. Scholars working in Africa (Cole and Thomas 2009) and elsewhere have observed tensions roiling beneath its surface. Below, I address four such tensions observable in Bamako, all of which, as I will explore later, also impacted polygamous marriage.

The Power of Elders

First, the cultural "old guard" had by no means conceded the struggle for influence over marriage formation. Patriarchal authority, while diminished, could still determine and even block many Bamakois' marriage plans (see Interlude 1). Fully twenty-three of the fifty wives in our interview sample reported that their marriages had been arranged for them; many had married before coming to the city, but even among those who had spent most of their lives in Bamako, nearly a third of unions were arranged. Men sometimes consented to marry brides they had never chosen, at least for their first marriages (we will explore their second marriages in chapter 2). Men lacking the means to attract a bride could be more or less compelled into marriages arranged and funded by their families. "Many men, when they married their first wives, didn't have much money," a married man in his thirties said of his peers during a focus group discussion. "Their elders found wives for them. And when these elders made these matches, [the young men] were obliged to go along with them." Even as young people of both sexes expressed their intention to choose their own spouses, Bamako families continued to complicate their plans and even impose arranged marriages in significant numbers.

Arranged marriage had its supporters. Some Mande traditionalists, citing an alleged thirteenth-century charter, claimed a father's right to choose a husband for his daughter at any age without the latter's consent (B. Camara 2011). For others, protecting family honor required marrying off a daughter before she might get pregnant (O. Koné 2015; cf. Cooper 2019). Resistance to notions of individual rights and emotional fulfillment also came from families, elders, and sometimes young people themselves (Whitehouse 2016). They saw efforts by the Malian state, foreign governments, and NGOs to eradicate forced marriage and promote women's rights as unwelcome intrusions into family affairs. They also rejected the assumptions that love ought to be the primary basis for marriage and that decisions about marriage are best left to young people themselves. Their objections stemmed from cultural and Islamic values and from concern that sidelining elders from the marriage formation process had led to fragile unions and social decay. Yacouba (M, 67, market vendor, three wives), a husband in our interview sample said:

> These days, young people meet each other, then inform their parents [of their intent to marry] without asking questions first, like "Are his or her parents good Muslims? Are they nobles?" They don't get these details. A guy just sees a woman with big breasts, a nice ass, and falls for her—but it won't last. You can't just meet a girl in the street and marry her! Among those who do, the unhappy outnumber the happy ones.

Customary approaches to marriage in Bamako rested on different philosophical underpinnings than companionate marriage. Over the uniqueness of the sovereign individual, conservatives and traditionalists valued the inherent duality or "twoness" of living things, foregrounding the person's embeddedness in webs of social obligation (Burrill 2015, 32).[14] Wary of the individualism implicit in romantic ideals, they saw spousal choice as a poor substitute for the wisdom of kin in marriage decisions. A report by a Bamako women's association evoked a reason for such wariness: "Until recently, the omnipresence of kin in every matrimonial transaction acted as a safeguard. The husband respected his wife and stayed in the marriage because he was bound by solid obligations, by an engagement contracted not between him and his wife but between his family and hers. Mutual choice makes all of that disappear. Parents are no longer consulted and no longer wish to intervene" (Miseli 1998, 31).

Elders in one rural community saw marriage as "too serious a matter to be founded on the caprice of youth who often do not truly know what they want or what is good for them" (I. Camara 2002, 194). Allowing young people to choose their own spouses, many Bamakois believed, had made the courtship process more opaque and vulnerable to false promises, misrepresentation, and betrayal, leaving marriages more prone to conflict and divorce.[15] Nor was it generally believed that love conquered all. While interethnic romances and marriages were commonplace throughout Mali, taboos still restricted marriage and dating across certain social distinctions, especially caste, though these strictures had softened somewhat under the influence of Islam.[16]

The notion that Malian society has been steadily evolving toward marital freedom of choice ignores the impossibility of disembedding choice and consent from economic- and kin-related imperatives. French administrators during the early twentieth century, viewing the practice of marriage in their African colonies as a form of women's slavery, thought it part of their "civilizing mission" to eliminate forced marriage by setting minimum age requirements and mandating the bride's and groom's explicit consent before a union could be formalized under law. But because African marriage remained "a messy engagement [that] could not be excised from other social obligations, labor and kin relationships, and political interests" (Burrill 2015, 158; cf. Cooper 1997 and Osborn 2011), these measures never succeeded. After Mali's independence, President Modibo Keita's nationalist regime similarly sought to modernize marriage and promote individual liberties, enacting laws to promote the nuclear family, end forced marriage, limit bridewealth payments, emancipate young people from domination by their elders, guarantee women's rights within marriage, and establish civil marriage as the sole legal form of marriage. These progressive measures were, likewise, widely defied in practice (see chapter 6).

Many Malian families, therefore, continued to arrange their sons' initial marriages, leaving those men free to choose their second or subsequent wives (see chapter 2). As for women, 61 percent of Malian females married before the age of eighteen (Diarra 2018). Throughout the Sahel region, fears of economic hardship and elders' retribution often combined to push girls into marriage. It is worth asking what "choice" means where social pressure is strong (cf. Dial 2008, 75; Paré 2018).

The Power of In-Laws

A second tension unsettling companionate ideals stemmed from the continuing role of kin in established marriages. A husband and wife might be compatible with each other, but what if she doesn't get along with his parents—especially when they live under the same roof? Many an engagement was called off after conflicts arose between the bride-to-be and her prospective mother-in-law. Owing to Bamako's patrilineal and patrilocal kinship pattern, the right of the husband's parents (and, to a lesser degree, his siblings and other kin) to have a say in his and his wife's everyday lives remained firmly entrenched, and wives bore the burden of their in-laws' constant surveillance, criticism, and demands for labor.[17]

A wife should "love the husband's parents the same way she loves her own parents," one female jeli told me in 2012; "They become her parents too." A woman's ability to get along with her future in-laws was a key criterion by which others judged her suitability as a wife. Fily, the thirty-year-old bachelor, told me that this ability was "the first thing I look at, because if she doesn't get along with my parents, she'll never get along with me." He expected that, once married, he would spend most of his time at work, while his wife would spend most of hers at home with his parents. Thus, Fily saw it as essential that he not marry someone who would sow division in his family. No husband could be seen to love his wife as much as he loved his mother (let alone more).[18] When husbands must make their parents' satisfaction their top priority, and when parents pressure sons on where to reside, when to have children, and whether to take additional wives, couples struggle to form solid, trusting companionate relationships. "Very often, when we have a case of divorce, the problem isn't between the man and his wife," said Issiaka, an imam in the Torokorobougou neighborhood who had mediated many marital disputes, during our 2012 interview; "It's between his mother and the new bride."

Romance and Finance

"Ever since marriage became a form of business, it has no dignity anymore," sang Bamako-born Oumou Sangaré, one of Mali's most beloved musicians.[19] Her lyrics addressed the tension between emotional intimacy and material needs. Around the world, many people have viewed romantic affection as intrinsically at odds with economic considerations, associating the former with selflessness and the latter with greed. Just as Americans generally scorned people who "marry for money," Bamakois decried young women's alleged tendency to marry for economic self-interest. They saw young single women as easily induced to trade sexual favors for money, whether in their romantic relationships or in commercial sex transactions; the distinction between these categories was murky (Castro 2014; Grange Omokaro 2009; Neubauer 2016). Young women's alleged materialism and sexual libertinage have been topics of perennial media moralizing since the 1960s (Burrill 2020; Mann 2015).

The problem is that romance and finance, affect and exchange, are not separate realms but "mutually constitutive" (Cole and Thomas 2009, 20). Even sincere romantic relationships are often structured by economic exchange, such as gift giving or payment of specific expenses by the male partner. Where poverty is rife, and where a young woman's acceptance of a marriage proposal could potentially transform her economic prospects, one can scarcely expect romantic attachments to be unaffected by material needs and incentives. Yet many Bamakois I spoke with believed that young people's desires for consumer goods and the trappings of modern life (cash, cars, and fancy houses) had eclipsed true love, pitting young women and men against each other in the pursuit of selfish interests, with women usually singled out as the villains.[20] "Money has messed up everything now" was among the most common observations about how marriage had changed over time, alongside remarks about increasing individual liberties. "Decisions about marriage didn't used to be based on money, but on values—what kind of family a person was from," said Safiatou (F, 22, market vendor, one co-wife). "But these days if you're rich, you can have any woman you want. I mean, we have abandoned our fundamental principles for money." Many women who agreed to become the second, third, or fourth wives of already-married men were singled out for special blame in this regard (see chapter 2).

Expectations of Infidelity

The final tension arose at the crossroads of love, marriage, and sexuality. Companionate marriage's emphasis on fidelity has always been difficult to meet. While many interviewees and focus group participants stated that Malian husbands and wives used to be faithful to each other in some fondly recalled past, they opined that marital infidelity ran rampant in present-day Bamako (see chapter 4). Many Bamakois associated romantic love with a relationship's courtship phase, leading anthropologist Anne Doquet (2014, 398) to observe that "men seem to pamper and respect their mistresses more than their wives. The notions of sharing and intimacy seem to vanish with the formal onset of marriage." Issiaka, the imam, echoed this observation: "The problem today is that after a wife enters [her husband's] home, she's abandoned. When the husband wants to go out to the cinema it will be with another woman. He's already forgotten about his wife at home. . . . You sense that six months or a year after the wedding, trouble has begun." And young Bamakois reported that fidelity had become unusual even during courtship, as unmarried men and women alike maintained multiple concurrent romantic relations to maximize their opportunities for sex, material gain, and, eventually, marriage.

After a bride moved in with her husband, she was expected to submit to the authority he and his family wielded over her. Under these circumstances, forging a strong pair bond based on mutual trust was especially difficult. "We speak of couples in Mali but that's not really what it's about," Aisha, a married interviewee in her thirties told me in 2012. (A recurring theme in this book is that marriage was often *not really about the couple* in Bamako.[21]) All these tensions undermined the couple and forced romantic ideals to take a back seat to more pragmatic marital considerations.

These factors seriously undermined the ideal of modern companionate marriage in Bamako, such that young people regarded it with ambivalence. On the one hand, they were enticed by the possibilities of liberation from burdensome collective duties to kin in general (and, for women, to their in-laws in particular) and of emotional fulfillment through the couple. On the other hand, they feared being deceived by their romantic partners, and they knew that defying their families by following their hearts into a love match might cost them valuable support and isolate them in the event of a breakup. Young women in particular had to reconcile their expectations of companionate marriage with their social context. The evolution of marriage toward mutual choice had not necessarily given wives a more equal footing with their husbands (see chapter 5; see, also, Miseli 1998). Malian society's patrilineal and patrilocal kinship structure, gender norms, homosocial expectations,[22] and economic precarity all worked against couples' autonomy, fostering a "climate of defiance between spouses that interferes with the development of relations of conjugal solidarity" (Hertrich 2006, 42; see, also, Adams and Castle 1994).

Yet despite its difficulties, marriage remained the best way for young Malians to acquire social status and economic security (Hertrich 2013; Schulz 2012a). Therefore, while marriage in Bamako in the 2010s was vastly different from what it had been a generation or two earlier, it had converged only superficially with Western companionate models. This generations-long tug of war between individual marital aspirations and family interests showed no sign of easing.[23] Meanwhile, young Bamakois downgraded their expectations of romantic love, enabling men and women alike to reconcile themselves more easily with polygamous marriage.

Gender Roles and Expectations within Marriage

In the Manding language, a sentence equivalent to "the woman married the man" would be nonsensical; a man may marry a woman, but not the other way around. As linguist Kassim Koné (2002, 24) pointed out in his study of Bamanan gender relations, such framings of marriage put wives "in the patient and subordinate position."

Patience and subordination were, indeed, among the qualities of a good wife that Bamakois frequently cited in interviews, conversations, and focus group discussions. The Manding verb *muɲu*, found in cognate form in several other West African languages, might be translated as "to bear patiently." A more colloquial translation would be "to suck it up"—to accept a difficult or painful situation and deal with it stoically. In many West African cultures and in Islam more broadly, the uncomplaining endurance of suffering and hardship has been represented as a virtue for both sexes (K. Ali and Leaman 2007; Ngom 2016). My research suggests that in the context of Bamako marriage, however, *muɲu* was hardly gender-neutral. Subjects cited it dozens of times in reference to wives, yet almost never in reference to husbands.

One woman in our interview sample applied this virtue to a wife "who puts up with the caprices of her husband, her in-laws, and her neighbors." A good wife was expected to put up with many such burdens. It was not that she was prohibited from protesting or complaining if her husband neglected her emotionally or materially, if he was sexually unfaithful or physically abusive. It was merely that she was supposed to anticipate such problems in marriage and bear them nobly. By doing so, she gained esteem in the eyes of society and favor in the eyes of God.

Here lay an important divergence in gendered expectations within marriage. While a woman patiently tolerating her husband's infidelity deserved social and religious reward, a man patiently tolerating his wife's infidelity was considered a fool. A husband would be fully within his rights to divorce an unfaithful wife; indeed, he could be criticized for not doing so. As interviewee Fatou phrased it ironically, "A woman doesn't have the right to make a mistake, and a man mustn't accept a woman who makes mistakes. But the wife must always tolerate it." (We return to this sexual double standard in chapter 4.) Women like Sira came to expect their husbands to stray and knew that those extramarital relationships could easily turn into polygamy.

The stakes for women were doubly high because, as mothers, they were seen as solely responsible for their children's moral character. A woman's ability to endure patiently—like other virtues such as obedience—brought long-term reward to her children, they believed (Ba Konaré 1993; de Jorio 2009). Aisha, a professional woman, told me that "whatever a woman does will come back to her children. When a woman behaves well, one way or another her children will benefit from that." A child enjoying good fortune or success would likely be hailed as a credit to her mother. Conversely, a child's misfortune could be considered proof of his mother's bad behavior and failure to *muɲu*. These notions found expression in the Manding saying *bɛɛ b'i ba bolo*—literally, "everyone is in their mothers' arms," but better rendered as "each man's destiny is forged by his mother for good and for ill" (A. Tounkara 2015, 199). By accepting suffering and submitting to her husband's will, a wife built up spiritual power (*barika*) that safeguarded her children's fates (Ba Konaré 1993; Kai 2014; M. Konaté 2010). "It's God Himself who made things this way, women must accept male domination for their children to succeed in life and become responsible men," a woman told sociologist Aly Tounkara (2015, 75); "A woman who acts like a man will give birth to villainous children who won't amount to anything in life."[24]

Bamakoises learned from girlhood to understand marriage as a tribulation to be endured as much as a partnership to be savored, an investment in their children's future more than in their own emotional fulfillment. Forbearance was their most important asset for withstanding this trial and raising good children, thereby redeeming their sacrifices and gaining social recognition.[25]

A shift in the timing of civil wedding ceremonies hints at the importance of *munu* as a wifely virtue in the early twenty-first century. More and more weddings in the city were being celebrated in the two months prior to Ramadan, the month of fasting. One municipal official told me that, in some parts of Bamako, two-thirds of the year's weddings took place during this short pre-Ramadan period. We could link this trend partly to increasing religiosity and partly to the construction of marriage as a woman's tribulation. During Ramadan, the new bride would rise earlier than everyone else in the house to start preparing the pre-dawn meal. From dawn to dusk she (along with other adults) would abstain from food and drink and would bear these burdens while going about her usual chores, acclimating to her husband's household, and often learning to live with demanding in-laws.

Regarding sexual relations, a wife was expected to be available to her husband unless she was menstruating or ill. This expectation was framed as both a cultural value and an Islamic obligation. Sometimes the expectation was voiced in reciprocal terms, as with one participant in a focus group discussion of unmarried males: "Conjugal satisfaction is required of the wife by her husband, and required of the husband by his wife," the young man said, immediately adding, "A wife who must be beaten before accepting her husband in bed cannot be considered well raised." Wives were not supposed to say no to their husbands; those who did faced a higher risk of gender-based violence. Yet the conjugal reality could be more nuanced, as Aisha suggested in our interview:

> You can refuse him, but there's a way to do it. You're not a machine, either! There are days when you're tired out from housework, but there's still a way [to say no]. It all depends on your way of proceeding that determines whether things will get serious or not. I have my own manner. In religion you're told never to say no.[26]

A wife had to be careful in refusing her husband, given the possible sanctions. A wife's protracted refusal of conjugal relations would be legitimate grounds for her husband to divorce her (A. Tounkara 2015, 72).

Domestically, a wife's duties included such tasks as "cooking, shopping, housekeeping, fetching water, doing laundry, [and] keeping watch over the home and the upbringing of the children" (A. Tounkara 2015, 90). Although most households with sufficient means employed at least one girl domestic worker (see introduction), and many women shared domestic duties with co-wives, even well-off Bamakoises could not entirely outsource these duties. Wives could not escape the obligation to prepare meals for their husbands, since women feared that poorly fed husbands were more likely to stray (de Suremain and Razy 2011, 260), an insecurity fueled by constant television commercials warning wives against letting their husbands' appetites wander (cook with Maggi spice cubes, one ad suggested, and your man will be content to eat at home).

Domesticity, thus, remained at the core of daily life for married women, whether they worked outside the home or not. Even though more than half the city's women reported being employed (DHS 2013 and 2019; INSTAT 2018), the largest occupational category for Bamako women was "housewife" (in French, *ménagère* or *femme au foyer*; see Rondeau 1996).[27] A woman's own economic activity in no way diminished her incentive to represent her domestic role of wife and mother as her primary responsibility; such representation justified her participation in the labor market to her husband and in-laws (Bertrand 2004).

A wife might use her own money to pay for her cooking utensils, clothing, and social and personal expenses. Eighty-eight percent of Bamako women reported that they alone decided how to spend the money they earned (DHS 2019). Husbands, by contrast, were supposed to be their households' primary or even sole providers. Under a "patriarchal bargain" (discussed further in chapter 4), Bamako residents tacitly accepted a set of gender relations leaving women with reduced autonomy in exchange for economic protection. It was incumbent on husbands to acquire and maintain their families' dwellings, give their wives money for all purchases of food, and cover dependents' health care and school fees (Miseli 1998). Household heads had to receive guests, including relatives from out of town, with hospitality. A man's duty to house his dependents was central to his identity, and a married woman was always at least nominally housed by her husband. A polygamous husband had to house all his wives, often in separate dwellings (see chapter 3). Asked to cite the qualities of a good husband, most interviewees began with "good provider," making this quality the masculine counterpart to wives' stoic submission. Men also were supposed to control the mobility, labor, and marriages of their households' younger members (Bertrand 2013; Meillassoux 1981). Men were the official arbiters in all important matters concerning their households and wives. Most Bamako women reported that they lacked final say over their own health care, major purchases, or even making visits to family and friends; that power lay with husbands (DHS 2013 and 2019).

If the husband's formal role as decision-maker and authority figure held relatively constant, his capacity as breadwinner was undermined by Bamako's economic conditions. The high unemployment and rising costs of living put tremendous strain on men's ability to earn incomes and provide for their families (especially if they had multiple wives), jeopardizing the terms of the patriarchal bargain. Husbands struggled to meet dependents' demands for hospitality and economic support, leading many wives to contribute their own earnings toward household expenses such as food and housing (Bertrand 2013; Marie 2011; Miseli 1998; Rondeau 1996). They had to be careful, however, not *to be seen* to supplement, let alone usurp, their husbands' roles as economic providers (de Suremain and Razy 2011). Moreover, wives feared that their household contributions could end up subsidizing husbands' extramarital affairs. With enough savings, a wife might invest in her own house to hedge against her husband's future betrayal, such as his taking a mistress or additional wife (Dougnon 2020; Miseli 1998; cf. Boltz and Chort 2016).

Women's increased economic importance was clearly altering the city's gendered political economy. "Women have changed completely!" exclaimed a radio host in 2011 when I asked how marriage had changed since her parents' generation. "Now, if a woman doesn't have means, men don't want her anymore. You must have resources, a car. . . . If you don't, he'll leave you. Now women are buying clothes for their men, cars even, everything." This scenario, alarming to many traditionalists, suggested that wives were gaining the financial upper hand. Men continued to dominate their households economically, overall, but interviewees agreed that men had lost much of their influence over their dependents' marriages, and that women had gained.

Men had seen their authority erode, especially in their dependents' marriage formation process. "There are household heads who, when someone comes to ask for their daughter's hand, say 'Go with her mother to agree on it,'" said Madou (M, 46, civil servant, two wives). "This means that men have really given up, may God preserve us!" Ali (M, 39, unemployed, one wife) concurred: "Men sit at home today and are in control of nothing. It's women who manage the household, that's clear. Parental authority has been chipped away, and the consequences have been enormous and dramatic." Several women in our interview sample opined that senior men's role in marriage had narrowed to approving a match, while female elders increasingly handled everything from initial negotiations to bridewealth payments and wedding-related expenses (cf. Buggenhagen 2012).

Yet, although the ideal of a husband as both economic provider and ultimate authority in family matters no longer matched marital reality for many Bamakois, women continued to pay tribute to it (A. Diallo 2009). Only under exceptional conditions—if her husband was deceased, or durably absent—could a woman claim the title of household head. Growing numbers of women became de facto household heads when men came up short as breadwinners (Marie 2011).[28]

As women's greater household responsibilities impinged on male authority, a new figure emerged at the end of the twentieth century: the nominal husband of an economically self-sufficient woman. Their union helped the woman conform to gendered social expectations regarding marriage but made minimal demands on her time and, by providing the social cover of matrimony, preserved her de facto independence.[29] Such a husband of convenience typically had multiple wives who lived separately and seldom encountered each other (Rondeau 1996). Having wives who did not depend financially on him left his true status as household head open to question.[30]

Polygamy, Remarriage, and Polygamy Again

Divorce and remarriage were common and helped maintain polygamy's prominence throughout West Africa, where up to half of women were no longer in their
first union by age fifty (Dial 2008; Kaufmann, Lesthaeghe, and Meekers 1988).
Some of my Bamako informants framed divorce as a product of the many challenges confronting marriage in the culturally and morally degraded conditions
of the neoliberal era—particularly materialism, selfishness, and a lack of respect
for custom. Interviewees and focus group participants frequently evoked divorce
as a sign of everything wrong with modern marriage, in contrast to an imagined
earlier time when husbands and wives stayed married for life. "In the past, our
mothers were submissive, there wasn't so much change, and people lived in
peace," said Keletigi (M, 56, researcher, one wife). "Now, there are all these problems, there are too many divorces. Everything has changed because there are
too many divorces."

But such views, while widespread, were tinged with more amnesia than nos-
talgia. The temptation to decry divorce as a recent or alien phenomenon overlooked its deep historical roots throughout Mali (Burrill 2015) as well as its place
in Islamic legal tradition (initiated by either the wife or the husband). A wife's
degree of economic autonomy correlated with her odds of divorce: the higher
her own income, the likelier she was to get divorced (Antoine 2006).

Although divorce was perceived to be widespread in Bamako, it carried
stigma as well as serious economic and social consequences for women, making
them reluctant to choose this option. "Divorce is like a failure," said Batogoma,
a women's rights activist I met with in 2012:

> When you marry, you're told, "You must submit, you must accept every-
> thing in order to stay in this marriage." Why do women in Mali stay in
> households where they're victims of violence? Because once you leave your
> father's home you no longer have a place there; it's taken by someone else.
> And if you ever do go back to your paternal family, it's like revisiting your
> failure, and the people there will keep reminding you of it.

In Bamako's patrilineal system, a divorced woman forfeited considerable control over the upbringing of her children, who would remain in their father's kin
group. Divorce often also meant having to support herself economically.

Most importantly, divorce was intimately tied to polygamy in Bamako. Taking a second wife raised a husband's likelihood of divorce with his first wife by
over 400 percent, making polygamy the city's leading cause of divorce (Antoine,
Djiré, and Nanitelamio 1998). And women's quick remarriage following divorce
or widowhood remained a prominent feature of West African marriage systems:
any woman without a husband was pressured to remarry.[31] Because few men

took previously married women as their first wives, many such women had to enter polygamous unions—in other words, they had to swap one polygamous husband for another (Dial 2008 and 2014). Fifty-five percent of Senegalese women's second marriages and 72 percent of third marriages in the early 1990s were to polygamous men (Antoine and Nanitelamio 1996). In urban Mali, survey data showed that while about 25 percent of women in their first marriages had co-wives, 38 percent of divorcees and 69 percent of widows did (D. van de Walle 2013). Divorce and widowhood were major drivers of polygamy. A woman's marital career might begin with monogamous marriage before moving to polygamy, widowhood, or divorce followed by polygamy (cf. Jennaway 2013; Wittrup 1990). Women's remarriages, therefore, sustained high rates of plural marriage.

In Senegal, a type of union known as *takkoo* wove together the threads of remarriage, women's autonomy, and the husband of convenience discussed above. Antoine (2018, 28) defined takkoo as a woman's "symbolic marriage to an already married man, often a friend or someone close to the deceased [husband]. This form of marriage seems to liberate women from suspicion of not wanting to remarry, while allowing them to remain in their dwellings, maintain their routines and keep their independence." Because takkoo generally concerned older widows and divorcees, sociologist Sadio Ba Gning (2011) likened it to "retirement polygamy" (see also Dial 2008). It originated as a form of levirate marriage wherein a man "inherited" a wife from his deceased brother—another example of the needs of the patrilineal kin group overriding those of the individual. But amid urbanization and women's growing economic autonomy, takkoo acquired new qualities: the woman might be a divorcee; her new husband was usually unrelated to her former husband; she need not reside with her new husband and might not even be expected to sleep with him (Gning and Antoine 2015). This arrangement allowed an older woman to maintain the social respectability that came with marriage while retaining the freedom to run her own household in every meaningful way—even if her husband might still be its titular head.

There might be no Manding equivalent of takkoo, but as more Bamakoises carved out autonomous financial spaces, I heard about many older women's remarriages in Bamako conforming to this pattern. Its appeal lay in its capacity to help older, economically self-sufficient women use the socially mandated cover of marriage to preserve their hard-won personal independence. By the early 2000s, a third of home buyers with the Malian government's subsidized housing agency were women. While Monique Bertrand (2004) ascribed some of this activity to financing by "sugar daddies," Bamako women were increasingly buying homes in their own names and with their own money—both as an investment and as refuge if ever widowhood, divorce, or the arrival of new co-wives drove them from their marital homes. Some viewed this trend with anxiety. A Bamako newspaper claimed that "virtually all" the newly built homes in the fast-growing neighborhood of Yirimadio were owned by women, and that these women were "almost all single mothers or divorcees automatically becoming household heads" (*Inter de Bamako* 2009). Still, only a small minority of women bought houses. By the end of the 2010s, barely 10 percent of Bamakoises age fifteen to forty-nine claimed to own a house either individually or jointly, and most of those lacked legal title (DHS 2019).

Conclusion: Enduring Universal Marriage

All over the world in the early twenty-first century, the institutional edifice of marriage was crumbling as people delayed marriage or eschewed it entirely. "Post-marriage" cultures emerged in which getting married was no longer a dominant feature of the human life course. Yet for most Malians, and most Bamako residents specifically, marriage remained the surest path to adulthood and social respect. Despite a range of social transformations underway, especially economic dislocation, shifting gender roles, changing conventions about romantic love and individuality, and rising age at first marriage, the city's residents had not subverted marriage or its cultural centrality. The local marriage system, including the practice of polygamy, remained resilient. To conclude this chapter, I will briefly recap this system's components encountered thus far and their impact on the experience of marriage in modern Bamako.

First was marriage's universality. Getting married was a powerful obligation for both sexes. Males married in their late twenties, on average, while females married in their late teens and were expected to stay married throughout their lives. "We've drilled into every Malian's head that a woman's place is in marriage, nowhere else," said Batogoma, the women's rights activist quoted earlier. Universal marriage helped sustain high levels of polygamy by pushing women into marriage sooner than their male peers and keeping them in marriage throughout their lives. It cast unmarried females, including those divorced or widowed, as a destabilizing presence in society, leading women to make marital choices that undermined their relative autonomy and life chances.[32]

The next component of Bamako's marriage system was the influence of kin groups over marriage formation and married life; quite often, marriage was *not really about the couple*. Despite some movement toward spousal choice and the companionate ideal, extended families continued to exercise considerable power over marriage formation. Wives felt patrilineal and patrilocal kin groups' power at every stage of marriage. Parents or other kin frequently determined whom an individual could marry and where they could live; their demands often undermined the spousal bond once a marriage was established. These same demands could lead to a husband taking an additional wife.

The final component concerned the gendered allocation of rights and duties within marriage. Many young people idealized marriages in which a husband

and wife loved and respected each other and made decisions mutually with minimal outside interference, the faithful husband fulfilling his breadwinner duties and the faithful wife focusing on domestic tasks and childrearing (Schulz 2002). The reality was seldom so neat. While economic constraints required many households to rely on wives' incomes, gender norms led wives to continue holding up their end of the patriarchal bargain, acquiescing (at least outwardly) to male domination. Economic and social pressures challenged vows of fidelity. As a result, gendered responsibilities within marriage were under pressure as Bamako residents struggled to reconcile aspirations for modern companionate marriage with disenchantment over its broken promises.

Perhaps my analysis in this chapter is tinged with more egalitarianism than relativism. As an egalitarian, I look for signs of unequal power. Bamako's marriage system disadvantaged females compared to males, and youths compared to elders; polygamy was a frequent expression of those disadvantages. In the following chapter, we will look at who formed polygamous unions and why.

2

Polygamous Marriage Formation

We women, none of us wants our husband to take two wives.

—Female interviewee (Bamako, 2011)

I think it's never a woman's choice to be the second or third wife, because each wants her husband to herself.

—Male interviewee (Bamako, 2012)

Who Becomes Polygamous?

I began fieldwork in Bamako with the mistaken assumption that polygamists and monogamists were intrinsically different, harboring distinct values and attitudes. But monogamy and polygamy are never definitive states. Either can be curtailed by death, divorce, or (in the case of monogamy) remarriage. Nor is it helpful to think of Bamako's monogamists and polygamists as distinct populations. Dividing our interview sample into people who happened to be monogamous and others who happened to be polygamous at the time, then comparing those two groups, would be pointless. When we ascribe entry into polygamy using solely individual-level factors, we overlook the marriage system's influence, including the power of elders and in-laws, the role of economics, and the importance of marriage to achieving adulthood and social respect. We will see that even Bamakois who never sought multiple wives could find polygamy thrust upon them. In this chapter, I consider why men and women enter polygamy, paying attention to individual preferences but also to larger societal forces that influence such unions.

Few factors predicted which husbands became polygamous in Bamako. A man's level of education, his ethnicity, whether he participated in the formal labor force, and even whether he was Muslim or Christian had little apparent effect on his likelihood of taking multiple wives (Antoine, Djiré, and Nanitelamio 1998; cf. Clignet 1970 and 1987).[1]

Socioeconomic status was another story. Men's socioeconomic status correlated everywhere with their likelihood of entering a polygamous union. All other things being equal, one might expect to find more polygamy among wealthy men than among poor ones. Evolutionary biologist David Barash boldly claimed that "in all of human history, it has never, ever, been the landless peasant, the struggling laborer, the hard-working down-in-the-dirt farmer or the lowly and anonymous spear carrier in a large army who ends up with multiple wives" (2016, 73).

While many scholars presume that polygamous men are well off, in Mali, I met plenty of struggling laborers and hard-working farmers who were polyga-mous (though, admittedly, no spear carriers). In fact, polygamy was *negatively* correlated with Malians' socioeconomic status. There, rates of polygamous mar-riage were lowest in the higher economic strata (DHS 2019; see, also, Diamou-téné 2015). Impoverished Bamako husbands might seek out polygamy to benefit from their wives' diverse income-generating activities and hedge their households against economic risks (de Suremain and Razy 2011; Miseli 1998). The widespread "impoverished polygamist" phenomenon in Africa (Timaeus and Reynar 1998; Tabutin and Schoumaker 2020) scuttles the "consumption hypothesis" ascribing polygamy to women's choice of wealthier husbands. While there were certainly well-off polygamist husbands in Bamako, including both Oumar and Malik pro-filed in this book's introduction, there were more poor ones.

Barash's claim, by emphasizing individual preferences and endowments in marriage markets, obscures the larger structures of power and constraint in which spousal selection occurs. In Bamako's marriage system, the needs of kin often trumped the desires of individuals and couples during marriage forma-tion (see chapter 1). A woman might become a poor man's second wife because of her parents' long-standing obligation to him or his family. Such relations off-set wealthy men's tendency to attract more wives.

Some men in our interview sample challenged the notion that polygamy was only for elites. "If polygamy prevented a man from meeting his needs, I wouldn't have been able to handle the last two [wives]," said Bakary (M, 53, market ven-dor, three wives). "Polygamy doesn't depend on the difficulties linked to your dependents. That's an old story but it isn't true," he continued. "According to some, a rich man is one who has many people." Bakary articulated a common view that having many children and other dependents is an asset, not a lia-bility. He illustrated his view with another adage: "Don't fear the man who has money; fear the man who has people." Malians measured wealth in more than money; a man who could support many dependents signaled his status as a "big" person.

Other Bamakois saw such pronatalism as suited only to rural farming households. To these urbanites, the cost of housing, feeding, and educating each additional household member negated whatever value could be gained from their work—and, in any case, they felt that children in the city should be going to school, not working. "Bamako is tough these days, taking two wives is really hard," said Ousmane (M, 47, market vendor, two wives). "If you know that you don't have the means to marry two wives, be content with just one, as long as she bears children for your peace of mind. Because if you don't own a house, you'll have to pay the rent and feed your family."

By this reckoning, only wealthy men could *responsibly* practice polygamy in the city. "Polygamy used to have advantages but doesn't anymore, because people used to marry in order to have many children," added Habib (M, 64, tailor, one wife). "A father of many children was a *faama* [powerful or wealthy person], especially in the village where he'd be happy to see so many children working in his fields. The harvest was there for everyone, but this is no longer the case; everyone must take care of themselves." Given that some Bamakois, like Ousmane and Habib, saw polygamy as outdated and affordable only to a select few, I wondered why so many men, including poor men, choose to enter into polygamous marriages.

Why Do Men Take Additional Wives? The Seven D's

Men cited many different rationales for entering into polygamy, and I group these rationales into a set of categories I call the "seven D's": domestic factors, duty to elders, distinction, desire, discipline, divine will, and demography. While some of these are influenced by individual choice, many illustrate the marriage system's effect on men's marital choices. Note that these categories, which seldom are clear-cut or mutually exclusive, consist of men's rationalizations and justifications for their *own entry* into plural marriage. As with any spoken account, we cannot take these rationalizations at face value. Nor can they explain the persistence of the *institution* of plural marriage in the way the components of Bamako's marriage system do. I discuss the first five categories of justifications below, reserving divine will and demography for chapters 4 and 5, respectively.

Domestic Factors

This category includes factors pertaining to household management, production, and reproduction. One such factor, having children, was a primary rationale for marriage in Bamako. When a couple was unable to conceive after some time, the husband might seek another wife, resorting to so-called "interventive polygamy" (Nwoye 2007). Most of our interviewees blamed childlessness on women and saw infertility as legitimate grounds for polygamy (cf. Dierickx et al. 2019). "In our culture, the social environment is such that when a couple is barren, if I can say that, there's so much pressure that men tend to get second wives," said Malik (M, 45, office worker, two wives). Madou (M, 46, civil servant, two wives) spent a decade trying to have children with his wife. "My home was like a hive without bees—it was sad, horrible, for those ten years," he said. "We should have had children and that's how I thought of taking another wife, the same year. With the second, I now have three children." But some married women could find themselves either supplanted by co-wives or divorced if unable to conceive after a year of marriage (Castle 2003). And although informants recognized that a man could be infertile, none suggested that this might justify his wife taking an additional husband to conceive a child.

Another major domestic factor was female labor. Tasks such as cooking, cleaning, and caring for children and elders were constructed as women's work in Mali, and many informants said that a man might need another wife to handle these tasks when his first wife was unable. Alassane (M, 35, market vendor, two wives) spoke of a monogamous household's vulnerability. "In my experience, [monogamy] has many consequences: a wife might get sick, or even die, heaven forbid." Polygamy built redundancy into the household and, from the husband's perspective, enabled sexual release when one wife was unavailable due to recent childbirth, menstruation, illness, travel, or nursing a child.[2]

Duty to Elders

I subdivide this category into two types. In the first, a man's kin would directly insist that he take another wife. Some parents, especially mothers, urged a son to do so if they viewed his first wife as too possessive, demanding, or emotionally attached to him (Brand 2001). It could be very difficult for him to refuse. For many, saying no to parents carried the risk of social isolation and even a dreaded parental curse (see Whitehouse 2012a). In other examples of this type, parents of an absent son (usually a rural-to-urban or international migrant) would ask him to take another wife to look after them in his absence (cf. Buggenhagen 2012). Lacking a state- or market-run social safety net, Mali's elderly parents relied on their children for support in the forms of money and labor. And since domestic chores were defined as women's work, aging parents might ask a son to send his wife to do them. "If you tell them you can't send her," said one male focus group participant, "they'll say, 'All right, now you must take another wife. One will stay with us for a year, then she'll join you and the other one will stay with us.' That's how I came to have a second wife. You can't say it was about desire." A migrant son could, thus, find himself with two wives trading places between the city and his parents' rural home at regular intervals.[3]

Communities with strong preferences for endogamy (marrying within the group) encouraged such imposed unions. Ngolo left his village as a young man to work in Bamako in the 1970s. Rather than accept the bride his parents chose for him, he wed a Bamako woman and dispatched a cousin to win his parents' blessing for the union, expecting them to accept this *fait accompli*. But Ngolo's mother made her approval conditional on his marrying the village girl, whom the village community would regard as his first wife. Ngolo accepted this condition. Later in life, the process repeated itself after he took a third wife, also from Bamako; his parents demanded he take his fourth wife from their village to maintain balance (see Whitehouse 2012b). Ngolo could have refused these arranged marriages, but judged the potential costs of doing so—alienation from kin and vital support networks—to outweigh the costs of acquiescing.[4]

As Hélène Neveu Kringelbach (2016b, 164) found in Senegal, after male migrants "married out" of their home communities, their parents could impose additional brides on them "in part to ensure that the migrants' resources were not completely absorbed by their new households" outside the village (see also Brzezińska 2021). Keeping one wife in the village while residing with another in town kept many sons connected to their rural communities (Hagberg and Koné 2020).

In the second subcategory of duty to elders, a man's kin imposed his first marriage on him, after which he could pursue a second marriage by choice. By accepting arranged marriages, men gained freedom to marry women of their own choosing.[5] They, thereby, fulfilled "dual marital aspirations," as Katherine Charsley and Anika Liversage (2013, 67) found among Muslim immigrants in Europe: first, to be dutiful sons by accepting marriages arranged by their parents, and second, to enjoy modern, companionate marriages to women with whom they felt more compatible.

Consider Issa, a native of Mali's Dogon country who won a coveted foreign university scholarship upon completing secondary school. Issa spent several years studying engineering abroad. Soon after he returned to Mali, at age twenty-nine, his mother told him it was time to get married. His protestations that he wasn't ready for marriage were to no avail; she fixed him up with her fifteen-year-old niece (his maternal cousin), who was from the same village but had never gone to school and spoke no French.

"In spite of my level, my understanding of life and everything, I didn't want to defy my mother too much," he said during our interview in 2012, some thirty years after his marriage. "So I had to marry this woman, who is my first wife." Issa's second wife, unlike his first, was a Bamakoise whose outlook and education were more aligned with his own and whose age was closer to his. "My relatives could not say no because I'd agreed to marry the first one," he said. By fulfilling his dual marital aspirations, Issa could satisfy his kin and his desire for a love-based marriage. Reflecting on his first marriage, he said, "I think, to be honest, it is more about respect for family than love. But we do what we have to do."[6]

Having seen several men in Bamako take multiple wives over their senior kin's strong objections, I hope not to exaggerate the importance of "duty to elders" as a factor for men becoming polygamous. Perhaps some men claimed it as a justification while secretly having other, less socially acceptable motives. But cases like Issa's suggest that duty was a genuine factor.

Distinction

Men derived status and prestige from having multiple wives. These benefits also could accrue to a married man with a girlfriend, mistress, or so-called "outside wife" (i.e., a woman in an informal but durable sexual and romantic relationship with him). In the eyes of his male peers, a man's multiple wives signified his virility and guaranteed descendants (A. Tounkara 2015; cf. D. Smith 2017). It also signaled socioeconomic status. As sociologist Wambui Wa Karanja (1994, 203) wrote of urban Nigerian men, taking an outside wife was "akin to acquiring a Mercedes-Benz or building an elegant house." In societies where formal polygamy was illegal, restricted, or socially stigmatized, having outside wives was an informal version of polygamy. In Bamako, of course, formal polygamy was both legal and socially validated, making "outside wives" unnecessary.[7] A Bamako husband might hesitate to display a mistress too openly, but once he *married* her, he could flaunt her without reservation.

None of our male interviewees listed distinction as motivating their own decisions about marriage, but females saw this motivation as widespread and harmful. "Not all men are cut out to be polygamous," said Ami (F, 28, accountant, no co-wife). "They do it because their friends are polygamous, or they think they have the financial means to manage multiple wives. I'd say 98 percent of polygamous men I've seen are not exemplary or encouraging. This isn't what God expects of us." Women did not always accept men's personal justifications of polygamy, and sometimes used Islam to challenge them (see chapter 4).

Desire

Like distinction, the category of desire was one to which few men attributed their polygamous marriages.[8] Yet desire for sexual variety and satisfaction underlay many second and higher-order marriages. Some male interviewees framed polygamy as a way to avoid extramarital "fooling around" (see discussion in chapter 5). Affairs also could initiate polygamy, however. Several polygamous men I met had, like Oumar, engaged in extramarital sexual relationships with women whom they later married, and several of the second wives I interviewed had similarly engaged in sexual relationships with their future husbands prior to marriage. It was when some of these women got pregnant that their extramarital relationships formalized into marital ones; their male partners preferred to convert such relationships into marriage rather than carry the stigma of having "outside" women and children.[9] A Malian professor in his thirties told me that his married male peers started seeking extramarital romance during periods of tension with their wives. For these men, taking new sexual partners to feel a renewed sense of manhood embodied what sociologist Robert Wyrod (2016, 174) has called "compensatory sexuality."[10]

An older husband might evoke desire to justify taking a younger wife after his other wife or wives lost interest in sex. "A wife at 50 tends to be done with sexual life," said Ali (M, 39, unemployed, one wife). "The second or third [wife], same thing. So it's very often the fourth wife who becomes her husband's faithful companion, because the others no longer have sex."

Desire and distinction also sometimes intertwined. A man finding economic success after his first marriage might seek a more desirable wife whose hand he could never have won in his younger, poorer days.

Discipline

This category concerns the effect that taking another wife could have on a man's relationship with his existing wife or wives. A husband could use polygamy to bring a recalcitrant wife to heel. By adding another woman to his marriage, he pitted his wives against each other in competition for his time, resources, and affections (S. Camara 1978; de Jorio 1997; A. Tounkara 2015).[11] Some men frankly described using polygamy as a tactic to keep wives on their best behavior:

> There's a certain kind of happiness with a woman that you can't have with only one wife. Because the wife can do certain things, like not taking good care of your parents or not taking care of you—so if you take a second wife, it can lead [the first wife] to take good care of you.
>
> —Mahamadou (M, 23, market vendor, two wives)

> I have a friend: since he took a second wife, his first wife has become the best wife in the household today. But before his second marriage, she was a viper!
>
> —Madou (M, 46, civil servant, two wives)

> With your second marriage, you really benefit from greater respect from the first wife; it changes completely.
>
> —Fousseyni (M, 55, civil servant, two wives)

> If you enjoy peace 20 percent of the time as a monogamous husband, once you marry a second wife you have peace 60 percent of the time. It multiplies your happiness. The peace you have in a polygamous marriage, you can't get that in a monogamous one. It took me some time before I remarried, and after I did, I regretted not remarrying earlier.
>
> —Sambou (M, 41, market vendor, two wives)

Co-wives could find common cause, however. "My father had three wives who lived in the same compound and all of them had children," said Amira (F, 19, housewife, no co-wife). "The atmosphere was nice. They didn't fight—to the contrary, they often formed a coalition against my father if he argued with one of them. This way my father was forced to be fair with them." Research in diverse African settings (Clignet 1970; Kilbride and Kilbride 1990; van Beek 1987) has suggested that an odd number of wives frequently leads to coalition formation.

But polygamy could even benefit *monogamous* husbands. The mere threat of being joined by a co-wife might suffice to make a wife obedient. As Malik (45, office employee, two wives) put it, "The very fact that there is this possibility of having a second wife, the fact that it's there calls her to order." This preemptive disciplinary effect might leave monogamous wives in high-polygamy settings with less bargaining power than polygamous wives.[12]

These categories, further emphasizing that marriage in Bamako was often *not really about the couple*, concerned only men's motives regarding plural marriage. Many men took brides chosen by their parents, or were motivated by household and extended family factors, contributing both directly and indirectly to polygamy. But while men had various reasons behind their choice to enter polygamy, women were less often able to make such a choice.

Women and Polygamous Marriage

We will analyze women's reasons for entering polygamous unions in later chapters, but here we explore their feelings about the institution. Did women ever *want* their husbands to take additional wives? While a few researchers have rejected this notion (anthropologist Inge Wittrup [1990, 131] called it a "male myth"), others have supported it. Among the Nyakyusa of colonial Zambia, first wives helping recruit second wives was the "mark of successful marriage relations" (Wilson 1950, 124). An older wife might particularly benefit from a young co-wife handling many domestic chores. In colonial northern Ghana, Tallensi wives seeking help with household chores lobbied their husbands to take more wives (Fortes 1949). A similar tradition was observed among Bamanan and Fulbe villagers in Mali (Brett-Smith 2014; Madhavan 2002).

Some Bamakoises cited domestic reasons in claiming to want co-wives. We asked each of the twenty-five monogamously married wives in our interview sample whether she would like to have a co-wife. Four, none of whom had surpassed primary school, cited pragmatic reasons for wanting one.

> I'd like a co-wife; this would mean I could do less housework and spend less time caring for children and husband.
>
> —Khady (F, 18, petty trader, no co-wife)

I'm the only daughter-in-law in an extended family, so there's plenty of work to do. A co-wife would enable me to rest and have more time for my children.

—Massaran (Γ, 29, housewife, no co-wife)

I'd like to have a co-wife, because although I'm my mother's only daughter, my half-brothers and half-sisters are like my own brothers and sisters. So I'd like my own children to have half-siblings to expand the family.

—Aminata (F, 21, housewife, no co-wife)

I'd like a co-wife, because I haven't been able to have a child since I was married, and my husband is in his forties.

—Nafissatou (F, 20, housewife, no co-wife)

These women clearly prioritized aspects of marriage (offspring, help with domestic labor, time for "rest," playmates for their children) other than the "deeply intense relationship between husband and wife" mentioned in the introduction.

The remaining twenty-one monogamous wives in our interview sample emphasized different marital priorities. They evoked polygamy with a mix of opposition and resignation, as in these examples:

Nobody wants a co-wife. Polygamy holds women back in every regard, upsets family tranquility, and utterly destroys children's futures.

—Doussou (F, 37, housewife, no co-wife)

I wouldn't like my children to be in polygamous marriages, but in the Malian setting a woman has no choice.

—Djeneba (F, 22, housewife, no co-wife)

I wouldn't want a co-wife, but in Malian society a woman has no choice; if such is my destiny, I will accept it.

—Lallaicha (F, 30, birth attendant, no co-wife)

I wouldn't like a co-wife, but I can't do anything about it. No woman can prevent her husband from taking another wife.

—Bintou (F, 30, housewife, no co-wife)

Many Bamakoises echoed the sentiments of the woman quoted in this chapter's epigraph: "We women, none of us wants our husband to take two wives." Yet they rarely condemned polygamy as an institution. It was, after all, authorized by the Qur'an and was practiced by the Prophet Muhammad himself (see chapter 4). Without objecting to men's *right* to take multiple wives, women criticized the *practice* of polygamy, which they often saw as beyond their control.

TABLE 2.1

Polygamous Marriage for One's Child: Views of Wives (n = 50) and husbands (n = 50)

Question: "When you have children of marriageable age, would you accept that they go into polygamous unions?"

	No. of Wives' Responses	No. of Husbands' Responses
Ambivalent	3	1
Does not matter	3	0
I have no say	2	0
It's up to my child	7	22
It's up to God	5	1
Yes	2	21
No	28	5

Like the interviewees above, many wives feared polygamy's potential for rivalry and conflict while simultaneously feeling powerless to keep their own husbands from marrying other women.

While a few wives envisaged polygamy's benefits, then, many more hoped to avoid the practice. One question we used to gauge attitudes toward polygamy asked whether interviewees would agree for their children to be in polygamous marriages. Of fifty wives, twenty-eight answered no, while fourteen replied that it was not up to them (including seven who said it was up to the child and five who said it was up to God). Compared to wives, husbands were much more favorable toward the possibility of their child's polygamous marriage (see table 2.1).

We also asked interviewees to describe polygamy's benefits (see table 2.2). Twenty-six wives replied that it had none; twenty mentioned domestic factors (e.g., pooling household labor, compensating for a first wife's infertility, or having a large family), one mentioned religion, and four replied that the benefits were "only for the husband." Husbands most frequently cited domestic factors, and only eight said it had no advantages. These responses revealed widely divergent male and female attitudes toward polygamy in Bamako. Wives were wary of it but felt they had little control over whether they or their children ended up in polygamous marriages; husbands were much more positive in their outlook.

One could argue that second and higher-order wives choose polygamy. After all, they agree to wed men whom they know are married already. To the extent that any unmarried Bamakoise could freely choose in nuptial matters, then,

TABLE 2.2

Polygamy's Advantages: Views of Wives (n = 50) and Husbands (n = 50)

Question: Does polygamy have advantages? If so, what are they? (*Interviewee could list more than one.*)

	No. of Wives' Responses	No. of Husbands' Responses
Avoiding infidelity	1	6
Disciplining wives	0	4
Having a large family	2	6
Household labor and cooperation	13[1]	23
In case of infertility	5	4
None	26	8
Only for the husband	4	0
Status and respect	0	3
Other	0	4

[1]Five of these thirteen women added provisos—either "if the wives get along" or "if the husband is fair."

these women did "opt into" polygamy. Ordinary people and newspaper editorials expressed anxiety about young single Bamakoises perpetually pursuing economically successful or at least self-sufficient married men, hoping to become their second (or third, or fourth) wives. They accused these young women of stalking married men in their workplaces and on the streets, seeing a wedding ring on a man's finger as a sign that he was stable enough to provide for a family. Issiaka, the married, middle-aged imam quoted previously, complained to me of constantly having to fend off subtle marriage inquiries from single women in his congregation. Popular discourse often portrayed young women eager to wed married men as home-wreckers, intent, at best, on supplanting existing wives as the husband's favorite and, at worst, on driving them out of their marriages altogether. "What do [single] women here do when they know that a man only has one wife? They pursue him," said Moctar (M, 39, engineer, one wife). "For them, he's easy prey!" Such perceptions of single women aggressively seeking out already-married husbands fueled the perception that women became second wives by poaching husbands from happy monogamous unions; a second wife, by one local saying, was "always in the wrong."[13]

Aisha, a professional woman in her thirties whom we met briefly in chapter 2, was one of those second wives. While she had never exactly aspired to polygamous marriage, it always had been an option worth considering. She spoke at length about how she had viewed the issue while single:

> For me personally, as a Malian woman and a Muslim, I'm not fatalistic or anything, but since childhood I had prepared myself psychologically for this factor. My mother had never lived [in polygamy], but nonetheless I told myself, "You must prepare psychologically for this. The day it befalls you, you must be ready psychologically." Because it all comes down to psychology, for me. So, from an early age I figured polygamy could happen to anyone—nobody is immune. If you're a Muslim in Malian society, you can set yourself certain conditions like "I'll never, ever accept polygamy," and make that your choice. In other words, if you're a man's first wife and he decides to take another wife, you divorce him straight away. To say, "I'll never marry a man who already has a wife," that's a personal decision. But me, from a young age, it's as though I had an idea about the fact that I would be a second wife. I knew from a young age that I could be a second wife, or be the first and have a co-wife.

Aisha here alluded to women's lack of control over whether their marriages would remain monogamous. Their husbands (or in-laws) could impose additional wives at any moment. Seeing every monogamous Bamakois as a potential polygamist, Aisha readied herself even before marriage for the possibility of sharing her future husband.

While on an internship in her twenties, she became friends with a manager in her office. She knew he already had a wife, but after they struck up a flirtatious relationship, he declared his feelings for her; eventually, they started seeing each other outside of work. When she got pregnant, he recognized his paternity and they agreed to marry. At that point, Aisha recalled her childhood preparations for the contingency of polygamous marriage:

> I thought a bit about this story. It wasn't my biggest motivation to marry my husband, but it was among my motivations. The biggest motivation was that I would imagine myself at 30 with no child and no husband. I'd always said I'd get married at 25 at the latest, in my teenage plans. By 25 I would have my diploma, I'd be married and have a home. But I'd keep getting suitors and at the last minute, some little problem would get in the way.

Aisha described her marriage in terms of trust, communication, and emotional intimacy. She was one of the few wives who called her husband by his first name, ignoring the local taboo. Like Issa, the engineer profiled above, Aisha settled for polygamy as a step toward companionate marriage—but, in her case, only after missing a self-imposed deadline (marrying by age twenty-five) and falling out with other suitors. The sense of time slipping away helped her commit to a relationship with an already married man; this was, as she said, her "biggest motivation."

I spoke to other professional women who became second wives. Unlike Aisha, each had considered the prospect of sharing a husband with another woman unthinkable until finding herself in a romantic relationship with a married man. But like Aisha, these women had passed what they considered prime marrying age by the time they met their future husbands. "In our Malian society, once you reach a certain age you prefer being the second [wife] to remaining single," said Sali, a journalist in her thirties whom I interviewed in 2011. Like Aisha, Sali had married an already-married man she met on the job.

To sum up, some Bamako women chose polygamous marriage insofar as they formed unions with married men, and some were attracted to polygamy's potential benefits. But given the constraints to marital choice, the pressure on young women to marry, and female interviewees' wariness toward polygamy, polygamous marriage was rarely a Bamako woman's absolute preference. In any case, what good were a woman's marital preferences? If entering into polygamy as a wife in a formerly monogamous marriage, she had hardly any say. If entering into it as a single woman in Bamako's marriage market, the alternatives might be uncertain (see chapter 5).

Conclusion

We already can see that women and men in Bamako viewed polygamous marriage through very different lenses. While entry into polygamy was not always under men's control, men articulated various instrumental and practical reasons for taking additional wives. Some of these reasons, like duty to elders and discipline, might seem to confound the logic of companionate marriage. Men often married women with whom they lacked a preexisting romantic attachment, or because they sought to protect their own power within the household and keep an existing wife "in her place." Yet we saw in Issa's case that a man compelled by kin into one marriage might seek out a love match in another. Some men, like Malik, talked up polygamy's benefits while others, like Issa, showed profound ambivalence about it.

Women were far less effusive about polygamy's advantages and expressed far more concern about its burdens than men. More importantly, many women felt powerless regarding polygamy's entry into their own lives. Plural marriage was an institution to which women had largely resigned themselves. To explore these gendered disparities in outlook further, the following chapter considers some of the challenges associated with living in polygamy. It surveys men's and women's perspectives on these challenges, focusing particularly on the residential arrangements intended to mitigate them.

Virtual Monogamy in Practice

"The man is never sincere."

Kani was in her late twenties, working at an internship and finishing her university studies, when she met her mother's acquaintance Brehima, a married man fifteen years her senior. He lived in Niger but had family in Bamako and often traveled there on business. Brehima is dividing his time between his two wives in Niger and Kani when I meet her in 2012. At age thirty-seven, she has a job with a foreign company and lives on her own with their son. She wears form-fitting Western clothes, speaks French with an educated accent, and even switches to English (rarely spoken in Mali) to answer some of my questions. Her words below are edited from the interview transcript.

KANI: I never thought I'd get married to a polygamous man in my life. Never, never! For me, it's my husband and me, you know? And our children, the family. Not a man who already had a wife, it was unthinkable for me. But you know, there's such a thing as destiny. Nobody forced me into this! It's what I wanted. My mom had a big role, she said here is a serious guy, a good guy she knew who would never hurt me. I wanted someone who would love his family and who is sociable. My husband is like that, he loves people, he loves to joke around.

When I met Brehima, he had two wives. . . . He came over for a meal, we talked and joked. I found him so friendly, he was likable, you know? I was going out with a man my mother didn't want me to marry because he wasn't from here, he lived in Niger. . . . And like that, each time Brehima came we'd hang out, we'd go out to a restaurant, joke a lot. He'd bring me gifts and everything. I found him very nice. And the next year he said, "I want to marry you." I was like, "What are you talking about? You want to marry me?" I hadn't finished my studies, I didn't want to get married. He said, "Yes yes yes, I want to marry you, because I love you so much and I don't want some other man to marry you."

So after he sent some people [marriage intermediaries] to my family, my dad said, "You have to take some time to get to know each other because you don't know each other well enough." Brehima said, "No, I don't need to get to know her, she's my family, my 'niece,' I don't want to hurt her, we're certain to understand one another." And I said, "Let's marry," and just like that we got married! [claps hands and laughs] Just like that. It was great, he's super, he's really a jovial guy, and he studied abroad. . . . He's good, he doesn't have any problems.

But the thing is, polygamy is difficult because the man is never sincere. I discovered that later, after two years of marriage. It was hard for me to see him coming and going, and to know that he had other wives—even though I knew consciously that he had other wives! But I married him thinking, "Well, I'll master him, manage him, he'll spend a lot more time here, and I'll have him base all his business here in Mali."

My problem is forgetting that he has other wives. While he's here, I take care of him 100 percent—I don't do anything else. And I didn't want him to talk about his other family over there. In the beginning that would hurt me, I didn't want it. I said, "You take care of your life there, and take care of me here," all that. And then, little by little, I thought, "No, I might hurt him, he'll become hypocritical and will never be sincere with me. He won't be open with me, confide in me if I don't open myself to him and let him speak about his problems."

So little by little, I let him start talking about how he married his wives, how things were between them. He said, "That's why I married you—I found you so sincere, so nice, you like people, you're sociable. I like that you're such a dynamic woman. And if I have problems, you can always help me . . . I love you because you're so ambitious. I have a wife who's a fighter, who's ambitious."

So, polygamy isn't easy because a man can never tell the truth. He'll tell this wife, "I love you, I love you," and when he's with another wife he'll say, "Oh that one, I don't care about her, she's like this, she's like that, she has these problems, she can't cook, she's dirty, she can't take care of her kids," all that stuff, it's hypocritical. To live polygamy well, you must keep your eyes and ears shut and do what feels right. You must always have a good heart and use it well. Otherwise, you'll murder each other, you'll see things that hurt you.

BRUCE: How do you communicate when he's away—when he's in Niger and you're here?

KANI: We talk on the phone all the time; every day he calls me or I call him. We send emails and text messages all the time. But when I'm angry, I can go a week without calling. When something hurts me I show it, and then we'll move on. These things happen in life. It's not all roses! Life has its ups and downs. Sometimes you're the best friends in the world, the best lovers in the world, and sometimes you're the worst enemies, you don't even feel like seeing each other and you're in the same house. All these things can happen. But when you have children, you look at those children and say, "Why are we fighting when we have this child who didn't ask to be brought into the world? He's our responsibility, I have to act right in front of him."

Polygamy's not easy! Each time he'd go away it would break my heart, tear my heart out. When he's here we're fine, like 16- or 18-year-old kids. We're so good together, we understand each other so well. But as soon as he says, "I want to go in two or three days," I start getting agitated and then I don't want to look at him. I tell him, "If you loved me you wouldn't leave"— because love is just for once, you cannot love twice. You can't divide your heart into a thousand pieces.

The disadvantage [of polygamy] is the home balance, especially for the children. Because my son, every time he's asking, "Where's my dad?" They organized a school party and he wasn't here. On Father's Day he made a nice gift for him, he asked "Where's Dad, I have a present, a surprise for him!" Sometimes it makes me cry because my son is so clever. I was raised in a friendly environment and I want the same for him. You know it's not easy. I'm always telling him, "Your dad is gone, he's traveling." He can't understand that his dad has a lot of families, you know? I think he's too small for me to explain all those things. He knows but he doesn't understand.

For me, [Brehima and I] were two, we were two. There was no other family between us, you know. I forgot about his family. When he was away [with his other wives], I came back to reality and said, "Oh, this man has a family." It wasn't easy because the second wife was calling him every day, bad-talking him, "You married this girl, the marriage will never last," blah blah blah. It was not easy. . . . This woman runs him down and he gets very sad, anxious, it's not easy. You can tell when he has a problem there, when he comes you can even feel it in his sexual performance. Because he cannot be like a normal man, he has problems in his head, he's completely dead, full of tension, you know? So he needs two, three, four days to get calm.

It's not easy in polygamy also, people are watching me, watching my attitude—

BRUCE: Who's watching you?

KANI: His second wife. She swore that she would break [up] my marriage. Yeah! From my wedding day, she said, "OK, this marriage will [last] two months." Then after one year, "OK, two years to finish." Three years, six years . . . she's always having people follow me to bring gossip and that kind of thing. I don't care, I tell him, "If I do something bad I'll do it—nobody comes to make me do something I shouldn't do. I'll do whatever is on my mind." He knows it already, before he married me. I can't deny my pleasure because he married me, no! It's not the end of life.

BRUCE: Do you think he will ever take a fourth wife?

KANI: If a man has two or three wives, he *will* take a fourth, there's no doubt about it. I'm waiting for that. And the day he does it will be the day that I leave, because I cannot accept it. And I've told him that since the beginning. For me, if you want to find a fourth wife, it must mean that you're not satisfied with three wives. No! I don't even care about the first and second; with me, it means that I'm not able to satisfy you. So why stay with him—it's hypocrisy that I will never accept.

My husband, in general, if it's just him and me, we don't have so many problems between us—our couple is so strong. When I take care of him and he goes away, then whether or not he phones me, that's fine, I forget. I forget that I have a husband who's gone. I tell myself he's traveling, he's on business.

3

Polygamous Household Dynamics

In the polygamous family in indigenous African society, a particular living arrangement is observed and respected. The man lives in the *same compound* with *all* his wives and children. Usually, boundaries of marked spaces are respected; the man has his own house and each wife lives in her own house with her children; the man is responsible for the general welfare, maintenance, and operation of his compound while each wife is directly responsible for her children. Sexually and materially, the man seeks to maintain fairness, equity, and justice among the wives. The children all grow up together and the man is *always there* for his family.

—Nnaemeka (1997, 173; emphasis in original)

During my research, I frequently encountered a cultural model of how a polygamous household was supposed to function in most of Mali (excepting its northern regions). This model, resembling the "indigenous African" pattern described above by literary scholar Obioma Nnaemeka, informed many Bamakois' thoughts about polygamous marriage, kinship, and households in general. I couch my description of this model below in the "ethnographic present" because it is an enduring ideal type:

A family inhabits a large residential compound with a central courtyard surrounded by sleeping huts, kitchens, and outbuildings. A wall rings the compound's perimeter. Each wife in the compound has her own separate dwelling, in which she and her children sleep. The husband might have his own dwelling or might rotate among his wives' chambers following an established nightly schedule.

All his children grow up playing, doing chores, and farming the fields together amid both solidarity and rivalry. The Manding word *badenya*, meaning "mother-child-ness," denotes solidarity among full siblings, children of the same mother. (In francophone Africa, a full sibling bond is often marked by the phrase *même père, même mère*—"same father, same mother.") By contrast, the word *fadenya* ("father-child-ness") describes the rivalry associated with half-siblings, as each set of full siblings competes for their father's attention and regard. Fadenya, an outward-driving force linked to competition, individual aspiration, and social disruption, is tamed or offset by badenya, an inward-driving force linked to social harmony and submission to authority.[1]

Badenya and fadenya are, in this model, essential for the household and society to thrive; a successful head of household learns to manage and harness both for the collective good (see Bird and Kendall 1980; cf. Gaibazzi 2019 and Osborn 2011). Like the man's children, his wives experience periods of cooperation and periods of conflict, with each working sometimes for herself and her children and sometimes for the household's advancement. But everyone within this cultural model regards this household as a single unit and its members' destinies as bound together.

This model of household organization, which I call the "traditional model," emerged from rural Mande communities over the past several centuries to become a prominent feature of Bamako's marriage system. Like all ideal types, it obscures the messiness of real life. For example, some co-wives might live separately, even in different villages, and their children might rarely meet. Moreover, the equilibrium between badenya and fadenya, between social harmony and disruptive innovation, might be elusive, and the unchecked forces of fadenya sometimes tear families apart. In many respects, the traditional model has proven poorly suited to sprawling cities like Bamako, where housing is limited and children's labor less valuable. Yet this model has remained important to many Bamakois for suggesting what polygamous family life ought to be.

Over the years, polygamous households found ways to domesticate the forces of fadenya. Husbands in Bamanan communities might assign the children born to one wife to be raised by a co-wife and vice-versa, thus discouraging mothers from pitting their children against one another (Brett-Smith 2014; Keller 2021; Madhavan 2002). Some of our interviewees experienced these arrangements. "The atmosphere was really good," recalled Madou (M, 55, civil servant, two wives) of his boyhood in the central Mopti region. His father had four wives, and "although our mothers had some rivalry among them, we hardly knew about it as children. I was raised by a co-wife of my mother, and some of my brothers were also raised by other co-wives up to the age of 10 or 15. We couldn't say 'That one is my mother in this family.'"[2]

Many an interviewee who grew up in a polygamous home referred to a father's wives collectively as "our mothers" (Manding *an baw*, French *nos mères*). In our interview sample, Malik (M, 45, office worker, two wives), claimed to have minimized rivalry among his wives' children by replicating these arrangements in his Bamako household. "I could invite you to my home, you'd come in and not be able to tell which child belongs to which [wife] if I didn't tell you," Malik said. "What's more, I have adopted children whose mothers aren't in the home, and you couldn't tell which ones they are either."[3]

Such arrangements, however, had fallen into disuse in Bamako. Assigning a woman's children to her co-wife could arouse resentment; in rural Bamanan households, this practice was an early casualty of modernization and its accompanying individualist ethos during the latter decades of the twentieth century (Brett-Smith 2014; cf. Dierickx et al. 2019). Most interviewees opined that mothers simply wouldn't entrust their children to co-wives anymore. As Ladji (M, 50, civil servant, one wife) put it:

In our society, customs have degraded and everyone wants to say, "My child is my child," and especially with competing interests, and wickedness [la méchancété], and lack of clarity between people, problems can often arise and get very bad, even affecting the children. Today, between these problems [and] the lack of resources, it's hard to manage polygamy.

Under the traditional household model, hierarchy prevailed among co-wives. The first wife held seniority over the others and could act as her husband's deputy in certain respects. Tiemoko (M, 50, civil servant, one wife) recalled growing up within this structure. "We understood in our grandparents' time that the first wife was always like the household head: she directed all the wives, she took charge of bringing up the children and integrating them into the family. She was the moral conscience of the setting. This is where the first wife plays a very important role." Yacouba (M, 67, market vendor, three wives) described a similar arrangement in his own marriage:

I have three wives and all my business is connected to the first. I consult her in all my undertakings and she gives her view, even if the decision is really mine on matters of family relations, my own problems or my children's. Even in my absence, if there's a family quarrel when she makes a decision, upon my return I give my view and very often it's the same [as hers]. That's how it is between my first wife and me.

Bamako's polygamous households frequently diverged from this practice, however. A husband's religious obligations (see next section) undermined his first wife's special status. Moreover, some junior wives sought ascendancy over senior wives. As Tiemoko said, "These days it's the newest [wife] who has the advantages. Especially when there's a husband who [remarries] to hurt his [first] wife, then the wife arriving later becomes the cherished wife of the family and benefits from all the advantages she can get from her husband." Men's reasons for taking multiple wives had shifted, many believed, from practical domestic or economic concerns to more selfish ones. A husband taking another wife for prestige or sexual desire was more likely to favor his new wife.

The Importance of Being Equitable

This brings us to the thorniest issue of polygamous practice: the husband's duty to treat his wives without favoritism. This issue acquired special importance as Malian society increasingly Islamized; Muslim law conditions a man's right to practice polygamy upon his equitable treatment of his wives. The requirement often was interpreted in terms of *equal* treatment. If a husband gave a bolt of cloth to one wife, for example, he had to give one of the same size and quality to every other wife. He could not spend five nights a week with one wife and only two nights with another; for every night he spent with one wife, he had to spend one night with each of her co-wives. For Muslims, the insistence on fairness was backed by the Qur'an's only direct pronouncement on polygamous marriage, found in the third verse of the fourth sura: "If you fear you cannot be equitable to orphan girls (in your charge, or misuse their persons), then marry women who are lawful for you, two, three, or four; but if you fear you cannot treat so many with equity, marry only one, or a maid or captive. This is better than being iniquitous."[4]

This requirement of equity between a man and his wives "opens vast possibilities for grievances" (Abu-Lughod 1999, 229), due to uncertainty over what constitutes equitable treatment and even over whether husbands can meet the Qur'anic standard for it. Bamakois widely perceived favoritism as infusing polygamous households. The Manding terms *baramuso* and *galòmuso*, respectively, designate the "preferred wife" and the "rejected wife" (Brett-Smith 2014, 149n16), and a saying held that "the best way to convince a man is to influence him via his favorite wife" (S. Camara 1978, 46). Polygamous husbands' unequal treatment of their wives was a perennial theme in popular songs. But polygamy's defenders argued that certain forms of everyday favoritism did not violate Islamic standards of justice. Most notably, they claimed that a husband's greater affection for one wife over another was permissible, as long as it did not affect how he *treated* his wives. After all, they said, the Prophet's wife Aisha was clearly his favorite. In the words of Ousmane (M, 47, market vendor, two wives), "According to the principles, if you have two wives, no matter what you do, there will always be one who pleases you more than the other, but you mustn't let it show."

Some polygamists preferred to discuss equitable treatment in terms of *fairness* rather than equality. "Perfect equality exists only with God, but there can be the appearance of equality," said Mooro (M, 54, librarian, one wife), whose father had two wives. During his interview, Malik (M, 45, office worker, two wives) objected to the wording of the question about wives' equitable treatment, the French version of which asked if a husband could treat his wives "*de manière égale*" (in an equal manner).[5] "This equality of which we speak, even God didn't create it among us as individuals," he said. "These questionnaires like the one you're using," he told the interviewer, "those who write the questions are often rather feminist, and they tend to be against our culture." In talking about his responsibility toward his wives, Malik preferred *la justice* (justice or fairness) to *l'égalité*:

> Equality doesn't exist. But *la justice*—I think that's what we should want and abide by. You can be fair between two individuals without them necessarily being equal. Whenever you hear "equality," it's about equality before the law; take away the law and there is no equality. Two persons should be equal before the law, but the reality is that they are not equal. So let's speak of fairness, because everything we speak of in life today, whether it's happiness, peace, all of it, it's about fairness. You must be fair when you're responsible; you must be fair with those in your charge. But their equality is another matter.

Issa, the engineer who married his much younger cousin at his mother's insistence (see chapter 2), likewise found equality in affection an impossible standard. He was more conflicted than Malik, however, about what fairness toward his two wives entailed. "You cannot love your wives the same way, but you can *treat* them the same way," Issa told me, continuing:

> What do I mean by this? To my mind, [equal treatment] has a somewhat material nature. Whatever the wives' needs are, you meet them—whatever society imposes. Last year, I decided to send my two wives to Mecca [for the *hajj* pilgrimage]. If I sent one and left the other, or if I said, "You go this year, and the other will go next year," even there, I don't think there's equality. But if you send them at the same time, you can treat them equally. Whatever happens, you must avoid favoring one over the other. I think you can *treat* them the same way, but you cannot *love* them the same way. Equal treatment means that if you give one franc to one wife, you must give one franc to the other. You cannot give 10 francs to this one and give one franc to the other.
>
> You build a house and put one wife in it. The house for the other wife must have roughly the same conditions, even if it isn't the same type of house.[6] Whatever you do for one you must do for the other. Now, perhaps what you give to one wife will satisfy her, but does that mean the same thing will satisfy the other wife? That's an open question. If you give 100,000 francs to one, let's suppose that will be enough for her, but the same sum isn't enough for the other wife. Have you treated them the same way?
>
> So that's the dilemma: is being equitable toward my wives about meeting their needs, or is it about telling myself that what I gave to one, I gave to the other? It's a question I keep asking myself, and honestly, I have no answer—it's really difficult! For my part, I wouldn't

TABLE 3.1

**Equal Treatment in Polygamy: Views of Wives (n = 50)
and Husbands (n = 50)**

Question: Can a polygamous husband treat all his wives in an equal manner?

	No. of Wives' Responses	No. of Husbands' Responses
Ambivalent or no response	4	10
It is difficult/rare	13	13
No	27	12
Not in affection but materially	0	1
Yes	6	14

recommend polygamy to anyone. Honestly, you know that somehow, individuals being different, you can't put them in the same conditions. . . . You can treat them the same way, but will each of them find the same satisfaction in that? I don't think so, from my experience.

None of the wives we interviewed made this distinction between equality and fairness, and most doubted that men were capable of equal treatment—never mind equal affection—toward their wives or children. "A polygamous husband can naturally never treat his wives the same," said Coumba (F, 26, housewife, no co-wife). "I think this is a matter of human nature. He cannot love them the same way, so he cannot treat them the same way. He cannot treat his children the same way. Treatment of children depends on their mothers' position in the family." Sanou (F, 36, housewife, two co-wives) spoke bluntly of men's disparate affections: "It's hard to find a polygamous husband who treats his wives equally. Personally, I've never seen it. From the time a man decides to remarry, that shows that he has more love for the new [wife]; otherwise, why would he do it?"

Judging from responses to the equal treatment question (see table 3.1), women in our interview sample were much more skeptical than men about whether husbands could live up to a standard of equality: twenty-seven of fifty wives said no, and only six said yes. Many men were similarly skeptical, but men were more likely than women to see equal treatment in polygamous marriage as an attainable standard.

Many Bamako residents felt that men used to be more honest and fairer in marriage. By calling out husbands' inequitable treatment, interviewees positioned themselves as criticizing the character of contemporary men, whom they saw as corrupted by social and moral decay, not the standard of equitability itself or the institution of polygamy. Discussions of equitable treatment were important, partly because failing to meet this condition could exacerbate tensions and disputes between co wives.

The Teeth and the Tongue: Co-Wives in Conflict

Nalu, n di à lase alu ma, sinaya la gweleya man yi, a masilannin.

Ladies, let me tell you: the difficulties of being a co-wife are onerous and frightful.

—Bembeya Jazz, "Sino Mousso" (Guinea, 1976)

Some scholars have described relations among African co-wives as marked more by cooperation than competition (Anderson 2000; Sudarkasa 1973 and 1982). Others, however, have framed friction as the central dynamic between wives of the same husband, casting rivalry as "a structural given of the institution of polygamy" (Fainzang and Journet 1988, 124). Research in Nigeria (Barr et al. 2019) and Senegal (Hidrobo, Hoel, and Wilson 2020) has found polygamous unions less cooperative than monogamous ones. A cross-cultural review of polygamy research (Jankowiak, Sudakov, and Wilreker 2005, 95) found "a recurrent motif of strident co-wife hostility." A host of ethnographic observations also points to the prominence of conflict between co-wives. The word for co-wife in many African languages, noted anthropologist Jack Goody (1976), is etymologically related to the word for jealousy.[7] The Manding saying *sinaya jelen ye gala ye* translates as "Indigo is the lightest shade of co-wife relations"; in other words, even the friendliest of co-wives remain rivals.[8] According to a proverb with a different spin, "The teeth and the tongue are close, but they still quarrel" (Luneau 2010, 99). Some degree of conflict is inevitable between any two spouses, roommates, or others sharing a residence, and co-wives are no exception.

In many polygamous societies, household practices have arisen to contain co-wives' rivalry and limit friction between them. One example is the intrahousehold sharing of children described previously. Others include strict schedules apportioning husbands' time among their wives and systems of initiation apprenticing younger wives to older wives. In rural Bamanan communities, such practices could build a sense of mutual support and cooperation (Madhavan 2002). In Australian aboriginal and South African Zulu communities, a man might marry two sisters, using his wives' sororal bond to soften the competition between them (Chisholm and Burbank 1991; Gluckman 1950). Such sororal polygamy is rare in West Africa, however, and is absent in predominantly Muslim communities like Bamako because Islamic law explicitly forbids it (K. Ali 2006).

TABLE 3.2

**Polygamy's Disadvantages: Views of Wives (n = 50)
and Husbands (n = 50)**

Question: Does polygamy have disadvantages? If so, what are they? (*Interviewee
could list more than one.*)

	No. of Wives' Responses	No. of Husbands' Responses
Conflict, disagreement, or rivalry	43	34
Expense	4	11
Health risk to husband	0	2
Health risk to wife	2	1
Husband's unfairness	7	1
None	0	2

Co-wife hostility, despite practices intended to minimize it, was firmly rooted in Malian history (Golaszewski 2020), and most twenty-first-century Bamako residents associated polygamy with conflict. This was the most common disadvantage of polygamy cited by members of our interview sample (see table 3.2). As the practices that reinforced the traditional polygamous household model, like seniority and intra-household child fostering, declined (cf. Kilbride and Kilbride 1990), co-wife conflict intensified. Perhaps life in modern Bamako lacked safeguards to keep the teeth and the tongue from quarreling. Perhaps, as my informants kept suggesting, changing values had made men less fair and women less willing to bear stoically the injustices and injuries done to them by husbands, co-wives, and in-laws.

In addition to competing over their husband's affections, time, and resources, co-wives competed over the quantity and quality of their children—two factors that could strengthen their claims to social status and household resources (cf. Bledsoe 1993; Fainzang and Journet 1988). As Sarah Brett-Smith found in a Bamanan village, co-wives' competition could entail supernatural aggression and even "magical operations to kill each other's offspring" (2014, 168). Bamakois regularly evoked the danger of sorcery targeting co-wives or their children.

In Malian usage, the French word *marabout* (or its Manding equivalent, *moriba*) denotes a diverse array of ritual specialists, diviners, and healers using secret mystical knowledge to benefit clients, usually on a fee-for-service basis.

Marabouts were widely consulted throughout Mali, as well as by Malians abroad, who, by the 2010s, conferred with their marabouts back home via FaceTime and WhatsApp. Although men and women alike consulted marabouts, my interviews with marabouts and clients suggested that more women did so than men (marabouts estimated that 70 to 90 percent of their clients were women), and that clients' reasons for consultations were highly gendered. Men's visits tended to concern money, jobs, and promotions, while women's visits concerned marriage, fertility, and trouble with co-wives. A woman was most likely to enlist a marabout's services first to find a husband, then to have children, drive away rivals for her husband's affection, and—if the latter effort failed—strengthen her own position vis-a-vis her co-wife or co-wives (see also Djiré 2012, Edwards 2012; cf. Ammann 2020, Hannaford 2017).

None of my informants, marabout or client, claimed to have employed dangerous supernatural measures; in matters of *maraboutage*, they represented their actions as purely defensive. "I won't help a woman put a curse on her co-wife or rival," said one marabout interviewed about his work in 2012. "I won't accept requests to hurt someone else. If a client is set on harming another, I will take their money and pretend to work on their request, but I won't really do it." Yet women frequently suspected their co-wives or other rivals of using offensive maraboutage (such as spiritual aggression, harmful potions, and poisons) against them and their children. Men worried about unexplained deaths in polygamous households, for husbands, too, could become victims in these struggles. Ami (F, 28, accountant, no co-wife) said, "A polygamous husband these days can't have a long life: each of his wives will try to slip him some marabout's potion. That's why there are more old women than men in this country. The men die off due to problems over polygamy." Habib (M, 50, tailor, one wife) added: "When you have many wives, you're liable to die too soon because of the medicines your wives use to attract you to them. So long as each wife wants the husband for herself, he cannot have a long life."[9]

Doing Decohabitation

In light of these tensions, it is unsurprising that many wives in polygamous marriages preferred not to live alongside their co-wives. They wanted separate residences, ideally at some distance, perhaps in entirely different neighborhoods (as with Oumar's two wives in the introduction). This preference fueled further deviation from the traditional household model of a man's wives and their children sharing a common courtyard. Families and households around the world are full of non-coresidential domestic arrangements, from long-distance commuter spouses (Lindemann 2019) to transnational marriages (Hannaford 2017). Lacking an English name for a conjugal unit's division into separate residential subunits, I borrow a French term: *la décohabitation*.[10]

Decohabitation was nothing new in Malian polygamous marriage. In fact, the notion that co-wives ought to live together was alien to northern Malians when they first came to Bamako. "Up north, wives never live together; each wife constitutes her own household," said Hawa (F, 42, housewife, one co-wife), originally from the Timbuktu region. "It's really impossible to put a bunch of co-wives and their children together in the same house and claim to have a peaceful life."[11] For southerners, practical considerations sometimes stood in the way of achieving the traditional household ideal, as dwelling space might not be available for women marrying into polygamous unions (Cunningham 2014). Yet decohabitation was the standard most wives aspired to,[12] and in some respects, it resembled a form of polygamy discussed previously: a polygamous husband with strong kin connections to his rural community of origin often kept one wife there and another in Bamako, with wives periodically trading places.

Advocates of old-fashioned polygamous cohabitation cited a few factors in its favor, particularly family cohesion. "According to our tradition," said Maimouna (F, 55, housewife, two co-wives), "wives should live together in the same compound—this is the very meaning of polygamy. Without this cohabitation, there will be no affection among the children." Amira (F, 19, housewife, no co-wife) found the idea of separating co-wives and half-siblings unfathomable. "Personally, I can't imagine polygamy without cohabitation, because that allows the children and wives to live together in the same compound and to develop feelings for one another," she said. Others stated that maintaining transparency and ensuring fair treatment among co-wives depended on a wife's ability to observe her husband with his other wives. "When wives live apart, each one thinks the others are receiving more privileges than she is," said Safiatou (F, 22, market vendor, one co-wife). And just as wives feared that a husband with non-coresidential wives would go behind their backs, some husbands worried that it was easier for a wife living apart from her husband to have extramarital affairs. "I prefer that they share the same house because if they're separated, that can lead to infidelity," said Alassane (M, 35, market vendor, two wives).

In general, however, interviewees of both sexes strongly preferred separation of co-wives. Asked if it was better for co-wives to live together or apart, wives in our interview sample favored "apart" by a three-to-one margin, and husbands favored it by a two-to-one margin. Several informants said that Islamic law requires a polygamous husband to house each wife on her own. Most framed decohabitation as an answer to the conflict problem, often describing peaceful cohabitation in Bamako as an impossibility:

> These days it's unwise to have your wives in the same compound because men's behavior doesn't allow it; they're not fair with their wives, which is at the root of all the problems between wives.
>
> —Ami (F, 28, accountant, no co-wife)

If you have the means, you don't want your wives in the same house because they'll be causing you problems every day.

—Suliman (M, 55, chauffeur, one wife)

Everyone knows that two wives in the same house will lead to all kinds of situations. That used to be done, because . . . back then, it was the role of the first wife, but that role no longer exists.

—Tiemoko (M, 50, civil servant, one wife)

Wives shouldn't live in the same house. Our forefathers used to do this because they could be fair with their wives, but men nowadays can never be fair, and we know today that the problems of polygamy are the problems of injustices by men.

—Niaghalé (F, 54, market vendor, one co-wife)

For decades, researchers in West Africa (e.g., Blanc and Gage 2000; S. Camara 1978; Fainzang and Journet 1988; Gning 2011; Le Cour Grandmaison 1971; Paré 2018) and beyond (Koktvedgaard Zeitzen 2008) have documented a developing urban preference for co-wife separation. Senegal's Ousmane Sembène depicted this practice, which he called "geographical polygamy" (1976, 61), in his novel and film *Xala*. While Bamako interviewees evoked a strong preference for housing co-wives separately, I cannot say how often this preference translated into actual practice.[13] With Hoffman (2012), however, I see the decohabitation of polygamous unions as a socially significant trend. In light of studies among groups as disparate as Bedouin (Slonim-Nevo, and al-Krenawi 2006) and fundamentalist Mormon (Bennion 2016) families, one might even describe decohabitation as an emerging global "best practice" enabling more tranquil polygamous unions.

But decohabitation also imposes economic and social costs. As interviewees reported, living in separate locations makes it very difficult to know whether a husband is treating his wives equitably. It divides formerly unified polygamous families into separate units (Antoine and Marcoux 2014; Gning 2011). Bamako husbands in decohabiting polygamous unions struggled to support these multiple units and, like Oumar in chapter 1, to remember which of their belongings they left in which of their wives' houses. Wives in this situation often maintained a "fantasy of monogamy" (cf. Bennion 2016; Dial 2008; Jankowiak 2023), as suggested by two professional women in non-coresidential polygamous unions whom I interviewed:

I really don't feel part of a polygamous marriage because the other [wife]—I don't know her, I'm not interested in seeing her, I'm not trying to get to know her. She's somewhere in town, and I'm here.

—Niellé (age 35, lab technician, one co-wife)

While [my husband] is here, I take care of him 100 percent. I don't do anything else. And I don't want him to talk about his other family over there. In the beginning, that would hurt me, I didn't want it. . . . when he's not here, I tell myself he's traveling, he's on business.

—Kani (age 36, office worker, two co-wives)

Notably, both Niellé and Kani resided independently rather than with their in-laws and co-wives, thus escaping the most extreme forms of domestic surveillance to which many wives of absent husbands were subject (cf. Hannaford 2015). Niellé had never once met her co-wife or visited her house. Decohabiting wives could fantasize about dyadic relationships with their husbands, and their children had minimal contact with their half-siblings. Some women visited their co-wives so rarely, usually on major religious holidays, that their offspring were practically strangers. "Now you have women who don't even know what their co-wives look like—they don't even want to know," sociologist Aly Tounkara told me in 2020.

Kani, at the time we met (see Interlude 2), had not yet told her five-year-old son that his father—a wealthy entrepreneur—had two other wives, each with children of her own, in different cities. She would say, "Papa is away on business" whenever he was gone. A decade later, I still wonder when her son learned the truth, how it affected him, and how he now relates to his half-brothers and half-sisters. His polygamous family will be quite unlike the polygamous families his father and grandfather had grown up in. The three sets of half-siblings will share little mutual solidarity (badenya), and perhaps little rivalry (fadenya), either. Even if decohabitation should remain an elite privilege—it is expensive to own and maintain multiple houses, after all—the rise of unions like Kani's will alter Bamako's kin relations, and its marriage system along with them.

Conclusion: Polygamy as Institution and as Practice

While Bamako's "traditional model" of polygamous household organization was under strain, polygamy endured as an important arrangement evolving with urban conditions. Women and men tended to see it from very different perspectives. While everyone advocated a husband's equitable treatment of his wives, fairness in polygamous households remained elusive. Men and women alike perceived two major threats to proper polygamous practice: 1) a general erosion of morality; and 2) a weakening of the cultural safeguards that once curbed co-wife rivalries. This perception informed a strong preference for housing co-wives in separate residences, with each wife's dwelling becoming a semi-autonomous household. The preference for decohabitation threatened to nullify a commonly cited justification for polygamy: co-wives' ability to work together to lighten one another's burden of domestic tasks (Anderson 2000; Marcoux 1997). The "labor-saving hypothesis" cannot apply to co-wives who do not reside or spend time together.[14] Through decohabitation, Bamako wives renounced the traditional polygamous household model in favor of what Nnaemeka (1997, 176) derided as "monogamized polygamy."

To make sense of these dynamics, we must distinguish between the *institution* of polygamy (the formal rules and social norms governing the formation and conduct of polygamous unions) and the *practice* of polygamy (the actions of individuals within polygamous unions). Bamako residents tended to view polygamous marriage more positively as an abstract institution. They held out hope that polygamy could be fair and beneficial, even as they criticized men's abuses of it in everyday practice. Women's criticisms of these practices were especially strong, yet as we saw in the previous chapter, wives often said they lacked control over their own marital situations and thus felt they had little power to alter them. While they voiced strong preferences for having their husbands to themselves, they also felt they had little say over the outcome (see chapter 2)—a clear indication of their insufficient agency in this regard. Many a woman who didn't already share her husband with another wife fully expected a co-wife eventually to disrupt her marriage and her life.

Choosing from limited options, women exercised their restricted agency to lessen polygamy's disruptions in their lives. They might enlist the aid of ritual specialists to keep their husbands faithful, ward off romantic rivals, or even inflict supernatural aggression on co-wives. They might insist on decohabitation, minimizing the potential for conflict by minimizing contact with their co-wives. As mentioned in chapter 1, they also might accumulate their own savings to afford their own home where they could take refuge against co-wives' insults and provocations. In this manner, they did their best to make an institution about which they were deeply ambivalent work for them.

Given women's concerns about the practice of polygamy, how had the institution of plural marriage remained so well entrenched in Bamako society? To begin to answer that question, we must consider the role of social structures and social norms. The next chapter shows the powerful structures and norms maintaining polygamy's prominent place in Bamako.

4

What's Culture Got to Do with It?

Religion, Gender, and Power

Is the Malian man viscerally polygamous? Is he condemned to it, as some despairing wives predict?

—Adame Ba Konaré (Mali, 1993)

Historian Adame Ba Konaré penned these questions around the time she became first lady of Mali. They emerged from perennial discussions about polygamy's place in modern urban life. Polygamy was a deeply embedded yet contested masculine marital ideal among twenty-first-century Bamakois, many of whom represented it as central to their identity and culture. Polygamy had a formative influence on local society, family structure, and marriage systems, and figured prominently in centuries-old Mande legends whose cultural templates continued to shape Malian lives. In this chapter, we consider polygamy's association with religion, customs, and other cultural factors. To what extent can these factors explain polygamous marriage's persistence in contemporary Bamako? What does it mean to say that polygamy is deeply rooted in local culture?

Culture is a slippery concept. Even anthropologists, whose discipline brought the term to prominence, disagree on its definition; some (e.g., Abu-Lughod 1991; Trouillot 2003) prefer to abandon the concept altogether. In this chapter, I operationalize culture as shared norms, narratives, attitudes, practices, ideologies, and social structures. After introducing the concept of normative polygamy and explaining how it illuminates Bamako's marriage system, I discuss Islamic customs alongside Mande cultural narratives and gender ideology. As a case study illustrating gender ideology, I examine marital infidelity and the gendered double standard surrounding it, then consider how social structures limit women's autonomy through the so-called "patriarchal bargain." I also reflect on women's alternative sources of power in Mande society, raising a critical question: How much is polygamous marriage an expression of social hierarchy and patriarchal institutions—in other words, of dynamics of inequality and power relations that play out similarly around the world—and how much is it an expression of specific social structures only grasped within Bamako's particular cultural context? A related question: Does power manifest itself similarly all over the world, or might it have culturally specific forms? These questions bring my relativist and comparativist goals once again into tension.

Making Polygamy Normative

In some twenty-first-century nation-states, polygamy has been lawful yet marginal, even stigmatized, in everyday life. Among city dwellers in Malaysia and Indonesia, for example, polygamous unions were described as not "fully socially approved" despite their legality (Koktvedgaard Zeitzen 2018, 36), and many people viewed these unions as conflicting with their cultural ideals. Elite Malaysian and Indonesian men who pursued polygamous marriages sometimes sought to keep them secret, even from their first wives and their children; knowledge of these men's "outside wives" and children, if made public, could cause a scandal (Nurmila 2009).

Throughout the western Sahel, by contrast, polygamy bore no social stigma. In Mali, while the rate of plural marriage was higher in some segments of the population than in others, the practice cut across class, educational, ethnic, and religious distinctions (Antoine, Djiré, and Nanitelamio 1998). Early twenty-first-century Bamako, where roughly one in four wives shared their husbands with co-wives, was a place of "prevalent polygyny," the highest level of anthropologist Douglas White's (1988) classification of polygamous marriage systems.

Polygamy shaped all marital experience in Bamako to some extent. The late Moussa Konaté (2010, 157), a longtime commentator on city life, wrote: "Nobody is safe from what one could call 'the spirit of polygamy.' The parents or grandparents of a monogamous person today were in many cases polygamous. The relations thus induced have become, to an extent, a heritage, such that even a monogamous household is affected by the spirit of polygamy." Konaté's "spirit of polygamy" recalls the condition political scientist Stephen Macedo (2015, 150), referring to fundamentalist Mormons, dubbed "normative polygamy," in which plural marriage was understood as not merely a possible outcome but a mainstream, socially legitimate, and perhaps preferred practice. As we saw in chapter 2, some Bamakoises even considered polygamy inevitable in their own lives. The possibility of husbands taking multiple wives played a large part in determining how Bamako residents perceived the options available to them and their partners before, during, and after marriage. This was true to varying degrees throughout the entire region. As demographer Thérèse Locoh (1988, 460) wrote in an overview of West African family structure: "Polygamy, while far from generalized, remains the "perspective" of all unions. Even when it is not realized, it is present in the partners' minds, and gives a distinctive character to conjugal relations and to alliance relations more generally. The latter are always lived and interpreted in light of the potential option for polygamy."

In a marriage system characterized by normative polygamy, every union is potentially polygamous. This fact influences how people understand the rules of kinship as well as marriage (Goody 1976). It also shapes hierarchies of power and status. "He with only one wife is older brother to the bachelor" [Muso kelen tigi ye cɛgana kɔrɔkɛ ye], states a Manding proverb, suggesting that a man with only one wife suffers from many of the same challenges an unmarried man would. It thus frames monogamy as an inferior state, exposing husbands to various privations, particularly when their wives are away, ill, or otherwise indisposed to care for or engage in sexual relations with them (Luneau 2010, 89). Spared such domestic inconveniences, the polygamous husband sits atop the social pyramid, "older brother" to bachelors and monogamists alike. He enjoys his marital status as a form of social distinction.

In a personal sense, I encountered normative polygamy in Bamako most directly whenever someone (a taxi driver, an aikido teacher, a clerk at the neighborhood pharmacy; it was always a man) asked me when I would take another wife—not "whether," but "when." To respond that one wife was plenty for me, or even that taking an additional wife would violate the law in my country, seldom put the matter to rest. The notion that polygamy was simply impossible for me was alien to these men. "You can leave one here and take the other to the United States," a vendor selling me a used television set helpfully suggested.[1] Having grown up in a context of normative monogamy (or "mononormativity," as some label it), I had to learn Bamakois' implicit assumptions and expectations if I was to understand their marriage system.

To grasp normative polygamy in Bamako, consider these statements about monogamy made by three polygamous husbands from our interview sample:

> It's really when you know that you can't support two, then you limit yourself to just one. There's no problem.
>
> —Ousmane (M, 47, market vendor, two wives)

> Monogamy is a bit difficult. Unless you're really unable to, you should take two wives. That's what's best for you. If you cannot, there will come a time . . . a woman ages faster than a man.[2] If you don't remarry, there will come a time when your wife won't be able to continue meeting your needs. That's what brings a lot of discord into monogamous marriage.
>
> —Makan (M, 35, market vendor, two wives)

> Monogamy isn't worthwhile. Oneness is fitting only for God [Kelenya ka di Allah dɔrɔn de la]; where men are concerned, it's only the lack of means

that keeps them monogamous. Otherwise, they should take two, even if they must borrow money to do so. That's what is best.

—Yacouba (M, 67, market vendor, three wives)

For these husbands, polygamy was the default marital type—something all men should practice if they're able. Not that there was consensus on this. We have seen that many Bamako men did not aspire to polygamous marriage, and some were categorically opposed to it. Yet those in the latter camp still had to contend with normative polygamy in the form of peer pressure and cutting remarks at their expense. As Joseph, a fifty-year-old schoolteacher and the lone Christian husband in our interview sample, said, "Often, when you're not polygamous, you're treated like a weak man, yet it is not a weakness." Still, it was not the views of men like Joseph but of "older brothers" like Ousmane, Makan, and Yacouba (who, not coincidentally, shared a similar socioeconomic background) that set the tone on polygamy in the city.

What made polygamy normative, even for Bamakois who did not practice it? The answer lies partly in the cultural and historical roots of the people who have populated Bamako over many generations and in the hierarchies that have characterized their society. After examining religion, specifically Islam, we will look at gender ideology and the ambiguous nature of gendered power structures in Mande culture.

Islamic Perspectives on Polygamy:
From Recommended to Licit to Discouraged

Chapter 2 discussed five categories of justifications of polygamous marriage. The sixth category, divine will, refers to discourses grounded in Islam that represent polygamy as not merely licit but laudable, a fulfillment of God's plan. Unlike the first five rationales, this one (along with demography, the seventh category, discussed in the next chapter) was supported by men and women alike. Bamakois tended to frame taking multiple wives as a Muslim man's absolute prerogative. While we should not generalize such discourses to Muslims everywhere, they were quite widely dispersed. Historian Judith Tucker (2008) found similar ideas in the writings of early Muslim jurists, as did scholars in twenty-first-century societies from The Gambia (Dierickx et al. 2019) to Saudi Arabia (Yamani 2008).

I showed in chapter 2 that Islamic approaches to polygamy stemmed from one particular verse of the Qur'an (sura 4, verse 3): "If you fear you cannot be equitable to orphan girls (in your charge, or misuse their persons), then marry women who are lawful for you, two, three, or four; but if you fear you cannot treat so many with equity, marry only one, or a maid or captive. This is better than being iniquitous." For centuries, Muslims justifying polygamy through "divine will" have found in this verse an unambiguous authorization for men to take multiple wives, as long as they limited themselves to four. Proponents of "divine will," such as this husband in our interview sample, understood polygamy as an unconditional right granted by an omniscient deity:

> If you see that God authorizes man to take four wives, the meaning of that—God Himself knows us better than we know ourselves. It is He who created us, knows what we are made of, our needs, it is He who knows us better than we ourselves do. . . . If one wife doesn't satisfy you, take a second; if you aren't satisfied, take a third; if that doesn't satisfy you, take a fourth. Where's the problem? It's very simple, I take four wives if I have the means.
>
> —Ali (M, 39, unemployed, one wife)

Such scriptural interpretations led some women to conclude that, as Muslims, they could support nothing less than men's absolute entitlement to polygamy— indeed, that they *had* to submit to polygamy even if they understood it as inimical to their own interests. One wife responding to an interview question about the advantages and disadvantages of plural marriage said:

> The advantage I'd name for polygamy is based on religion, since polygamy is authorized by the Muslim faith. Beyond that spiritual authorization, I see only disadvantages. . . . In light of how I've suffered in mine, I wouldn't want to see my child in a polygamous marriage. But since religion requires a woman to accept polygamy, I can only accept it for my child.
>
> —Djelika (F, 33, market vendor, one co-wife)

While Islamic jurisprudence and custom have often buttressed normative polygamy, Muslim societies' stances regarding polygamy have varied from "permitted absolutely" to "permitted but not encouraged" to "prohibited" (Waines 1982). The stance of absolute authorization rested on the perspective of "traditional literalism" (Majeed 2015, 69 ff.). This perspective interpreted the Qur'an and the hadith (recorded sayings and traditions of the Prophet Muhammad) as endorsing polygamy almost unconditionally, elevating it as a valuable service to society (an idea we will explore further in the next chapter). The literalist perspective dissuaded many Malian women from criticizing polygamy as an institution, but they critiqued men's *practice* of it, especially in song lyrics (Durán 2017).

But does the Qur'an make polygamy an absolute right for Muslim men? Verse 129 of the fourth sura begins, "Howsoever you may try, you will never be able to treat your wives equally." To reconcile this verse with the one requiring equitable treatment, literalists have restricted a husband's duty of equitable treatment to measurable domains like time, housing, and money, while exempting his allocation of affection from the rule (K. Ali 2008). Alternative interpretations, particularly since the nineteenth century, have stressed the impracticability of equitable treatment. Reformist Islamic scholars, like Muhammad Abduh (b. 1849) of Egypt and Rashid Rida (b. 1865) of Syria, while recognizing polygamy as lawful in the Qur'an, wrote that Muslim governments could, nevertheless, justifiably curb the practice because of its associated social ills (K. Ali 2006; Stowasser 1994; Tucker 2008). Muslim women in Middle Eastern societies were not necessarily "required to accept" polygamy in their own marriages, and many insisted on monogamous marriage contracts (Baugh 2021). In Mauritania, Mali's Arab-majority neighbor to the northwest, Muslim jurisprudence recognized a "right to monogamy" that many women invoked (Fortier 2011).

During the late twentieth century, Muslim feminists like Fatima Mernissi (b. 1940) of Morocco and Amina Wadud (b. 1952) of the United States advanced scriptural interpretations lending normative weight to monogamy. They cast polygamy as justifiable to ensure social justice for orphans, never to quench male sexual desire (Mernissi 1987; Wadud 1999). So-called "contextualist" readings of Islamic scriptures by Pakistani scholar Fazlur Rahman (b. 1919) and others (see Nurmila 2009) have stressed the social and historical specificities of early seventh-century Arabia, where the Qur'an was revealed to the Prophet Muhammad, including a shortage of men due to high male mortality in warfare (K. Ali 2006). Accordingly, contextualists have framed polygamy as licit under circumstances similar to those, but not otherwise permissible, let alone generally recommended (Hasan 2019; Mashhour 2005). Unlike interviewee Ali, quoted previously, contextualists believed that a husband was *not* justified in taking an additional wife merely because his existing wife or wives "didn't satisfy" him. During the late twentieth and early twenty-first centuries, contextualist readings motivated a spate of reforms to marriage and family laws in countries throughout the Muslim world (see chapter 6).

Some people in Bamako favored limits on polygamy. "Islam allows polygamy, but not at any price," said Issiaka, the imam. "It gives reasons: for example, there must be a need for multiple wives—that is to say, you cannot take many wives just because you want to. Islam requires a reason, because when you're married in Islam, you cannot be running all over the place" (i.e., having extramarital affairs, even if they lead to marriage). Issiaka set out specific conditions in which he considered polygamy justified: "Perhaps you'll take a wife who is sick or who cannot have children; instead of divorcing her, instead of rejecting her, Islam allows you to take a second wife." Sali, a journalist in her thirties who shared her husband with one co-wife, also set a high bar for permitting polygamy under Islamic law:

> The Qur'an says a man can take two, three, or four wives, each of whom constitutes a household. You must give each wife a home, a roof over her

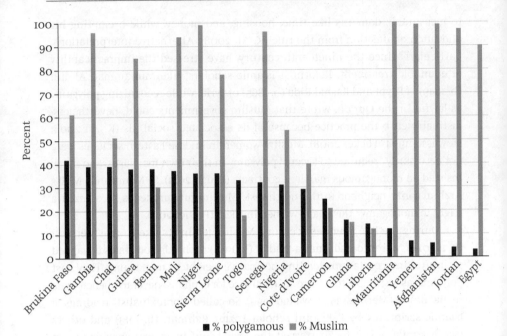

FIGURE 4.1 Islam and polygamy rates in twenty countries.
Source: DHS reports.

head, money for food, the same for each of your wives. But reality is completely different. If you know that you can't do all that, you have no right
to take more wives. . . . The Qur'an doesn't require polygamy of men; it
says that if you decide to marry multiple wives, you must be fair. If the
Qur'an is clearly followed, it's a manner of discouraging [polygamous
marriage].

Such critical perspectives defied the literalist narrative about the relationship between polygamy and Islam. That narrative is further discredited by
comparing the respective presences of polygamy and Islam across countries. In
figure 4.1, for each of twenty African and Middle Eastern countries, I have charted
in blue the portion of married women in polygamous marriages (arranged in
descending order), juxtaposed with the portion of Muslims in the population
in green.[3] This chart reveals no clear correlation between these two variables:
some countries with fewer Muslims (e.g., Benin and Togo) have very high polygamy
rates, while some countries with Muslim populations approaching 100 percent
(e.g., Afghanistan, Egypt, Jordan, and Yemen) have very low rates. Muslims in
Sahelian countries like Mali were much more likely to practice polygamy than
their coreligionists in North Africa and the Middle East, and polygamy was
nearly as common among Sahelian Christians (Antoine, Djiré, and Nanitelamio

1998; Diamouténé 2015; Paré 2018). In Mauritania, 100 percent Muslim, 4 percent of wives in the Moorish Arab majority were in polygamous marriages compared to 55 percent of wives among the Soninke minority. Polygamy rates varied little, moreover, between African Muslims and followers of African traditional religions (Fenske 2015).

Reviewing the demographic data, Youssef Courbage and Emmanuel Todd concluded that "mass African polygamy owes nothing to Islam" (2011, 42). I wouldn't go that far. After all, Islam provided a legitimizing framework as well as a code of conduct for polygamous marriage. But given the contrast between Arab and West African rates of plural marriage, religious doctrine could not be a primary factor underlying normative polygamy in Bamako's marriage system.

Gender Ideology and Patriarchy

In Western feminist analysis, the concept of gender ideology concerns "normative beliefs about the proper roles for and fundamental natures of women and men in human societies" (Philips 2001, 6016). Each society is characterized by a gender ideology composed mostly of unquestioned assumptions about what it means to belong to a gender category and how members of the different gender categories should relate. Such assumptions might include gender dualism (the notion that gender differences must conform to a binary division of traits), heteronormativity (the view that heterosexual relationships are the only "normal" or "natural" sexual relationships), and ideas about which tasks and types of labor are appropriate for people in each gender category. Gender ideologies both model and reflect social reality. A patriarchal gender ideology, more specifically, entails "a cultural understanding that men should have power and authority over women that women should not have over themselves or men" (Philips 2001, 6019).

By this standard, much evidence suggests that Bamako, and Mali in general, was subject to heavily patriarchal gender ideology. Most Malians surveyed have voiced opposition to equal rights for women and support for the idea that women should remain bound by "traditional laws and customs" (Afrobarometer 2013). With regard to sexuality, 54 percent of women in Bamako agreed with the statement that husbands should beat wives who refused sexual intercourse (DHS 2019).[4] In Bamako, only 36 percent of wives reported being able to ask their partner to use a condom, and just 28 percent reported being able to refuse sexual intercourse (DHS 2019). While Malian women had a culturally legitimated right to request and enjoy sex with their husbands, they also were socialized to satisfy their husbands' sexual needs and to accept the imposition of unwanted intercourse. "Women's sexuality is about giving and pleasing, whereas men's sexuality emphasizes experience and power," wrote sociologist Assitan Diallo, while "men's virility is praised and also presented as something out of their control: it is up to women to avoid being victims of their own sexual impulses, and to use the necessary means to enhance their own sexual capabilities" (2004, 183).

Such attitudes, when combined with male provider ideals and expectations of male authority over women, fostered what Robert Wyrod (2016, 25), drawing from fieldwork in urban Uganda, called "masculine sexual privilege." Men used their (increasingly uncertain) ability to dispense money to dependents as a justification of their right to maintain multiple sexual partners. As Wyrod found, this claim established a "reservoir of privilege that men could draw on when their relationships became stressed, often due to financial problems" (2016, 119).

Politically speaking, Malian women were discouraged from taking part in formal community decisions (Bleck and Michelitch 2018), while, at the national level, they were historically all but excluded from most governing bodies. While the number of female elected officials has grown in recent years, men still dominate national and local politics.[5] All these facts would qualify as manifestations of patriarchal gender ideology by S. U. Philips' definition: they enabled males to exercise forms of power over females that females could not exercise in return.

Mande historical epics, transmitted through oral traditions over many centuries, offer additional evidence for patriarchal ideology. These narratives shaped how Mande people (and Malians more broadly) understood their own past and its role in forming their modern cultural identity. Mande legends, folk tales, and sayings often portrayed women as weak, treacherous, and full of artifice as well as dangerous spiritual energy. These oral texts framed women's positive contributions to society in terms of their domestic duties and mothering abilities (Ba Konaré 1993; Hoffman 2002). In the Mande tradition of historical epics, while males were the protagonists and antagonists of history and the holders of formal political power, women often appeared as wicked stepmothers, dangerous sorcerers, and *femmes fatales* (Ba Konaré 1993; Conrad 1999).

Polygamy played a key role in the lives of this tradition's male and female characters alike. At the heart of the Sunjata epic, the master narrative of Mande history (Austen 1999), lies jealousy between co-wives. Sunjata Keita, before founding the Empire of Mali in the thirteenth century, must overcome the spells and curses of Sasuma Bereté, his father's first wife. To see her son Dankaran Tuman succeed his father on the throne, Sasuma stops at nothing to prevent Sunjata from fulfilling his royal destiny. Her unrelenting aggression eventually drives Sunjata, his mother Sogolon, and her other children into exile until Sunjata returns to claim his father's title and transform his kingdom into a mighty empire (Gomez 2018). Such accounts of medieval Mande "give weight to a view of relationships between co-wives and their respective children as intrinsically combative" (Brett-Smith 2014, 168; see, also, Kai 2014). In more recent history, some of the western Sahel's most prominent leaders of Islamic renewal and anti-colonial resistance were noted for accumulating many wives: El Hajj Omar Tall

(b. 1794) had at least fifteen, while Samori Touré (b. 1830) may have had up to eighty (Ba Konaré 1993).

As Philips (2001, 6020) cautions, however, the power of gender ideology usually resides less in myths and legends and more in an "implicit, pervasive, and diffuse semiotic gendering of all of social life" (see also Grosz-Ngaté 1989). Gendering of this sort manifests in kinship systems. As we saw in chapter 1, Bamako families were largely patrilineal and patrilocal, meaning that, after marriage, brides had to move into their husbands' homes and, in many cases, live under their in-laws' close supervision. Since polygamy has been closely associated with patrilineal, patrilocal cultures (Clignet 1970), local rules of kinship probably had a greater role than Islam in maintaining normative polygamy (Courbage and Todd 2011).

We also saw in chapter 1 that Malian marriage systems were thoroughly structured by patriarchal ideology and characterized by deep inequalities. Only males could be the subject of the Manding verb "to marry" (*ka furu*), while females had to be the object. Men tended to marry much younger women, and most wives observed an unreciprocated taboo against calling their husbands by name (chapter 1). In rural Bamanan communities of the Segou region, elders told anthropologist Maria Grosz-Ngaté (1989) that a man's wife had to be his social inferior. A man of noble ancestry could marry a woman of slave ancestry, for instance, but a man of slave ancestry could never marry a woman of noble ancestry. Normative polygamy could be considered a prominent manifestation of patriarchal ideology, since it enabled only males to take multiple spouses and reinforced male power over women within marriage. Anthropologist Sory Camara characterized polygamy as an instrument of male power. "The discord that results," he wrote, "conceals from the wives their common cause and makes their husband into the all-powerful arbiter" (1978, 46)—hence, husbands' view of polygamy as a disciplinary tool within marriage (chapter 2). Polygamy, kinship structures, and Bamako's wider marriage system clearly fit Philips's definition of patriarchal gender ideologies in all these respects.

Infidelity and the Sexual Double Standard

"All cultures may not be monogamous," wrote anthropologists Lionel Tiger and Robin Fox (1998, 117) in their review of human biology and cultural adaptation, "but they are all certainly adulterous." Discourses about sexual fidelity in Bamako illustrate how the patriarchal structures outlined previously reinforced normative polygamy. Bamakois used the Manding terms *tilenbaliya* and *tilenɲɔgɔnyebaliya* (literally, "lack of being honest/lack of being straight with each other") to refer to sexual infidelity; a related term, *ko lankolonw* (literally, "empty/worthless things"), referred more generically to "naughty acts" or "fooling around"—a category that encompasses flirting and other séductive behaviors as well as sexual intercourse. Bamakois' most common French euphemism for infidelity was *faire les bêtises* (literally, "to make mistakes" or "to do foolish things").

The problem of sexual fidelity generated much concern and debate among Bamako residents. In their dating and marital relationships, lack of mutual trust could foster preemptive cheating (Castro 2012; Doquet 2014). We have no accurate way to gauge the proportion of husbands or wives who actually participated in extramarital sexual relations; survey data on such behavior, when they exist, are based on self-reported responses and, therefore, suspect. But the *perception* among men and women in Bamako was that marital infidelity was rampant and rising.

> [Men and women] have changed. Before, wives would be faithful. Infidelity wasn't so widespread. But where we are now, infidelity has become a national scourge.
>
> —Sambou (M, 56, teacher, two wives)

Many interviewees described marital infidelity as part of the broader dynamic of moral decay in their society and bemoaned the erosion of taboos against adultery. Imams told me that accusations of spousal cheating were among the most frequent family problems in which they were asked to intervene.

Bamakois often attributed the spread of marital infidelity to socioeconomic factors, such as more women working outside the home, or the cost of urban living forcing wives to find lovers in order to meet their household expenses. Others blamed new childrearing and media environments for encouraging immorality among the youth:

> What has changed is that more and more children are not being raised right; we've allowed enough freedom for children to say that they need their input on everything, plus they have access to information from TV, radio, cell phones, the internet and everything, so a lot has opened up at the young people's level [and] sexual relations have been demystified. . . . What this all means is that we ruin those other values that dictate that an unmarried woman shouldn't have relations with a man. This is contrary to religion: a married woman should stay faithful to her husband, a husband should stay faithful to his wife. These values have practically all been abandoned.
>
> —Lamine (M, 55, public health specialist, one wife)

Perceptions of rampant adultery reflected deep-seated anxieties about Mali's direction in the era of neoliberal globalization. Three significant developments affecting urban life starting in the first decade of the twenty-first century deserve emphasis in this regard. Two of them, at least on the surface, were positive new technologies. First, mobile phones came into wide use, making telecommunications accessible to virtually every adult. Second, affordable Chinese-made 110-cc motorcycles facilitated travel around town. Known locally as *djakartas*, they cost about one-fifth the price of the Yamahas that had previously dominated the local market (Lambert 2006). Whereas only 28 percent of Bamako households owned a motorcycle in 2001, nearly 70 percent did by 2018 (INSTAT 2018).

A third change was of a different sort. In neighborhoods throughout Bamako, private entrepreneurs began opening small, discreet establishments selling alcohol and offering rooms by the hour (Bourdarias 2009). One journalist estimated that the city was home to over a hundred of these so-called *bars chinois*, so named because many belonged to expatriate Chinese entrepreneurs (Tembely 2017)—another product of globalization. If the hotel room tryst had once been a privilege of elites in a few pricey locations downtown, the humble *bar chinois* (see figure 4.2) brought it, along with inexpensive commercial sex (Neubauer 2016), to the masses where they lived. "And it's not just young people going there either, it's older ones too, married people," fretted Issiaka, the imam. "It's very serious. [Infidelity] has always been there, but the *bars chinois* have added to the gravity of the situation—it's become the style now. These last few years, there's truly been a degradation of morals."

Taken together, these changes had indelibly altered Bamakois' social landscape by the time I began fieldwork in 2010. Thanks to these developments, people who once had little choice but to submit to the mutual surveillance system of the extended family household and residential neighborhood now could escape that system's gaze, at least for a few hours. The mobile phone provided the means to communicate in complete privacy—one Bamako journalist described it as a "vector of infidelity" (Gnimadi 2009)—while the djakarta facilitated lovers' covert liaisons, usually at bars chinois outside their own neighborhoods. And city residents had the impression that these developments encouraged mass participation in once-rare illicit behaviors.

Male infidelity was believed to be the most common form. In our focus group discussions, participants' estimates of the percentage of Bamako husbands who cheated on their wives ranged from 60 to 100. Impressions were just as bad in our interview sample: "Out of 100 men, well, you might find 100 unfaithful ones," said Ali (M, 39, unemployed, one wife). Many women described a penchant for straying as an essential male characteristic. "Infidelity is in men's nature, nobody can do anything about it," said Niaghalé (F, 54, market vendor, one co-wife). Mamou (F, 31, secretary, one co-wife) made a direct connection to polygamy: "Men's infidelity is natural for them, for they think that they cannot limit themselves to one wife." Such explanations were often grounded in notions of a biologically determined male sex drive casting polygamy as the only responsible answer. If a woman refused to share her husband with a co-wife, this

FIGURE 4.2 Signs for a *bar chinois*, advertising food and beer (2010).

thinking went, she would end up sharing him with a mistress (Blanc and Gage 2000; cf. Wa Karanja 1994).

Some Bamakois blamed wives for their husbands' sexual dalliances in terms that underscored masculine sexual privilege:

> With men, if you can't manage to have regular relations with your wife—she's always making problems—well, this can push a man to look

elsewhere. When you're always unhappy with your wife, you'll go out chasing skirts [draguer]. And if you're always staying in with your wife, she might even underestimate you. She has to know that you're going out, even if you're just going out for a walk.

> —Souleymane (M, 55, driver, one wife)

Wives also might blame themselves:

> The primary cause of infidelity is us, the wives. A wife who takes good care of her husband at home, avoids conflict with him—[that husband] will never be tempted to cheat on his wife because he has no reason to do it.

> —Amira (F, 28, housewife, no co-wife)

Husbands were not alone in seeking out extramarital partners; many Bamako residents believed infidelity had become common and even overt among wives as well. "There are unfaithful wives who don't hide it anymore," Nantené, a twenty-five-year-old single female entrepreneur, told me in 2012:

> I know a woman who cheats on her husband and he's fully aware of it. He *knows* his wife's lover who gives her everything, who even had a house built for this man's wife, who bought cars for this man's wife, who furnished the house. And this guy lives in that house with his children. It's not something hidden.

People ascribed wives' infidelity to their growing consumerism and materialism (particularly their need for money to spend on glamorous clothing for the weddings and naming ceremonies that were a fixture of women's social life in Bamako). They also blamed infidelity on wives' growing independence from the domestic surveillance of in-laws, and on women's growing desire to challenge the double standard that condemned unfaithful wives while ignoring unfaithful husbands. As Fatou, a single twenty-eight-year-old office worker, told me, "Wives are thinking, 'My husband's cheating on me, why should I stay faithful? I can cheat on him too.'"

But cases of Bamako wives overtly taking lovers remained exceptional and infidelity's potential consequences remained very much gendered. As noted in chapter I, a wife who caught her husband cheating would be expected to forgive him, while a husband who caught his wife cheating would be expected to divorce her. This social attitude influenced the legal system. In 1985, a Bamako court declared that a husband's adulterous behavior did not render continued marriage to his wife impossible; five years later, the same court ruled that a wife's adulterous behavior rendered continued marriage to her husband impossible.[6] Many Bamakois, judges included, saw male infidelity as natural, even inevitable, while attributing female infidelity to weak moral fiber and poor upbringing.

Moreover, some people believed that Islam, and specifically its scriptures allowing men to practice polygamy, effectively gave husbands *carte blanche* to engage
in extramarital affairs:

> A man can be unfaithful because religion authorizes him to take up to
> four wives. But he should do it respectfully, in such a way that his wife
> never crosses paths with his girlfriend. In my own case, I know that my
> husband is cheating on me, but he has always kept it secret and I see
> this as a sign of respect. He could have done it openly, without respect-
> ing me.
>
> —Aminata (F, 21, housewife, no co-wife)

A single woman could be tempted by a married man's romantic overtures, given
the prospect that their affair might be legitimized into marriage. "A man can
easily have a *deuxième bureau*,[7] a mistress, because he tells her, 'Act properly, and
if I'm happy I'll marry you,'" Penda, a female journalist, told me in 2010, "There
are many cases of married men with mistresses who really take advantage of
many women like that." As Inge Wittrup (1990, 134) found in The Gambia, husbands' ability to take additional wives made having girlfriends "a legal and
acceptable part of the marriage system" (cf. Olaore and Agwu 2020). Acceptable,
that is, as long as men pursued their affairs discreetly and never accumulated
more than four wives.

Women resented this double standard. "Married men can hang out with as
many women as they want, even pick up girls, abusing their positions of power
without anyone taking offense," an unmarried Bamakoise protested in a blog
post (Touré 2018): "If a married man is caught cheating on his wife, he will say
that he has a right to four wives and that he is getting ready to take a second
wife. But even if this were true, we often forget that religion strictly prohibits
intimate relations with someone who will be the second wife prior to marriage.
We forget that it was to avoid unfaithfulness that Islam allows polygamy."

When I spoke to the post's author, Sadya Touré, in 2020, she highlighted the
gendered disparity between men's and women's marital infidelities. "You rarely
see a couple that reunites after the wife commits adultery and her husband for-
gives her; I've never heard of such a case," she told me. "I've never heard a
Malian religious leader discuss men's adultery."

There were some who did. The popular charismatic preacher Chérif Ousmane Madani Haïdara, notably, asked his followers to swear a public oath to
avoid six major sins, including adultery (Chappatte 2018). Members of the conservative Salafi movement, for their part, advocated strict punishments, such as
death by stoning, for those convicted of adultery and other forms of fornication,
seeing such measures (based on their interpretation of Islamic law) as a deter-
rent against sinful conduct. In describing these so-called *hudud* punishments, a
young Salafi imam I met named Abdoul Wahhab, who led prayers at a mosque

in the Badalabougou neighborhood, said that Mali would not truly be a Muslim country until it adopted this approach:

> There's a punishment which is supposed to be applied under sharia; that's when you will know it's a Muslim country. For example, if you have never been married at all, you are flogged [for committing fornication]. If you have been married and you are caught in fornication, you are put to death. That does not happen here.[8]

Indeed, armed Islamist insurgents enacted hudud punishments in some of the northern towns they occupied in 2012. But no mass movement in Bamako openly advocated similar punishments during the 2010s.[9] Bamako's philanderers had little reason to fear social or legal sanction; if caught with a woman not his wife, a husband could claim he planned to marry her. Supported by dominant patriarchal ideology, the persistent sexual double standard worked in tandem with masculine sexual privilege and normative polygamy, each one strengthening the others and facilitating men's entry into polygamy.

Bargaining with Polygamy

While patriarchy clearly structured many aspects of relationships in Mali, this is not to say women exercised no power within this system. I find the concept of the "patriarchal bargain" (Kandiyoti 1988) useful for contextualizing women's choices pertaining to marriage and polygamy. This concept, introduced in chapter I, assesses women's agency within the household, where husbands and wives often have conflicting interests due to their assigned roles within marriage. While wives in Bamako worked to protect their interests within marriage (see previous chapter), many also submitted to patriarchy when they perceived benefits from doing so. They accepted reduced autonomy in exchange for full womanhood and other purported social and economic benefits.

Bamakoises lived in some respects under a system fitting Kandiyoti's "classic patriarchy" model of the Muslim Middle East, North Africa, and Asia (1988, 278). They married at a young age into multigenerational, patrilocal households where they remained subordinate to senior women; their husbands' patrilineages claimed their children; and few inherited wealth from their fathers (patrimony being generally reserved for sons). But Bamako's system also had traits in common with Deniz Kandiyoti's sub-Saharan African model of patriarchy: wives traditionally kept their earnings separate from their husbands' money, allowing them some autonomous space within marriage. Most also had considerable leeway in conducting their own income-generating activities and setting their own domestic priorities, for example in decisions about how to spend their earnings and raise their children. Polygamy could expand this leeway. A wife in a non-coresidential polygamous union enjoyed significant freedom of movement, especially if she lived apart from her in-laws. And because marriage in Bamako often was not really about the couple, many wives sought to avoid financial dependence on their husbands.

Bamako's patriarchal bargain played out, ideally, on the following terms. Upon marrying and entering their husbands' homes, women adopted a code of conduct that they understood as contrary to their own interests, at least in the short term: in exchange for limited autonomy, they secured the promise of economic and social support from their husbands and in-laws over the long term—even if this promise was frequently broken. By embodying the virtues of patience (*sabali*) and forbearance of suffering (*munu*) described in chapter 1, a wife put her husband and his kin under a publicly acknowledged moral obligation to support her. This obligation was all the more powerful when a husband had multiple wives. A first wife who welcomed a newly arrived co-wife into her home without complaint, or a second wife who placidly ignored the first wife's many barbs and provocations, built up esteem in the eyes of her husband, in-laws, and neighbors. One of Mali's most popular female singers, Babani Koné, described life in a polygamous household as "a constant competition, where the wife who has the qualities of respect, humility, tenderness . . . etc., comes to triumph. She usually is the one that draws the admiration of her husband" (quoted in Durán 2017, 170; cf. Gilbert 2018). Over time, such a "good wife" could convert this esteem into assistance from those around her because, as Schulz (2012b, 55) put it, "only endurance [*munu*] puts a woman in a position where she might request support in situations of difficulty."

For Bamakoises, then, the polygamous patriarchal bargain was not necessarily about trading an exclusive relationship with their husbands for greater social status and economic security, as Nurmila (2009) described for wives of wealthy Indonesian polygamists. Instead, even wives of poor Bamakois could use the bargain to accumulate a gendered form of symbolic capital (Bourdieu 1986), a durable asset that could benefit them and their children in the future. For women to collect this gendered symbolic capital, they had to fall in line with the patriarchal bargain.[10] Women, thus, clearly exercised agency within their polygamous marriages, but their options for garnering symbolic capital were circumscribed by their husband's control.

By the 2010s, decades of economic insecurity had weakened men's capacity as providers, unbalancing Bamako's patriarchal bargain. Even when husbands failed to hold up their end of the bargain, however, their wives were still expected to abide by it and usually did, fearing the social sanctions for breaking that bargain (e.g., by leaving their husbands and setting up their own independent households). If a woman became her household's main breadwinner, she had to maintain the bargain's pretense, quietly passing her earnings to him so he could preserve his dignity (Schulz 2012b), not to mention his masculine sexual privilege.

Bamakoises bargained with patriarchy from positions of weakness. Unable to get what they preferred, they tried to secure conditions that were at least minimally acceptable. This explains why women expressed strong dislike for the practice of polygamy without contesting men's right to engage in it (chapter 2).[11] Khadidja, a female public intellectual in her forties who provided Islamically inspired commentary on the phone-in radio program described in Interlude I, exemplified this conflicted stance. When I spoke to her in 2012, she described herself as personally opposing polygamy despite being in a polygamous marriage herself:

> When I say I'm against polygamy—I'm in it, and one can't change one's destiny. But men are often dishonest, so polygamy is never honest. From what I've learned, from my own marriage, I saw that the people who complained about it were right. A man is never honest with his polygamous household. That's why I say I don't agree with it. But it was my destiny and I can't change it. I don't think a polygamous man can be honest—maybe just one out of 100, which is not enough. If it was 25–30 percent, that would be acceptable. But one percent, this is dire![12]

Khadidja's use of the concept of destiny to justify being in a type of marriage that she found inherently objectionable is striking. By calling out the polygamous husband's chief challenge—that is, the near-impossibility of being honest, hence equitable, with his wives—she came close to providing a religious rationale for invalidating plural marriage as an institution. That Khadidja refused to take this additional step, settling, instead, for a polygamous marriage she experienced as dishonest, reveals both the strength of normative polygamy and women's limited bargaining power within Bamako's marriage system. Women were disadvantaged within this system. And yet, they were not powerless.

"Any Man Will Kneel before a Woman": An Alternative View of Gendered Power

Before we get too comfortable with the notion that women in Bamako have been uniformly oppressed by patriarchy, let's consider male-female relations under a set of assumptions shared by many Malians. Rather than stressing gendered structures of domination, these assumptions stressed the existence of gendered spheres of activity and influence that were complementary even as they were hierarchical. The distinction between these spheres might be best understood not as public versus private or public versus domestic (cf. Rosaldo, Lamphere, and Zimbalist 1974) but as visible versus invisible. While Bamako men held a near-monopoly on positions of visible, formal authority, according to this way of thinking, Bamako women commanded hidden forms of power that offset their exclusion from formal mechanisms of household and state decision-making.

Some scholars found support for the idea that Malian men's dominance was more illusory than real. They followed the lead of anthropologists Susan Carol Rogers (1975) and Peggy Sanday (1981), who framed male dominance in various pre-industrial settings as a "myth" obscuring important domains of female power from public view. Rogers, for instance, studied a French peasant community in which men and women occupied "partially divergent systems of perceived advantages, values, and prestige." "The members of each group," she wrote, saw themselves "as the 'winners' in respect to the other" (1975, 729). In a similar way, anthropologist Barbara Hoffman (2002, 16) has noted, the "acceptance of and submission to a public ideology of subordination [gave Mande women] the cultural space in which to cultivate substantial quantities of actual power and effective authority."

Evidence suggests that male dominance among the Mande people, and in Mali more generally, was less ironclad than it appeared, and that local gender ideology was suffused with hints of women's invisible power that may have survived from an earlier, less overtly patriarchal time. Historical accounts indicate that fifteenth-century Mali was home to a matrilineal kinship system (Ba Konaré 1993; Thiam 2020). "The public performance of the patriarchal ideology" in contemporary Bamanan life, linguist Kassim Koné (2002, 28) wrote, "is challenged by the private matrifocal behavior. The matrilineal challenge is mute but obvious and can even be found in aspects of language when it subverts the dominant patrilineal ideology." Some analyses of the same Mande legends described above as representing patriarchal gender ideology have stressed the fact that women, while rarely exercising political authority, commanded spiritual powers essential to male leaders' successful exploits. Heroes acquired much of their occult force via their mothers. If men in these epics were "instruments of conquest and destruction," wrote historian David Conrad (1999, 191), women were "the sabuw (sources, providers) of all that men accomplish." Mande epics portrayed Sogolon, mother of Sunjata, as endowed with potent supernatural abilities of her own that stemmed from her spirit animal, the buffalo; without Sogolon's spiritual assistance, her son could never have conquered his enemies (see figure 4.3). This portrayal led historian Michael Gomez to describe women in medieval Mali as "alternative sites of power" (2018, 76).

Observers of modern Mande society found similar signs of hidden female power that defied and even counteracted male authority. In marriage and sexual relationships, Malian women employed ruses designed to "turn men's own weapons against them" (Broqua and Doquet 2013, 293), setting traps into which their male partners would be led by their masculine sense of pride and honor. In the bedroom, women could use sexual wiles (known in Manding as taafe fanga, literally "skirt power") to manipulate their male partners (Schulz 2012b, 52).

FIGURE 4.3 Place Sogolon, a traffic circle in Bamako featuring a statue of Sogolon's spirit animal, the buffalo.

Photo: Wikimedia Commons, 2008.

Men deeply feared and were even intimidated by women's childbearing ability, which they saw as both miraculous and inherently dangerous (Conrad 1999; cf. Grillo 2018; cf. Liogier 2020). And in a society where secret knowledge was highly valued (Roth and Jansen 2000), a wife had another weapon: as an outsider to her husband's household, she could leave in the event of marital conflict, taking with her sensitive information that could lead to her husband's downfall. As one Bamanan villager told Réné Luneau (2010, 122), "A woman is never the wife of one man. She can divorce and later marry your worst enemy. If she knows all your secrets, you will be utterly helpless."

In the domain of politics, it is true that women were usually excluded from formal power in colonial and postcolonial Mali. Yet even here they managed to wield hidden influence. Leaders of the women's wings of Malian political parties saw their role less as making demands through direct confrontation (which they described as an alien tactic), and more as devising nonconfrontational approaches to shape decisions. Malian women, by this logic, chose not to challenge male political dominance because they knew how to circumvent patriarchal authority by pursuing their goals in less overt domains where they enjoyed greater autonomy. In light of this approach, we might conceive of power more expansively than its official or legal exercise (de Jorio 1997).[13]

Then there is the question of sorcery, specifically the version known in Manding as *subaya*, the most dangerous form of supernatural power. Historians have noted that women faced no disadvantage relative to men in this arena, and, indeed, many of the most powerful sorcerers were reputed to be women (Conrad 1999; Kai 2014). Anyone seeking to understand Malian male-female relations from an insider's perspective should not dismiss sorcery's importance. Alongside women's spells and curses cast that many men genuinely feared, the category of subaya included the use of poisons (Conrad 1999). The deadliest poisons in Bamanan villages were reportedly known only to women. From her Beledugu fieldwork, Sarah Brett-Smith (2014, 181) concluded that "in the world of the 'night,' women [had] the advantage, and men [were] often pawns in a game played in the unfamiliar territory of the darkness." Women's reputed mastery of subaya was, perhaps, the ultimate expression of their invisible power. Bamanan belief also ascribed to women the strongest ability to place curses on other people; fear of this ability gave women "a very robust role in the internal politics" of their husbands' families, according to Kassim Koné (2002, 26).

In its most extreme form, women's resistance in the domestic realm could manifest as overt violence. Bamako newspapers occasionally reported on women who attacked their husbands or co-wives with physical weapons—typically knives, wooden pestles, boiling water, or other kitchen items. The headlines often revolved around polygamy: for example, "Stabbed to death for wanting to take a second wife," or "Wife kills co-wife and her son."[14] While rare, such domestic dramas garnered more media attention than cases of husbands attacking wives. They reminded readers that there were limits to what women would tolerate in their marriages, and that women were anything but helpless in the face of male efforts to dominate them.

Many people in Bamako even objected to characterizations of Malian women as victims of oppression. Of our interview sample participants, Malik (M, 45, office worker, two wives) did so the most explicitly, and his remarks deserve quoting at length:

> In our society, in fact, it's women who have the biggest share, women who influence men's decisions, just not in the open. . . . Those white people do their surveys and things, but in reality, these are the depths of the culture that we preserve, that we don't speak about, and these so-called feminists often don't look into those depths. I think this is very important—everyone should consider these aspects, otherwise women will have lost something. That's why, generally, in these meetings where they talk about gender and the like . . . people tend to mislead women, to minimize the things they've already won. There is not one man who can beat his chest and claim, "No woman can change me," that's nonsense, just nonsense! Because a woman who really knows how to use her

femininity—not her sex, I mean, just her way of sticking up for herself, of speaking with a friend, with her husband, using respect and everything—she can take everything from him, influence his decisions, lead him to change his mind about anything, this is clear. I would go so far as to tell you something that we also say, culturally: Any man—no matter his size or build—will kneel before a woman. There is not one man who doesn't kneel for a woman, if only for sexual relations. That's how God Himself created things; woman is very, very great. God Himself made it this way; if only through the sexual act, you'll find yourself on your knees somewhere. . . .

You'll notice in our cultural milieu, I will never talk about certain aspects of a woman's sexuality. I'll never speak of childbirth; I can't even listen to media reports about it. I was trained as a biologist originally, I can speak about all the organs and everything I was taught. But in my upbringing, I was forbidden from speaking of some things regarding women. Menstruation, I can't talk about that; childbirth, I can't talk about that, because it diminishes me. Culturally, I know that a man who takes these things lightly is diminished. . . . That's the truth, women occupy a very important place in our society—contrary to what I often hear.

A number of important themes appear in this excerpt. Alongside the fear of the female body and its reproductive capacity, Malik expressed men's anxiety of being overpowered by women, an anxiety deeply ingrained in Mande society (Brand 2001, 145).[15] He saw men and women as inhabiting separate but complementary domains. He saw women's power as capable not merely of opposing male dominance but of dismantling it, undoing men's power so subtly that people might not even notice that only its hollowed-out husk remained. Malik saw outsiders—in particular, white people and "so-called feminists"—as oblivious to such hidden power.

Can we afford to judge male-female relations by a single standard in every culture? From a Western feminist perspective, patriarchy in Bamako (and most everywhere else) is an objective fact, and its consequences are evident in global indexes of gender inequality. From the perspective of many in Bamako, men and women draw their powers from different sources and wield them in different arenas, and it does women a great disservice to assess their power using a standard that is, in fact, particular to men.

Conclusion: Culture and Power

Culture is notoriously difficult to define. Even as it shapes human society, human behavior reshapes it. Ben Cislaghi, researching social change in Senegal, described cultures not as self-contained worlds but rather as "markets or public squares where the leading values are continuously bargained" (2018, 19). In other words, culture is in constant flux, transformed by social, economic, and political factors. In Adame Ba Konaré's elegant metaphor, "Culture bathes in history like the fetus bathes in amniotic fluid" (1993, 18).

In this chapter, I have toggled between two approaches to analyze polygamy's links with culture in Bamako. One approach is universalist and comparative, viewing behavior from an outsider's perspective; for example, by comparing the distribution of polygamous marriage and Islam in different societies and assessing marital behavior using universal categories such as social structures, male dominance, and patriarchy. The other approach is place-specific and relativistic, examining gender relations from the viewpoint of Bamakois themselves by exploring local notions of normative polygamy, gender attributes and roles, and invisible power. While these approaches risk generating incommensurable findings, both are necessary in ethnographic research. The ethnographer must be able to hold these contradictory ideas simultaneously.

Much evidence suggests that women in Mande society, including Bamako, were more powerful than outsiders often realized and that women commanded largely unacknowledged forms of power.[16] While I would not characterize male dominance in Mali as a myth, I contend that supposedly universal rankings and indexes of gender inequality tend to overlook important aspects of Malian gender dynamics. At the very least, the concept of "mythical male dominance" should remind us of women's capacity to oppose and subvert male agendas even in contexts of apparent patriarchal power; it should encourage us to be skeptical of one-sided narratives of female victimization. Malian women *never* have been powerless, nor should we understand them primarily as victims of oppression. They often exercised power in roles and spaces different from those in which men exercised it.

At the same time, my research in Bamako highlighted limits on women's power and agency regarding marital questions such as sexual fidelity and polygamy. In this domain, women's power was largely tactical, enabling them to react to the situations and conditions that men had created. As Raphaël Liogier (2020, 128–9) wrote about women everywhere, "Yes, women have learned to play men skillfully for their own comfort and survival. . . . But it's still never anything more than a negative, covert power, devoid of any positive recognition." Male power over marriage, by contrast, has been more strategic, shaping decisions from the household via domestic authority (chapter 1) up through the national level via law and policy (see chapter 6). In Bamako, a woman's ability to set the agenda for marriage, especially her own, was highly circumscribed (cf. Olaore and Agwu 2020). As a result, even if men's power relative to women's had diminished over time, marriage was one arena in which the city's men could exercise significant control. Women, particularly younger ones, were left with less autonomy and compelled to tolerate conditions they disliked within marriage. They could use invisible power to *undermine* and *resist* but rarely to *undo* male dominance in the marital domain. A woman could make her husband regret his decision to take another wife but usually was unable to prevent him from carrying out that decision.[17]

As a result, in Bamako of the 2010s, many women were unable to avoid polygamous marriages of which they wanted no part. Instead, as we saw with Khadidja, they acquiesced to these marriages. Bamakoises in polygamous unions could use their power to complicate (even, in a few cases, end) the lives of their husbands and co-wives but rarely to escape from polygamy altogether. Despite their distaste for polygamy, most wives, nonetheless, found themselves submitting to patriarchal bargains that maintained polygamy (whether real or potential) in their lives.

While women in Bamako are not best understood as victims of oppression, I find that cases like Khadidja's lend weight to the "oppression hypothesis." This is the hypothesis that women enter polygamous unions primarily because patriarchal institutions reduce their agency and restrict their marital options, driving them into polygamous marriages that run counter to their interests (see introduction). Mindful of the steep price—including social ostracism and physical violence—for challenging an entrenched gender ideology and its specific manifestations (including normative polygamy), most Bamako women had to make the best of the patriarchal bargain, embracing the virtue of stoic patience (see chapter 1). While they might criticize husbands' specific abuses within the framework of their polygamous marriages, they stopped short of calling polygamy itself into question. Judging from their unwillingness to contest or disrupt their society's dominant gender hierarchy and its supporting ideology (cf. Brzezińska 2021; Wyrod 2016), Bamako women faced real limitations on their agency within marriage. Those with the greatest agency were older, higher-status women, many of whom already had endured unwanted polygamous marriages themselves.

To return to the question of culture: this chapter's ethnographic and comparative analyses suggest that polygamous marriage's longevity in Bamako stemmed more from firmly embedded social structures than fixed cultural scripts or values. The institution of polygamy was supported by gender-based power disparities and a durable sexual double standard in the city. Patriarchal norms encouraged men to have sexual partners outside marriage and to seek additional wives. These same norms encouraged wives to tolerate their husbands' extramarital sexual activity, even when it could threaten their monogamous unions and material security, and to accept new co-wives arriving on the scene. For want of marriage on their own terms, women learned to tolerate both polygamy and unfaithful monogamy in hope of building up their own social standing (in other words, their gendered symbolic capital) and their children's life prospects.

In exploring these workings of Bamako's marriage system, we have seen the importance of bargaining. In the next two chapters, we will delve deeper into bargaining power, the relative ability of the parties in a negotiation to secure an agreement on favorable terms. We will see how the gendered disparities of Bamako's marriage market (chapter 5), along with the laws governing Malian marriage (chapter 6), weakened women's bargaining power and undermined their aspirations of entering marriage and living well within it. Women's weaker bargaining position helped maintain polygamy as a common marital option in the city.

5

Marriage Markets and Marriage Squeezes

The Demographic Underpinnings of Polygamous Marriage

Polygamy, when tried under modern democratic conditions, as by the Mormons, is wrecked by the revolt of the mass of inferior men who are condemned to celibacy by it; for the maternal instinct leads a woman to prefer a tenth share in a first rate man to the exclusive possession of a third rate one.

−George Bernard Shaw, *Maxims for Revolutionists* (England, 1903)

Seeking Truth in Idiosyncrasy

In the rainforest of Papua New Guinea, anthropologist Don Kulick (2019) observed a belief in one village that a human being's emotions emanated not from the brain or heart but the liver; a villager experiencing romantic rejection might be said to suffer from a broken liver. Most Icelanders in the late 1990s claimed to believe in elves, and folk wisdom blamed a range of everyday troubles—from freak accidents to mechanical breakdowns—on elven interference (Hafstein 2000).

Every society has taken-for-granted notions that outsiders find idiosyncratic, even downright ridiculous. Learning about these notions can help us perceive and even question some of our own societies' strange notions. After entering the field of anthropology, for example, I came to recognize my own people's collective belief in something called "the Economy"—an abstract, all-powerful entity demanding human sacrifices to further its expansion. As American writer Ayad Akhtar wrote in his novel *Homeland Elegies* (2020, 240), "No longer ruled by a personified abstraction, Zeus or Yahweh, we appeased a material one: the Economy. We feared its humors . . . we tended to its imagined well-being with our ritual purchases." My people see the Economy like a deity ruling over our bank balances, our professional prospects, and our destinies. Our economists, like missionaries, have exported the belief in this strange deity all over the world (see Appel 2017).

One might be tempted to chalk up strange beliefs to the irrationality and ignorance of those who harbor them, or to write them off as signifying only humanity's capacious gift for imagination. As a cultural anthropologist, however, I hesitate to dismiss these beliefs as "wrong." Whenever an idea finds broad purchase in a population, those of us seeking to understand that population should start from the assumption that we have something to learn from it, however false it may seem. A relativist stance helps uncover useful truths inside apparent falsehoods.

This chapter explores conflicting Western and African beliefs about the demography of polygamy, and considers what we can learn from them. According to one, polygamy results in too many potential husbands and not enough potential wives, an imbalance allegedly causing a host of social and political problems. Another belief holds that without polygamy, a society would have too many potential wives and not enough potential husbands, causing a host of different problems. Neither belief accurately describes Mali's demographic reality, but each has adamant supporters. I will discuss the first belief briefly before moving on to the second, which I have encountered again and again during my years in Mali and elsewhere in Africa. I have come to see both these beliefs as *myths*—not mere fictions but narrative frameworks providing "ways of expressing and constructing complex political and cosmological schemas" (Ferguson 1999, 203). As we consider why polygamy endures in Bamako, we can learn a great deal from these two myths about the demographic and social structures shaping Bamako's marriage system.

First, however, let's consider some key terminology. Economists define a *marriage market* as "the process that determines how men and women are matched to each other through marriage" (Foster 2008, 8341). This definition masks who is doing the matching (remember, marriage in Bamako is often not really about the couple) and reduces that selection process to a series of rational choices by consumer-like actors. I use "marriage market" here to designate the social space in which people seeking marriage in Bamako were matched with marital partners, whether at their own initiative or that of their families and other intermediaries.[1] This matching process did not play out only according to participants' personal preferences and endowments, of course; parents and other elders also had their say. The relative supply of males and females of marriageable age in this market, I will show, affected how people found partners and entered marriage, particularly plural marriage.

Polygamy, War, and Male Marriage Squeezes

A myth distorts Western views of polygamy. One recent embodiment of this myth comes from an article in *The Economist* (2017) titled "The Perils of Polygamy." This article asserted that polygamy "destabilizes society, largely because it is a form of inequality which creates an urgent distress in the hearts, and loins, of young men. . . . Every time a rich man takes an extra wife, another poor man must remain single." This simple rule constituted, *The Economist* maintained: "one of the reasons why the Arab Spring erupted, why the jihadists of Boko Haram and Islamic State were able to conquer swathes of Nigeria, Iraq, and Syria, and why the polygamous parts of Indonesia and Haiti are so turbulent. Polygamous societies are bloodier, more likely to invade their neighbors and more prone to collapse."

Commentator Jonah Goldberg (2018), defending monogamous marriage, conceded that it is not "natural" to *Homo sapiens*. But he contended that limiting each man to just one wife, thereby affording every male a chance to reproduce, "introduced a good deal more social peace and stability to primitive societies. In this way, primitive monogamy may be the driver of mankind's success as a species. By taking the need to fight with other males out of the equation . . . males became much more cooperative and willing to make sacrifices for their tribe" (2018, 264). While, according to Goldberg, polygamy distorted marriage markets by forcing men to compete over a limited supply of potential wives, leading to runaway inequality and violence, monogamy was a pacifying, civilizing force.

Such arguments in the popular media have echoed similar arguments made by scholars. Psychologist Jordan Peterson echoed Goldberg's assumptions regarding what, in interviews, he called "enforced monogamy": applying strong monogamous social norms makes marriage accessible to more young men, thus solving the problem of involuntarily celibate males ("incels") as each wealthy man no longer attracts multiple female partners (Bowles 2018). Biologist David Barash described polygamy as fostering competition among males for females, "predisposing societies toward social disruption, increased violence, and possibly even war, ultimately because the reproductive prospects of these 'excess' men are limited or even foreclosed altogether" (2016, 126). In her book *The Evils of Polygyny*, political scientist Rose McDermott wrote: "Many men, often a majority, have no wives at all in societies where polygyny is prevalent. This imbalance is the crux of what precipitates widespread societal effects of violence based on individual patterns of sexual behavior" (2018, 12–13). These scholars and many others, in disciplines from evolutionary psychology to economics, have seen polygamy as inherently destabilizing to society.[2] And they have tended to assume that polygamy distorts marriage markets, specifically by causing a "marriage squeeze" barring significant numbers of men from matrimony.

Demographers define a "marriage squeeze" as the effect of an excess supply of one sex relative to the other in a human population (Bhaskar 2015; Meekers and Gage 2017). Marriage squeezes result from sex-specific changes in fertility, mortality, or migration that alter the population's sex ratio. In the African American population, for instance, mass incarceration of men and the preference of

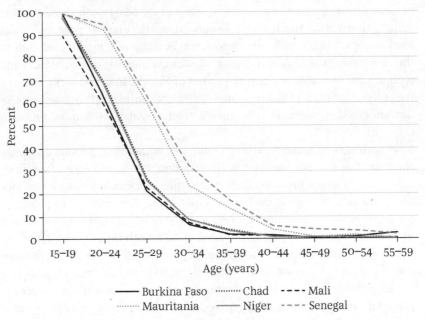

FIGURE 5.1 Percent of never-married males by age in six Sahelian countries.

Source: UN World Marriage Data.

some men to marry outside their racial group generated a marriage squeeze on women, such that some African-Americans saw polygamy as a justifiable, even indispensable marital option (Dixon-Spear 2009; Majeed 2015). The writers quoted above on polygamy and war, without using the term "marriage squeeze," based their arguments on the notion that widespread polygamy creates a male marriage squeeze. This notion is expressed above in Shaw's epigraph about polygamy condemning "the mass of inferior men" to celibacy.

If this assumption looks like common sense—surely, as *The Economist* reasoned, every man who marries two wives leaves another man with no wife at all—it overlooks a stubborn fact: despite high polygamy rates, the vast majority of men in Mali and throughout the Sahel marry (see figure 5.1). No mass of "inferior men" to see here; marriage has remained universal for both sexes (see chapter 1).

Moreover, comparing male rates of marriage between Mali and a sample of developed countries, we find Mali's rate significantly higher at every age (see figure 5.2). In other words, even though Mali's marriage system caused men to spend much less of their lives within the bonds of marriage than Malian women did, Malian men were, nevertheless, much more likely to be married at any point in their adult lives than men in wealthy countries. If marriage is a civilizing force that diminishes male sexual competition and dampens the risk of violence, and

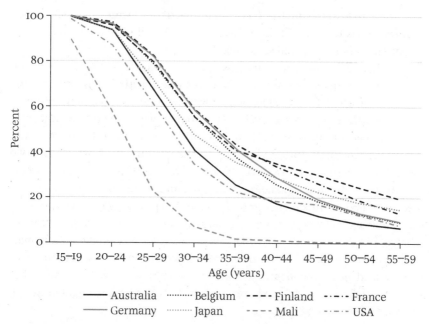

FIGURE 5.2 Percent of never-married males by age in eight countries worldwide.
Source: UN World Marriage Data.

if this civilizing force has a powerful effect on society, why would male marriage rates be consistently higher in impoverished, politically unstable countries like Burkina Faso, Chad, or Mali than in prosperous, peaceful ones like Australia, Finland, or Japan?[3]

The fact is that polygamy usually coexists with universal marriage; even high levels of polygamy need not deprive young men of sexual partners (Reniers and Tfaily 2012), nor make them losers in a Darwinian struggle to reproduce. Widespread polygamy has not prevented men in Mali from marrying. Men married later than women, as we saw in chapter 2, but they nearly always married. Other scholars (Gleditsch et al. 2011; Renner and Krieger 2022; Schacht, Rauch, and Borgerhoff Mulder 2014) challenging the "polygamy and war" argument seem to assume that men's delayed entry into marriage constitutes a politically destabilizing male marriage squeeze. The roots of political turmoil in the region, however, lie less in marriage markets than in generations of exploitative and often brutal governance dating back to colonial rule, recent floods of narcotics and small arms into the region, and other political-economic disruptions (Whitehouse 2021). Whenever we ascribe this turmoil to polygamy, we take our eye off the ball.

Ethnographers and demographers have long known that marriage in most polygynous systems is universal.[4] Yet decades after the scientific evidence should have laid it to rest, the myth of polygamous marriage squeezes and their associated social ills lived on. More curiously, it continued to find adherents even among eminent natural and social scientists. Why?

The likeliest explanation concerns the Western tendency to categorize non-Westerners, particularly Africans and others who practice polygamy, into the so-called "savage slot" (Trouillot 2003). Polygamy has long served as the ultimate marker of difference, a tool for policing the boundary between the civilized, progressive, peaceful, modern "us" and the primitive, backward, violent, traditional "them" (Taiwo 2010). It has proven the ideal tool with which to make invidious comparisons between the West and the rest. This distinction discourages Westerners from considering nagging questions about the violence, inequality, and oppression in our own societies. "By keeping the focus on *them*, we are able to distract ourselves from hard questions about *us*," as Lori Beaman (2014, 6) put it. It is simpler to condemn polygamy for blocking men from marriage than to unpack the origins of postcolonial conflict or the impact of decades of misguided aid and economic policies imposed by the United States and other Western governments and the harm these institutions have wrought on young Africans' life chances.

Perhaps, then, the myth of polygamy's male marriage squeeze has served too many uses for its believers to dispense with it. The argument that polygamy excludes men (perhaps even a majority of them!) from marriage rests on the assumption that there are not enough women in the marriage market and that men base their decisions about marriage on this alleged shortage. I should emphasize that I have never met anyone in Mali who presumed a shortage of marriageable women in their society. In fact, most Malians I knew perceived a *surplus*.

Demography and Female Overpopulation

Chapter 2 listed the "seven D's," categories grouping the local justifications men used for taking additional wives; these included domestic factors, duty to elders, distinction, desire, discipline, and divine will. The final "D" is demography. Birth rates matter here, but we will focus on sex ratios and how popular perceptions of them affected Bamako's marriage market. If you asked people in Bamako how widespread polygamy could coexist with universal marriage, the most likely answer you got was that *women far outnumbered men*. This notion was every bit as obvious to Bamakois as the male marriage squeeze was to proponents of the "polygamy and war" narrative. Both narratives concealed the demographic basis of plural marriage.

The belief that there are more females than males in societies that actually have balanced sex ratios—a phenomenon I have dubbed "the myth of female overpopulation" (Whitehouse 2018, 304)—has appeared again and again in the West African ethnographic record over the years. For example, in Senegal during the late 1950s, Luc Thoré found a conviction that women outnumbered men. He described this belief as a predominantly elite phenomenon:

> It is "intellectuals" more than illiterates who use this stereotype to defend the institution of polygamy and build upon it a whole series of moralizing rationalizations: if polygamy is banned, given that there are two or three times as many women as men, many [women] will never be able to marry; if they stay single, the desire for motherhood plus their sex drive will inevitably lead to situations condemned by family and morality. There is but one way, established by tradition, to avoid general debauchery: polygamy. (1964, 820)

Decades later, in the magazine *Jeune Afrique*, demographer Jacques Vallin (1999, 36) recounted a conversation with a Togolese doctor who swore that polygamy was necessary because his country had "seven women for each man." Anthropologists have observed similar—if usually less extreme—local perceptions of imbalanced sex ratios throughout the region: in Benin (Falen 2011), The Gambia (Wittrup 1990), Guinea-Bissau (Temudo 2019), Senegal (Fainzang and Journet 1988), and Sierra Leone (Dorjahn 1959). Some Malian scholars writing about polygamy in their own country (e.g., Diallo and Diarra 2009; Dissa 2016) have taken for granted a significant surplus of females there.

Human populations with female-skewed sex ratios—often stemming from increased male mortality in warfare—have always been more likely to practice polygamy (Ember 1974; White and Burton 1988). We saw in chapter 4 that polygamy was written into Islamic law following a time of warfare in the Arabian Peninsula; assumptions of a female surplus still undergirded pro-polygamy discourse in early twenty-first-century Saudi Arabia (Yamani 2008). Unequal sex ratios stemmed from other factors, as well. When Mormonism was established in the United States, for example, polygamy may have emerged in response to a surplus of marriageable female converts (Koktvedgaard Zeitzen 2008).

Skewed sex ratios are by no means a requirement for high polygamy rates, however (Leach 1991). In 2020, population sex ratios in the western Sahel were generally close to parity, ranging from a low of ninety males per one hundred females in Senegal to a high of 101 males per one hundred females in Niger; Mali's ratio was 100.4.[5] Mali's 2009 census put the ratio at 98.4 males per one hundred females for the country, and one hundred males per one hundred females in Bamako. In short, demographic data contradicted the notion of a general surplus of women in these populations. But, as with the myth of the male marriage squeeze, what interests me about the myth of female overpopulation is more than its counterfactuality. I also am interested in the myth's productivity—the work it performed and the social realities it helped fashion.

Like the myth of "excess men," the myth of female overpopulation survived despite an abundance of contrary evidence. Whereas the myth of excess men persisted in the West because it helped maintain a particular ideological stance toward cultural Others, the myth of female overpopulation persisted in Mali and beyond because it fit into an interpretive framework with which people made sense of their societies' marriage patterns, gender relations, and power dynamics. Like all myths, it also shaped people's views and experiences. More specifically, it structured their perceptions of the marriage market, their decisions about when and whom to marry, and their relations with actual and potential spouses.

Encountering the Myth of Female Overpopulation

Truly, they're even troubling, the statistics! According to the latest statistics—when they say how many women per man there are, they say each Malian man must marry three and a half wives—that frightens me. Yes, that's what they said; it's complicated, hmm? Even surveys done in the hospitals, maybe if they bring them out—it's troubling, perhaps for four [girls] there's one boy, or for five girls there's one boy, that's how it is!

—Ali (M, 39, unemployed, one wife)

As depicted in figure 5.3, Bamako's population actually skewed in favor of *males* in nearly every age bracket (RGPH 2011). The only exception was the teenage years, a life stage during which many girls moved from rural areas to the city to work as domestic laborers prior to marriage (see introduction), when 6.5 percent of girls age ten to fourteen and 14 percent of girls age fifteen to nineteen were estimated to be domestic workers in the city (Pilon et al. 2019). As temporary residents, these workers did not typically participate in its marriage market. While Bamako's overall sex ratio was virtually 1:1, my research team's interviews with a purposive sample of 108 city residents, in twelve different neighborhoods and with men and women of various ages and levels of schooling, revealed a widely held belief that their society harbored a huge surplus of females. Among male interviewees, 86 percent maintained that Bamako had more women than men, 10 percent correctly said the sex ratio was at par, and 4 percent did not know. (All the men who characterized Bamako's sex ratio as being essentially balanced were educated through the post-secondary level, but we will see that this knowledge did not make them immune to the myth of female overpopulation.) Among female interviewees, 88 percent similarly evoked a female surplus, 6 percent said the ratio was at par, and 6 percent did not know. Interviewees who believed in a female surplus offered estimates of the female share of Bamako's population ranging from 60 percent to 80 percent.

The notion that females outnumbered males in Bamako and throughout Mali was something so apparently self-evident that Bamakois saw proof of it

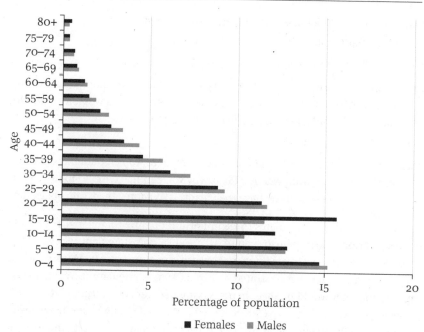

FIGURE 5.3 Age structure for Bamako, "present residents."

Source: 2009 census; total sex ratio: 0.996 males/female.

everywhere. When asked how they knew their city to have more women than men, people offered anecdotal evidence from everyday life. "Just look around when you're in the marketplace, or on public transport," they would say. "You always see more women than men." Abdoul Wahhab, the Salafist imam quoted in chapter 4, told me, "If you go to a maternity ward, you'll see more girls than boys, which is why we say there are more women than men." Residents with modern secular education were no less prone to this notion. "At the maternity clinics, statistics show that there are more births of girls than of boys," said Fatou, the twenty-eight-year-old single professional woman we met in chapter 1—echoing Ali's reference to "surveys done in the hospitals."

Statistics showed no such thing. Still, the myth of female overpopulation persisted as conventional wisdom. To understand the myth more fully, consider this excerpt of a 2012 focus group discussion with middle-aged, polygamously married men in the Boulkassoumbougou neighborhood:

BRUCE: Do you think there are as many men as women in Bamako?

PARTICIPANT 1: Statistically—

PARTICIPANT 2: It's a little hard to say, but a while ago a statistic came out saying that of the men and women who had reached the age of marriage, each man could marry two women.

PARTICIPANT 3: Which means there are more women.

BRUCE: Is that for all of Mali, or only for Bamako?

PARTICIPANT 2: Mali in general, the country.

PARTICIPANT 3: Not just Mali but everywhere. There are more women than men. If there was one woman for every man, how would women's share [of marriage] be managed [*musow ta bɛ kɛ cɔgɔdi*]?

BRUCE: Throughout the world?

PARTICIPANT 3: Throughout the world there are more women than men. Not just in one place, but everywhere. This is why you can marry up to four wives, if you have the means. If you have the means! If you don't, there's no obligation.

This exchange encapsulates three important qualities of the myth of female overpopulation. The first, also seen in Ali's and Fatou's statements above, is the tendency to refer to *purported statistical evidence* in support of it. Many believed that official statistics demonstrated a surplus female population. When speaking with me, they would preface their assessment of female overpopulation with phrases like "According to the latest survey . . ." A male radio host I interviewed in 2011 said that "in past years, in 2009 especially, I had the report, and women composed 66 percent for all of Mali." Again, official demographic reports disproved such notions locally and nationally. I asked Alimatou, a journalist who often wrote about demographic issues and family planning in the Bamako press, to explain my informants' frequent misperception of official statistics. She framed them as possibly a strategic misinterpretation of data showing very slight (i.e., under 1 percent) skews toward females:

> I think when the census results are released, there's a lack of communication. We have to know how to talk about population. We tell people, "There are more women than men." We're already in a country where most people don't know statistics, what a margin of error is or anything like that. And we just stop there. . . . But people will say, "No, they said it on television, they said it on the radio." It takes on a truth of its own, yet it's not true!

Another pattern evident in the men's group discussion excerpt is the *naturalization* of the perceived sex imbalance. Many informants (male and female, young and old) imagined female overpopulation not only at home but throughout the world. In their view, the sex ratio was skewed neither because males died at higher rates than females nor because more men emigrated than women, but because many more girls were born than boys. By casting female overpopulation as something God-given and global, rather than as the product of human action in a specific place, they framed sexual inequality as a natural and fundamental attribute of humanity.

The myth's third and perhaps most crucial quality is its *justification* of polygamy. In Mali, where everyone was generally expected, for cultural and religious reasons, to marry (chapter 1), depriving anyone of marriage was a serious violation of their social and spiritual rights. Rather than seeing polygamy as an impediment to universal marriage, as the Western critics cited above did, Bamako residents tended to see polygamy as an indispensable means of *achieving* universal marriage and contributing to the public welfare.[6] After all, without polygamy, in the words of one group discussion participant, "how would women's share be managed?"

According to this thinking, polygamy and sexual imbalance are intertwined aspects of the human condition. One begins with the existence of polygamy, authorized by the Qur'an (see chapter 4), then infers the existence of "excess women." If Muslim men are allowed to take up to four wives, the reasoning suggests, there must be a glut of potential wives for the taking. This assumption may have been valid for Muslims at the time of Qur'anic revelation due to excess male mortality in warfare, but it was not valid in Bamako.

Interestingly, the focus group participant's closing words quoted above implied that while men who lacked the economic means carried no obligation to take multiple wives, men of sufficient means were so obliged.[7] By this implication, marrying additional wives was a nearly sacred duty for senior men who could afford to do so, since these men's plural unions bestowed the "gift of marriage" upon women who would otherwise be shut out of the marriage market. By helping these ostensibly surplus women fulfill their marital responsibilities and, thereby, become full-fledged adults in society, polygamous men could claim to render a valuable community service. Rather than selfishly depriving other men of married futures, as critics would have it, these men saw themselves as enabling the extension of marriage to every eligible female. Thus polygamy, a practice which some interpretations of Islamic law framed as merely *licit* under exceptional circumstances (see chapter 4) became regarded as generally *recommended*, if not required, of any man who could afford it. This expression of normative polygamy, amply buttressed by the myth of female overpopulation, reinforced the privileges of males—especially senior ones—concerning marriage.

Bamakois of both sexes also feared that a mass of unmarried women would destabilize social mores and their own domestic security. As we saw in chapter 2, they were concerned that their city was already full of single women who, unable to find husbands of their own, set their sights on married men. Without polygamy, many of my informants felt, this surplus of women would destabilize otherwise secure marriages. "More women remaining *à quai* [literally, "on the dock," i.e., unmarried] would even endanger married men," said Mahamadou Diawara, a judge who had helped draft Mali's family and marriage legislation, when I interviewed him in 2020. "You can expect those women to go out looking! Adultery would be more apparent, perhaps the women themselves would be much more exposed—the ones already in marriage who would be forced to fight every day to keep their man." This argument inverted the male marriage squeeze myth articulated by Jonah Goldberg and others. Later in this chapter, I will show that although Participant 2 in the focus group above was incorrect about the total number of men and women, he wasn't too far off regarding Bamako's marriage market.

Countering the Myth

I asked Alimatou, the journalist, why Malian government officials had not tried to raise public awareness about their society's demographic realities or bust the myth of female overpopulation. Her answer evoked the myth's power to rationalize polygamy:

> But we come back to the fact that this serves their interests [ça les arrange]—because it strengthens the notion that a husband must have two or three wives, because there are more women than men. It's an after-the-fact justification for that. And I don't know if, on the communication side, they thought about this issue. If they thought about it, I think it was to take advantage of it, not to confront it head-on.

Local beliefs about sex ratios cast polygamy as useful, necessary, even inevitable in Malian society. "Currently we can't avoid it," said Ladji (M, 50, civil servant, one wife). "There are too many women, more than there are men, so oftentimes polygamy really becomes necessary here so that at least those girls can find a husband." Yet Ladji was one of our few interviewees (six of fifty-eight men) who estimated Bamako's sex ratio with reasonable accuracy. Even he, a former teacher with an advanced degree who moments earlier had said there was only a tiny difference between the male and female share of the population, believed that without polygamy, many women would be unable to marry.[8]

The generally balanced sex ratio in the total population—of Bamako, Mali, and the world at large—was an "inconvenient truth" which Mali's male-dominated political and religious elites could not recognize or did their best to avoid uttering so as not to call their own prerogatives into question. If one had to speak about sex ratios and hard data, one did so in a way that reinforced (or at least failed to challenge) the myth of female overpopulation.

Even if the Malian government wanted to bust this particular myth, however, it would be difficult to do. As we saw in Ladji's case above, sound demographic knowledge was not always sufficient to bust the myth of female overpopulation and its justification of polygamy. When the topic of female overpopulation arose in my conversations with Malian men, I sometimes shared with them official survey and census results showing that the overall sex ratios for Bamako and Mali were essentially 1:1. Such evidence left them unfazed. Some took issue with the official studies and vital records, questioning the professionalism of Malian survey takers or alleging that these instruments systematically undercounted females. Consider this statement from "Moussa," a participant on a Malian online discussion forum, during a 2013 exchange about Mali's sex ratio in which I had cited 2009 census figures estimating Bamako's population to be roughly evenly divided between males and females. Moussa wrote:

> Censuses are carried out to the detriment of girls. In rural areas they take place in the village chief's courtyard, and women aren't "concerned" by paperwork. Besides, with the threat of a scolding [for neglecting their domestic duties] they don't have much time to go get themselves counted. And household heads already struggle to pay taxes on their sons (annual tax: 1000 francs [approximately US$2.00] per head). They don't want to add the names of girls, who will wind up in someone else's family.

> Many girls are domestic servants in Bamako, and believe me, the woman of the house will not give them the luxury of getting counted on the census. But the male servants, night watchmen, and laborers have a certain freedom of movement and can go get surveyed on their way past a counting place.

> That is why the demographic difference between girls and boys [in official statistics] is almost nonexistent. But the reality is that women are more numerous.

Moussa's allegations of systemic bias in surveys touched on familiar themes: how patrilineal and patrilocal kinship systems encouraged fathers to view daughters as temporary household residents; how females shouldered a heavier burden of domestic labor than males; and how gendered norms stigmatized certain forms of mobility for females but not for males. His depiction of the data-gathering process during census operations, recalling the legacy of French colonial head taxes (cf. Cooper 2019), became another "justification after the fact," to use Alimatou's phrase, of the assumptions underlying the myth of female overpopulation.

I have failed to persuade most Malians that no natural surplus of women existed in the total population, for those supporting the myth of female overpopulation invoked alternative facts or discounted my evidence's validity. They could not question a myth that propped up important frameworks for making sense of the world. In this regard, they were not unlike my own compatriots who believed immigrants accounted for a disproportionate share of criminality in the United States; or who discounted the medical consensus around vaccines; or otherwise accepted and propagated ideas in defiance of established expertise, official statistics, and scholarly research. (As Moussa did, they could always dismiss such evidence as "fake news.") These narratives did important social and political work in justifying their adherents' existing worldviews.

Pierre Bourdieu (2002) described symbolic violence as a phenomenon that by determining people's schemes of perception, normalizes social hierarchy while rendering it invisible. The myth of female overpopulation helped naturalize sexual inequality and shape popular perceptions of the marriage market. By both positing a significantly imbalanced sex ratio and framing that imbalance as a God-given, worldwide phenomenon, the myth of female overpopulation inflicted a form of symbolic violence on women. It was impervious to information intended to bust it, and as a component of prevailing Malian gender ideology (see chapter 4), it had powerful support.

A Female Marriage Squeeze in Bamako?

In addition to shaping perceptions, the myth of female overpopulation also shaped individual decisions about marriage, especially polygamy. Recall Fatou, twenty-eight years old, educated and single, who described unmarried women waking up and exclaiming "My God, I'm 25!" (chapter 1). Fatou went on to mention a schoolmate who had sworn never to go into a polygamous marriage.

> In our little group we all said that. But as time went by, some changed their minds. One was just visiting me yesterday. She said if she found a man who's already got a wife, but who wants to marry her, she'll accept. She's the same age as me. Personally I wouldn't, but that's what she wants, to be someone's second wife. So at a certain age the mentality changes. At 22 she's seen her parents suffer—her mother was in a polygamous marriage—so she refuses, and at that time she says it's best to be alone with one's husband and one's children. But after some time she doesn't find that single man, and so as not to be alone she accepts a man who already has a wife.
>
> I'm not yet 30, but already some are saying I'm old. In the US, I've been there, I saw girls my age who feel young. But in Mali I'm already considered old, because all my friends are married and have children. In this environment it's hard to feel young when you visit a friend and she's got children, you visit another and she's got children, then you start to wonder: what's wrong, why do all my friends have children but not me? Then there are girls who hold out, who want to find just the right husband, but if you're too choosy you'll remain single. That's very poorly regarded—when you want to take your time and choose, people will ask why you're not already married, they'll tell you just to close your eyes and pick someone who'll be the father of your children.

The perception of a female surplus only intensified young women's rush into matrimony. Many who might have otherwise preferred to delay marriage in hope of establishing a career or finding the ideal husband instead opted for men who were available, under the assumption that they were competing with a host of other single women for just a few eligible men. And, as Fatou suggested, some who might otherwise have preferred monogamous husbands eventually settled for polygamous ones out of fear that being too choosy could actually drive suitors away. "Naturally my daughters can be in polygamous marriages, whether as first or second wives," said Maimouna (F, 55, housewife, two co-wives) when asked if she would consent to her children marrying polygamously. "There are too many women for them to refuse to marry polygamous men." Sata (F, 34, housewife, one co-wife) similarly stated that while polygamy had no advantages, "women have no choice in Mali—we have to accept it given the large number of women in our society." (Sata estimated that Mali's population was 80 percent female.)

Prior to marriage, Bamako women commonly worried they might never find husbands (chapter 1). In interviews and group discussions, men voiced no corresponding concern that they would be unable to marry. They were confident that however long it took them to prepare for marriage, they would still find brides. This is how the myth of female overpopulation encouraged the belief in a marriage squeeze on women, with Bamako's allegedly skewed sex ratio making husbands hard to find.

But while there was, let me reiterate, no *overall* surplus of females in Bamako, and while researchers can never take beliefs at face value, we should not simply dismiss the myth as meaningless. My relativistic approach discouraged me from rejecting out of hand those beliefs about a female marriage squeeze. Choosing to take such beliefs seriously—not at face value, but as an indication of a sincere view grounded in something real—led me, instead, to ask, "Why does this perception of a marriage squeeze exist, and how does it shape women's marital options?"

Research around the globe has linked sex ratios to the gendered distribution of power. David Buss, for example, writing from the perspective of evolutionary biology, described low population sex ratios (i.e., with more females than males) as tending to destabilize the institution of marriage, endangering couples as men with more potential sexual partners become more inclined to stray.[9] He tied the rise of "hookup culture" on U.S. college campuses to the rising share of women in student populations. By contrast, Buss wrote, "When there are more men competing for fewer women, the balance of power shifts to women" (2016, 323; see also Uecker and Regnerus 2010).

Ethnographic research has documented the latter dynamic in China where, by the early 2000s, the government's One-Child Policy plus the lingering practice of female infanticide had generated a surplus of males. The resulting marriage squeeze gave "young women the upper hand in the marriage market," according to anthropologist Lihong Shi (2011, 95), and began to reverse the traditional preference for sons (see also Shi 2017). One Chinese economist even proposed that his government allow some women to marry multiple husbands to mitigate the country's marriage squeeze (Tatlow 2015).[10]

Just as a population's sex ratio affects the options that a man and a woman perceive before forming a couple, it also affects the options they perceive after forming a couple. (By "couple" here, I mean men and women in monogamous unions.) Social psychologists Marcia Guttentag and Paul Secord (1983, 22) wrote:

> A crucial feature that determines the balance of dependency and power in a relationship is the level of outcomes that is perceived to be obtainable in *alternative* relationships. In those instances where alternative relationships are not available or where alternative relationships are perceived to have low outcomes, dependency in existing relationships is high. . . . The level of what is expected within the existing relationship is raised when alternative relationships with high outcomes are perceived to be available.

When more "alternative relationships" are seen as available to one member of a couple, that member enjoys a specific type of bargaining power, dubbed "dyadic power" by Guttentag and Secord. He or she can more easily leave their partner to pursue a potentially more advantageous relationship with someone else.

Women in Bamako lacked dyadic power at least in part because information about the marriage market was filtered through the myth of female overpopulation. But Bamako women also lacked dyadic power because the myth of female overpopulation, while hardly accurate, was *not entirely wrong*.

Why not? Because what generates a marriage squeeze is a skewed sex ratio, not in the total population but among *participants in the marriage market*. To account for Bamakois' widespread perception of a female marriage squeeze, we must shift our gaze from the sex ratio of the city's total population to its "marriage sex ratio"—the ratio of men at marriage age to women at marriage age (Neelakantan and Tertilt 2008).

Recall from chapter 1 that Bamako men marrying for the first time were, on average, about nine years older than their brides. This differential marriage age worked in tandem with demographic growth driven by the city's high birth rate—4.8 children per woman (DHS 2019)—to lower marriage sex ratios. (Like a Ponzi scheme, Bamako's marriage market required constant expansion at the bottom of the population pyramid to enable males at the top to reap the rewards in the form of additional wives.)

Using Bamako's 2009 census data, I juxtaposed the number of females in each of three five-year age cohorts with the number of males in the cohort nine years older (see figure 5.4 and table 5.1), matching each group of young women to the men among whom they would be most likely to seek mates. The resulting marriage sex ratios ranged from approximately 0.73 (between twenty-four- to twenty-eight-year-old males and fifteen- to nineteen-year-old females) to 0.69

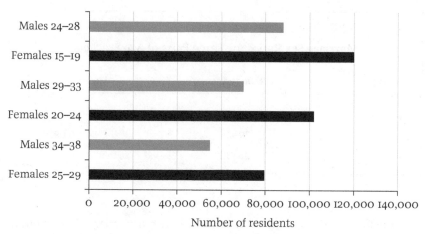

FIGURE 5.4 Size of Bamako age cohorts entering marriage.
Source: 2009 census.

(between thirty-four- to thirty-eight-year-old males and twenty-five- to twenty-nine-year-old females). The ratio for all marriage-age brackets combined (twenty-four- to thirty-eight-year-old males and fifteen- to twenty-nine-year-old females) was 0.71.[11]

This means that the Boulkassoumbougou focus group's Participant 2 was not wildly wrong in claiming that there were two women for every man reaching the age to marry. Assuming a nine-year differential marriage age, we find about 1.4 women of marriageable age (age fifteen to twenty-nine, for our purposes) per man (age twenty-four to thirty-eight). Bamako's high birth rate made each new birth cohort larger than the one preceding it (see figure 5.3). High birth rates plus high differential marriage age explains how widespread polygamy coexisted with universal marriage.

Cross-culturally, polygamy rests less on unbalanced total sex ratios (as in the myth of female overpopulation) than on marriage systems requiring women to enter the marriage market earlier than men (Hertrich 2006). This is precisely what Bamako's marriage system did, as we learned in chapter 1. Marriage sex ratios are, therefore, more useful than total sex ratios for analyzing marriage markets.

Marriage sex ratios also can help explain why the myth of female overpopulation persists in populations where total sex ratios are relatively balanced. In the age brackets in which young Bamako residents were most likely to get married, there actually was a "surplus" of females—though not for the reasons suggested by the myth. This surplus was an artificial byproduct of Bamako's high fertility and differential marriage age. Nevertheless, the fact that the marriage market was, indeed, glutted with women reduced both women's bargaining

TABLE 5.1

Marriage Sex Ratios for Three Pairs of Age Brackets

Male Ages	Female Ages	Marriage Sex Ratio
24–28	15–19	0.73
29–33	20–24	0.69
34–38	25–29	0.69

power before marriage and their dyadic power within marriage. Perceptions of a shortage of potential husbands encouraged women to accept suitors they might otherwise not have chosen—already-married men and bachelors refusing to commit to monogamy. In a society where marriage was an obligation, and where that obligation applied earliest and most forcefully to females, many women decided that sharing a husband with another woman was preferable to remaining single.

Yet dyadic power alone does not determine the relative advantages enjoyed in a marriage market or in society at large. Those advantages also are shaped by what Guttentag and Secord (1983, 26) called "structural power." Where social, economic, and legal structures distribute more rights and privileges to males than females, males enjoy a structural power advantage. And where women lack structural power, even a significant dyadic power advantage may be insufficient to free them from male domination. For example, Chinese women living in the western United States during the late nineteenth century, outnumbered by males in the Chinese immigrant population by a ratio of twenty to one, were by no means given an "upper hand" in marriage; they were, instead, forced into clan-controlled brothels (Guttentag and Secord 1983). Power emanating from a society's social and political structures can trump dyadic power emanating from its demographic structure. By the early twenty-first century, women in China enjoyed greater structural power than their mothers or grandmothers had, in part due to their government's long-standing commitment to abolishing various forms of gender discrimination (Shi 2011). These women were free to capitalize on their dyadic power to command marital advantages their grandmothers could hardly have imagined.

Unlike women in modern China, Bamakoises lacked structural power, not least with respect to marriage. Marriage was their primary means of attaining adulthood and economic security. But a wide age gap between husbands and their wives plus a high birth rate—each indicative of strong patriarchal structures—systematically skewed Bamako's marriage sex ratio, undermining women's bargaining power. A woman in the city hoping to find a husband who was both monogamous and a good provider would find the city's demographic deck stacked against her. To win the affections of such a man, she would have to compete against a "reserve army" of unmarried women. This outcome was anything but the inevitable product of differing sex ratios at birth; it was, instead, produced by a marriage system in which husbands married significantly younger wives and women bore many children. Bamako's marriage market pitted would-be brides against each other, intensifying competition for husbands, constraining their choices about when and whom to marry, and further fueling perceptions of a God-given surplus of females in the population.

Conclusion: Moving beyond the Myth

There is a long association between polygamy and West African sex ratios. Through an analysis of historical records and modern demographic surveys, John T. Dalton and Tin Cheuk Leung (2014) argued that the transatlantic slave trade, by capturing and exporting more males than females, left West African communities disproportionately female, creating a demographic environment conducive to polygamy, an institution that persisted long after total sex ratios in the region had equalized. This historical factor may account for polygamy's greater prevalence in West Africa than elsewhere on the continent. Perhaps in contemporary West African communities like Bamako, where polygamy rates remained relatively high, the myth of female overpopulation survived as a reminder of that bygone age.

The persistence of this myth owed its existence to other factors, as well. Aside from the fact that marriage sex ratios truly skewed toward women—sustaining the illusion that females outnumbered males in society—the myth had evident utility (at least to men) in justifying polygamy and in encouraging women to marry polygamous husbands. Through symbolic violence, the myth rendered gender inequality and gender hierarchy not just "normal" but taken for granted. By concealing both the effects of Bamako's marriage system and the intergenerational power dynamics the system embodied, the myth reinforced notions of female inferiority, suggesting the need for women's perpetual education and control by men (see chapter I).

The status of marriage as an essential element of womanhood served as another tool of male domination. As Kecia Ali (2016, 47) wrote in reference to African-American Muslims: "The justification of polygamy as giving all women the chance to be wives and mothers . . . reflects the normative centering of marriage—and the idea, partially real and partially a scare tactic, that there are surplus Muslim women and not enough good men to go around. This framing commodifies and devalues women." In the African American population, perceptions of a female surplus were grounded in reality (Dixon-Spear 2009; Majeed

2015). But similar perceptions have been noted in other settings, such as rural Indonesia and urban Malaysia (Krulfeld 1986; Koktvedgaard Zeitzen 2018), where total population sex ratios were balanced, and in Saudi Arabia, where there were actually more men than women (Yamani 2008). Is the myth of female overpopulation *always* present in high-polygamy settings, irrespective of actual sex ratios? I invite scholars studying other societies to consider this question.

The combination of a bottom-heavy age structure, low marriage sex ratio, and patriarchal gender ideology afforded men numerous advantages over women in Bamako's marriage system. The fact that women were encouraged and sometimes compelled to marry young helped maintain high birth rates, because women who married early also tended to start bearing children early and to have more children than women who married later. High birth rates fueled rapid population growth, which worked in tandem with the differential marriage age to perpetuate the marriage squeeze on women. With her options narrowed by these factors, as well as by the social and economic pressures described in previous chapters, a woman who became a man's second, third, or fourth wife rarely did so because she preferred polygamous unions over monogamous ones. More often, she feared being left with scant prospects for marriage and no way to become (or, in the case of widows and divorcees, remain) a respectable member of society.

This exploration of sex ratios and marriage markets leads to two conclusions. The first is that where polygamy is widespread, it is enabled by two intertwined power structures. We have reviewed the gender-related behaviors and ideology that limited women's marital options and bargaining power, pushing them toward marriages they would not otherwise choose (chapter 4). But gendered structures of power were not the only ones operating in Bamako; age-based hierarchies also were at work. Parents pushed their sons and daughters into marriages those young people did not want; senior females rendered the everyday lives of their daughters-in-law unbearable; and senior males demanded that young men pay exorbitant bridewealth for the right to wed their daughters, thereby forcing them to delay marriage and perpetuating their society's skewed marriage sex ratio. As historian Barbara Cooper wrote in her study of marriage in urban Niger, the institution of polygamy "reinforces the authority of senior men over junior men who have not yet achieved fully adult status through marriage" (1997, 131). If patriarchy has been a crucial factor behind polygamy's persistence in Bamako, so has gerontocracy.[12]

The second conclusion, not specific to polygamy, is that cultural relativism offers a valuable analytical approach to understand practices that initially seem irrational. Beginning research on this book, I regarded the myth of female overpopulation as quaint, perhaps even absurd. A commitment to a relativist mindset, however, led me to presume that the myth had something to teach me. I needed to dig deeper into these perceptions and the demographic realities they reflected. Further analysis helped me appreciate that this myth, while a distortion of reality, was actually closer to the truth than the alternative myth (propagated by many critics of polygamy) of a male marriage squeeze, and that it was based on the entirely legitimate perception that sex ratios in Bamako's marriage market restricted women's marital options. While both demographic narratives are erroneous and misleading in some respects, we also can find in them useful truths about the values and unquestioned assumptions of the people expounding them. As suggested at this chapter's beginning, we can learn much from strange beliefs.

The previous chapters showed that polygamy remained common in Bamako even though women there were quite wary of it. Dominant cultural norms and patriarchal logics pressured women into entering polygamous unions in spite of their reservations about or outright opposition to them, and women lacked the power to negotiate better outcomes. In this chapter, we have seen how public perceptions of the marriage market, shaped by inaccurate beliefs about sex ratios, further undermined women's bargaining position, leading many women to settle for polygamous husbands. How might women gain bargaining power in the marriage market? How might they gain structural power in society?

We have now covered three pillars of Bamako's marriage system: universal marriage, patriarchal gender ideology, and demography. Unlike the "seven D's," which are conscious rationales for polygamy, the components of the marriage system go largely unnoticed by Bamakois. Nevertheless, by shaping people's marital options and their perceptions of those options, these components help maintain polygamy as a common form of marriage. In chapter 6, we will examine the fourth and final pillar, consisting of the legal institutions of the postcolonial Malian state and their coexistence with alternative legal traditions. Mali's legal environment, I will argue, has had a determining effect on men's and women's marital choices. In its function, if perhaps not its intent, the law also shored up polygamy's central place in Malian life.

INTERLUDE THREE

Family Law, Identity, and Political Islam

"When the family is gone, the state is finished."

One morning in March 2012, I meet up with Julian Wyss, a student at Carleton College, and we share a taxi to Bamako's ACI 2000 neighborhood to interview Hassan (not his real name) about his role in Mali's Haut Conseil Islamique (HCI). The HCI is an organization set up by the Malian government ten years earlier to advocate for Muslim issues. Two and a half years earlier, it led the opposition to more progressive laws governing marriage and family life in Mali, and helped shape the conservative 2011 family code subsequently enacted.

Wearing brown robes and a brimless hat, Hassan welcomes us into his modest, exceedingly tidy office with an effusion of Arabic greetings. His large desk is bare but for a few sheets of paper, a set of prayer beads, some writing implements, an empty cup and saucer, and a lone cigarette. Our conversation, almost entirely in French, is interrupted by an incoming phone call, which Hassan answers, "Bonjour, Monsieur le Ministre!" When discussing Mali's long, contested process of family law reform, he speaks in terms of identity, anti-imperialism, and a clash between Islam and the West. He seems afraid that not only forced marriage and polygamy but even marriage in general will be branded "harmful cultural practices" by Western-led human rights campaigns, which he sees as an existential threat to Malian culture. What follows is edited from our discussion.

BRUCE: I want to ask about the public mobilization against the 2009 code. Why did the HCI choose to intervene in this area and not some other, like corruption, criminality, oppression of the poor, or others that are equally condemned by religion and that arouse equally strong reactions from Malians?

HASSAN: Leaving corruption, mismanagement aside—no, those reforms to the [2009] code were targeting the family. When the family is gone, the state is finished. It was to safeguard the family, because the law isn't just about marriage. . . . We struggle every day against corruption, we fight against all the problems in our society, including the political. But this time it was really too much, because once the family is destroyed the community is destroyed, the whole republic—the family is the foundation of everything. So when we protect the family, we protect our community.

The family has disappeared in Europe, and Europe wants it to disappear here too. There's no more family in France. You take a girlfriend, live with her, after a year or two you split up—we cannot understand this. Men marrying one another—we cannot understand this. Women marrying one another—we cannot understand this. So there is a cultural difference between us and Europe. The problem is that Europe wants to impose its culture, its civilization. If you refuse, they call you an Islamist, a terrorist, whatever. . . . We cannot accept this. If it's progress, I'm all for it—I'm for air conditioners, but I'm against colonizing our mentalities.

We live communally. If you come to my house, you'll find a hundred people eating together at noon, all in the same family. I live with my brothers, there are nine of us still alive, with all our wives and children, our sisters, aunts, uncles, in the same family. Does this happen in Europe? We want to protect the family, because the country is the richest in the world as long as we conserve the family, the solidarity among family members. If we let everyone go their own way, many people will die of hunger or sickness because there's nobody to help them. But when we stick together as a family—if I'm rich and he's poor, I give him something; if he's sick, I care for him, I bring him to the hospital. His child is my child. . . . This is a cultural difference: Europe cannot understand our culture, and we don't want European culture.

We reject it because it's not adapted to ours, to our religion. That's the truth. It's a war between cultures.

They pressured us to accept that law. . . . They want to impose their vision, so they fund feminist movements [and] women's associations. When foreigners give money, they want their vision to be applied in Mali, that's the problem. But when you refuse, they say all sorts of things about you.

JULIAN: Some accuse Islamic leaders of spreading false information to manipulate people against the 2009 reforms, such as the notion that they would have given homosexuals the right to marry.

HASSAN: That's true—it's called propaganda, and it happens all the time. Nicolas Sarkozy and Francois Hollande[1]—just tune in to France 24 [the international French TV news service], they're at war with each other. . . . We used disinformation to mobilize people, it's true. Because when they tell you that your family is threatened, you're going to stand up.

BRUCE: Of the changes made under the new family law, the version adopted in December [2011], which do you consider the most important?

HASSAN: The first was the recognition of religious marriage. We have our culture, we have our past, we have our civilization. . . . In the past, we had our ways to do marriage: customary marriage and religious marriage. Before 1962, during the French colonial period, it was France that brought another culture, another vision, another type of thought, a colonization of the mind and of culture. That is what we refuse. We don't want France, we cannot accept French culture. If it's for dominating us, we refuse. So recognition of religious marriage was an advance, because children born in religious marriages didn't used to be recognized since their mother's marriage wasn't recognized.

BRUCE: Without going to the *mairie* [municipal office] for a civil wedding, it wasn't possible to get birth certificates for one's children?

HASSAN: Unless [the father] went to make a declaration. But a wife with no marriage certificate, if her husband died, she inherited nothing because she had no paper. The wife with the paper would be the one to inherit; the other wife would be excluded. This isn't normal. . . . Now, with the legalization of religious marriage [in the 2011 code], first of all the wife can inherit because the mosque can issue a certificate. Her children have the same rights as the children of the wife who went to the mairie for a civil wedding. An imam would have been imprisoned under the 1962 law for performing a religious wedding before a civil one—two years plus a fine. Now the imam is innocent, he won't be punished. This is important for us. So religious marriage is the first advance. You can get married [in the United States], you go to the church, have your wedding, they give you your paper and you go, your marriage is legal. Why not here? Because French culture is a backward culture! French secularism is anti-God. In England, in Germany, in the US, [secularism] is pro-God.

BRUCE: Before the new law, men sometimes resorted to religious marriage to bypass state law, for example to marry a young girl or take a second wife after signing monogamy. With these new reforms—

HASSAN: That's over, it's not possible anymore. Civil weddings will stay the same, with the same papers. At the mosque you'll make a declaration two weeks ahead of time, like at the mairie. If you signed monogamy at the mairie, it will be the same thing at the mosque. The mosque and the mairie will work together. We will train imams to ensure that nobody can promise to take only one wife and then go to some marabout or imam for a second marriage. Now wives' rights are protected. I know many high-ranking bureaucrats who took second wives in secret whom they never declared to the state, by holding a religious wedding. That's not okay—it's betrayal!

JULIAN: Have you noticed a change in relations between the HCI and the Malian government since 2009?

HASSAN: Yes. We're not against the government. The HCI is here to advise the government, to tell it what's working and what's not, to tell the truth, to remain neutral. But sometimes there's an obstacle because our government is not independent. . . . A sovereign, independent country, if it's always going to the Americans asking, "Give me money, I want to build a school," and going to the EU, "Give me money, I need to dig a well for drinking water," and to the Japanese, "Give me food," and the Chinese, "Come build a bridge for me"—is that country independent? Someone without economic independence isn't independent these days, because you do the bidding of whoever gives you money.

No, we want to be independent—we're rich, we're not poor. We've got water, land, sun, and people. What's lacking is the will and the knowledge, that's all. But we're not independent because the white colonizer, France, hasn't left—it's still here. It runs everything . . . because on the independence deal we signed, it's written that France will be Mali's first partner. So Mali was chained up and given to France. If the Chinese and the Japanese want to do something here, and France doesn't agree, it won't happen. This is a sickness, we need independence from France—even if we must go to war with France, that's what we'll do. There's a link between the French language, French culture, and colonization. It's for keeping us in their grip forever.

In the HCI we said, "The legislative elections are coming, we'll get involved, choose our candidates so that not just anybody can join parliament, that's over. The HCI and Islamic associations are going to put an end to that. To be a legislator, you must be a man of integrity, you must know yourself, love your country and defend your country's interest." The people in the National Assembly only got there because of their money, they have no political training. They show up, some can't even write; how can they make the laws? How many laws did they pass without the people's knowledge? It's a rubber stamp, not a national assembly. So Mali needs a change—of everything. The schools have failed; if we don't change them, we're in trouble. The army needs a change. Health care needs a change. Look at the money the IMF, the World Bank send to fight AIDS: a few individuals steal it, or they send it to their foreign bank account, and the guy with AIDS here dies. Why? Is that Mali, how people are? We must change everything, and the HCI will change everything. That's a promise.

Postscript

At the time Julian and I interviewed Hassan, we never imagined that before the month was out, a coalition of armed militants would take over the northern half of

Mali, some proclaiming an independent homeland for the Tuareg people, others seeking to replace Mali's secular state with their vision of Islamic law. While a French-led offensive in early 2013 would drive these militants from the cities and towns they occupied, their violent insurgency would drag on for years. For the first time since independence, thousands of French soldiers (later joined by UN peace-keepers) would deploy on Malian territory.

Violence between Islamist militants and government security forces would become endemic in the country's central and northern regions, costing thousands of civilians their lives. In Bamako, unprecedented terrorist attacks would strike hotels, restaurants, and clubs frequented by Westerners. Mali's secular government, whether military- or civilian-led, lacked legitimacy and was manifestly unable to protect its people. The influence of the HCI and others interested in establishing an explicitly Islamic political system would grow along with anti-Western sentiment. Secular regimes in Mali, both civilian- and military-led, would advocate dialogue with armed Islamist groups, which the French government opposed. A decade into this crisis, the HCI's pledge to curtail misuses of marriage law would remain unfulfilled. Amid gathering public despair, many Malians who had hoped for a united, secular republic saw this prospect dimming further.

6

Marriage Law, Polygamy, and the Malian State

We should not hide the fact that our [native subjects],[1] quite attached to their customs, are loath to let us undermine their traditional social organization. . . . our attitude should be one of extreme circumspection when it comes to affecting their family organization.

—Auguste Brunet, Governor-General of French West Africa
(Dakar, Senegal, 1920; quoted in Rodet [2007, 3])

A Premature Requiem for the African Family

In July 1959, female delegates from five French West African colonies gathered at a Bamako technical college for the inaugural congress of the *Union des Femmes de l'Ouest Africain* (West African Women's Union). They met to discuss the role of women in the coming era of political independence. A major question before the group, the *New York Times* reported, was whether to ban polygamous marriage, with defenders of tradition arguing that such a ban would run counter to natural law and reformists stressing polygamy's incompatibility with egalitarian principles. The reformists prevailed. The first of the meeting's resolutions boldly called for abolishing polygamy by the following year. Polygamy, the *Times* correspondent ventured, "seems to be on the way out, however long its final disappearance may take" (Lengyel 1960, 116).

After the meeting, participants from what soon became the Republic of Mali set to work drafting legislation to define women's rights and responsibilities for their emerging nation. Their draft inspired Mali's first family law, the *Code du Mariage et de la Tutelle* (Law on Marriage and Guardianship), enacted in 1962. But their bid to outlaw polygamy—most of them were urban and educated—met with opposition from two camps. First, many illiterate, non-elite women saw the effort as proof that their educated peers were unwilling to share their husbands with less fortunate women[2]; they feared a polygamy ban would prevent them from finding husbands of their own (de Jorio 1997 and 2020). Second, elite men feared losing marital prerogatives. To cite one prominent example, President Modibo Keita, the father of Malian independence, already had two wives when he attended the 1959 women's meeting, and subsequently married a third. The only two provisions of the female activists' draft not included in the 1962 code were a ban on polygamy and a minimum marriage age of seventeen.[3]

Even without banning polygamy, however, the *Code du Mariage et de la Tutelle* (hereafter, the "1962 code") and similar legislation of the era promised to reshape society. Newly independent francophone West African states' laws aimed at modernizing family life and marriage were inspired by the Enlightenment-era egalitarianism of metropolitan French law. In an article titled "Requiem pour la Famille Africaine," Roger Decottignies, a French jurist and dean of the University of Dakar law school, anticipated the new laws' revolutionary effects on West African gender relations:

> Woman has emerged the big winner from these rules' assault on African mores. She has succeeded in escaping from the degrading system of bridewealth, shaking off the yoke of insatiable relatives, and finding her place in her husband's family, all while maintaining her legal independence and her share of marriage's benefits. . . . She has also managed to avoid competition from other wives, whether definitively through polygamy's suppression, or through a monogamous contract which her husband can only change with her accord. The African family of yesteryear therefore appears to have been destroyed. Its pillars have been dismantled. (Decottignies 1965, 274)

Decottignies warned, however, that "customary resistance to legal innovations in family affairs" could, ultimately, undo these new states' modernizing projects (1965, 275). Here, at least, his vision proved correct. Not only did Africans' opposition to lofty goals of gender equality remain strong half a century later, but progressive laws pertaining to marriage and women's rights had been challenged and even repealed. The "African family of yesteryear" was back—or, more accurately, it had never gone away.

Marriage is a core component not only of social reproduction but also of state-building, and Mali's 1962 code emerged amid a wider reimagining of the relationship between marriage and African states (Boyd and Burrill 2020). Postcolonial laws established formal marital protections, including some intended to strengthen monogamous unions. These laws' implementation, however, allowed for considerable ambiguity and abuse. This chapter examines the intersections between marriage, law, and the Malian state. It introduces Bamako's three-tiered legal environment and explores the gray areas around marital rights and responsibilities that helped maintain polygamy as a widespread practice in twenty-first-century Bamako.

Celebrating Marriage in Bamako

A Bamako couple's wedding could be celebrated in multiple ways, each stemming from a different aspect of Mali's cultural heritage, entailing a different type of wedding ceremony, and conferring different rights and duties upon wives, husbands, and their respective kin. These overlapping marital registers structured couples' lives long after their weddings were complete, and the lines between these registers blurred—even in cities and towns where state institutions were strongest.

Bamakois recognized three salient categories of marriage.[4] Each category entailed different rites to establish and celebrate the marital bond, as well as different rules and obligations for spouses to follow within marriage. Despite their disparate origins, these categories were seldom mutually exclusive; most people used more than one. Creative manipulation of the categories was an essential feature of Bamako's marriage system.

Traditional Marriage: Konyo à la Bamakoise

Bamakois considered the "customary" or "traditional" marriage category as their society's oldest nuptial type.[5] Traditional marriage was adapted from the many cultural groups whose members inhabited the city. Bamako had long attracted migrants from throughout Mali, with peoples of diverse geographic, linguistic, and ethnic backgrounds sharing space and intermarrying. The customs they observed might not be linked to their own ethnic ancestry or parents' places of origin. Rural-to-urban migrants retained many specific village customs, but these tended to fade among their city-raised offspring. Wherever their elders came from, young people in town generally conformed to the cultural patterns set by native Bamakois, with an increasingly standardized set of customs governing how marriage was contracted and celebrated. Even Bamako's Christians differed little from Muslims in their adherence to these patterns.

Traditional marriage often began at the initiative of families rather than individuals (chapter 1). In Mande communities, a family seeking a bride for their son would discreetly gather intelligence about a potential match—her character, personality, destiny, and luck, as well as her mother's conduct. If the signs were good, the family dispatched an emissary (usually a griot, and always male) to broach the subject with the girl's parents. A gift of kola nuts to her kin symbolized their interest in her as their son's future wife. If she was not already spoken for and if her kin approved, negotiations began between the two families over bridewealth and gifts. A period of nuptial engagement (*mamineli*) could then extend for weeks, months, even years until the bride was finally brought to the groom's house (B. Camara 2011). Bamakois followed many of these same steps, with young people themselves usually initiating the process.

The heart of customary marriage was a ritual sequence known as *konyo*. Derived mainly from Bamanan practice, konyo became a common way for Bamakois of many backgrounds to celebrate a union. In rural Bamanan communities of the Segou region (150 kilometers north of Bamako), konyo started with a series of bridewealth payments negotiated through intermediaries between the bride's and groom's families; negotiations and payments could play out over several years (Grosz-Ngaté 1988). According to anthropologist Rosa de Jorio, konyo's associated rites and transactions were often purposely left unfinished, prolonging "the relationship of mutual dependence between intermarrying families through time" (2002, 37). Konyo rituals could last up to seven days.[6] Some version of konyo was the defining nuptial event in rural Mali, from the southern Wasulu area (I. Camara 2002) to the central Mopti region (Cunningham 2014), and was equally dominant in Bamako and other cities.

By the twenty-first century, konyo *à la Bamakoise* often was simplified. Following multiple bridewealth payments over a period of weeks or months, a wedding ceremony usually took place in the groom's family home and required little or no participation by the couple itself until the bride was delivered to the groom's family. Praise singers and drummers performed in the family courtyard or the street outside while a group of maternal aunts and other female kin looked after the bride. Before she entered the nuptial chamber, the bride's head and hands might be washed as part of the Mande *kokoli* ritual marking her passage from single to married life (B. Camara 2011). Seven days of seclusion for the couple might follow (Brand 2001), but many urban newlyweds abbreviated or even skipped this phase, depending on their means or geographic origins.

A customary marriage ceremony demonstrated the commitment of both families (if not always of the bride and groom) to the union and conferred some social legitimacy upon the union and its offspring. In Bamako, however, this was almost never the sole form of marriage celebrated by a couple.

Religious Marriage

Religious rites, usually Islamic, constituted Bamako's most widespread type of marriage. One survey in the late 1990s (Miseli 1998) found that 96 percent of city wives had married through a religious ceremony. For Muslims, this entailed a short ritual known in Manding as *furusiri* ("marriage-tying") at a local mosque before male witnesses. An imam would ascertain that bridewealth (in Arabic, *mahr*) had been properly paid; in Bamako, as in many Sahelian communities, it was generally paid to the bride's father rather than to her. The imam then would lead prayers with both families' representatives, recite scripture regarding marriage, ask for divine blessings upon the newlyweds, and distribute kola nuts to those in attendance. *The couple was usually absent from this ceremony* and could not, therefore, express consent in person; male relatives affirmed consent on the bride's and groom's behalf.

This was an aspect of local culture not grounded in Islam, according to Issiaka, an imam in the Torokorobougou neighborhood. He opposed excluding a couple from their own wedding, saying:

> [The wedding] shouldn't even be performed in their absence. The problem now is that we're seeing child marriages [where] we don't even know the bride's age. If she comes to the mosque, the imam can observe that she's ready to be married or that she is not. It's really best that the families agree to bring the couple before the imam at the mosque, so he can ask them questions instead of having to ask their proxies whether the bride agrees to the marriage. Because the proxy can lie—that happens in many of our weddings.

Brides' poor representation at their own weddings may have stemmed from prevailing traditions of Islamic jurisprudence that treated women as legal minors requiring male guardianship in important matters (Cooper 2010)—a stance very much at odds with the postcolonial state's more egalitarian aspirations.

Nevertheless, an Islamic ceremony bestowed social legitimacy upon the newlyweds and carried considerable moral weight in the eyes of society. "The religious ritual [was] often sufficient to legitimize a union in the eyes of the majority of Malians," conferring "an aura of respectability upon an already existing relationship between a man and a woman" as well as their offspring (de Jorio 2002, 34). Indeed, a Bamako marriage was generally not socially valid until a religious ceremony had taken place (Miseli 1998, 24). While a groom might commit during the Islamic wedding ceremony not to take additional wives, such monogamy agreements—a common feature of Islamic weddings in other societies[7]—were unusual in Bamako religious ceremonies. Bamakois seeking to formalize such a pact could use the third marital category.

Civil Marriage

The institution of civil marriage in Mali was a legacy of colonialism. French legal decrees established a marital framework that survived, in modified form, into the twenty-first century. Unable to enforce civil law uniformly, the colonial state accommodated various customary laws and practices regarding marriage (Ba Konaré 1993; Burrill 2015 and 2020; B. Camara 2011; Lydon 2018). Regarding women's rights, administrators drafted laws based on elder- and male-friendly interpretations of local custom so as not to stoke opposition, trading their "civilizing mission" for political expediency (Rodet 2007 and 2019; Wing 2012). Colonial administrators saw African family structures as too dangerous to meddle with, as shown in this chapter's epigraph from a French official.

The civil marriage process that the Republic of Mali inherited from French law entailed two official steps. An initial declaration of the couple's intent to marry, filed with local municipal authorities, would precede a civil ceremony by two weeks. Both declaration and ceremony required explicit consent from the bride and groom, whose physical presence at the ceremony was officially required, though marriage by proxy was allowed here, too. Each wedding ceremony was performed by a public official, typically a mayor or other official of the local *commune* (municipal government). Most took place in a municipal office, known as a mairie.

Civil marriage was not for all. Many Malian couples, especially in rural areas, never celebrated one (Hertrich 2007). Some saw avoiding civil marriage an act of resistance against the postcolonial state (Soares 2011). But because unions lacking valid marriage certificates (*actes de mariage*) were unrecognized under the law and conferred no official benefits, civil marriage became widespread in urban settings. By the late 1990s, two-thirds of Bamako wives had married in civil ceremonies (Miseli 1998). Socioeconomic distinctions shaped Bamakois' choices. Uneducated people working in the informal sector were less likely to celebrate civil weddings, while civil servants and formal-sector workers were more likely.[8] But twenty-first-century Malian urbanites, especially women, wanted the validation and status that came with a civil wedding. The civil wedding ceremony became the pinnacle of the ritual marriage process for most Bamako residents, who added considerable pomp and frills. While the official ceremony required no expensive trappings, by the early 2000s, white bridal gowns, trendy hairstyles, videographers, praise singers, rented luxury cars, and accompanying motorcyclists driving in boisterous procession to the mairie were *de rigueur* for many Bamakois (figure 6.1).

The 1962 code introduced multiple safeguards to Mali's marriage system. It required the consent of both bride and groom; it barred girls under age fifteen and boys under age eighteen from marrying; it qualified civil servants and their spouses for state benefits; it granted legal recourse to wives repudiated, abandoned, or materially neglected by their husbands; and it established divorcees' right to financial support from husbands who had wronged them. Significantly, it also maintained colonial-era conditions under which a husband could lawfully wed an additional wife.

Having resisted the campaign to abolish polygamous marriage at independence, Mali's founding fathers preserved the civil recognition of polygamy established under colonial rule. Article 43 of the 1962 code required a groom to choose an *option matrimoniale* indicating his preference for a polygamous or monogamous union. This provision, adapted from a 1951 French decree, was intended to provide couples an escape from the pressures of normative polygamy. "By establishing monogamy alongside polygamy, Mali's legislators of 1962 wanted to leave free choice to spouses and enable them to deviate from customs and Islamized norms," wrote legal historian Bakary Camara (2011, 233). Selecting the polygamy option by no means required the husband to bring another wife into his marriage; it merely established his legal *right* to do so without

FIGURE 6.1 A bride arrives for her civil wedding ceremony.
Photo: Oumou Coulibaly, 2012.

preconditions. A husband who opted for polygamy in his civil ceremony had no obligation even to notify his existing wife (or wives) before marrying a new bride. Nor did choosing *la monogamie* definitively bar the way to polygamy. The law allowed husbands to change the option on their civil marriage contracts with their wives' consent. In the 2010s, Malian law still required grooms to state their matrimonial option publicly during their civil ceremony.

The 1962 code imposed just three other controls on polygamy. It limited a husband to four wives (Article 8); forbade him from spending one wife's revenues for the benefit of the other(s); and recognized each of his wives as constituting a distinct household (Article 35). The code also wrote male supremacy into marriage. Article 32 stipulated that husbands owed protection to their wives and that wives owed obedience to their husbands, while Article 34 defined the husband as the household's primary provider. This language, rooted in French civil law, constructed wives as jural minors dependent on their husband's authorization (Kombo 2021; A. Tounkara 2015). Although many of the code's provisions meshed with Islamic law, the code's framers declined to criminalize violations of a rule made explicit in the Qur'an: the polygamous husband's obligation to treat his wives equitably (Decottignies 1965). In crafting the 1962 code to build their new nation, Mali's male elite served its own interests, often at women's expense.

Legal Pluralism, Ambiguity, and Risk

Bamakois generally saw these three forms of marriage as complementary, not competing, and approached their timing and sequence in many different ways. One couple might marry through an Islamic ceremony alone; another might celebrate Islamic and civil ceremonies years apart; another might perform Islamic, civil, and customary ceremonies all on the same day. The 1962 code established civil marriage's formal preeminence, making it Mali's sole legally binding form of marriage, and prohibited a couple's customary or religious wedding until they performed a civil ceremony.[9] An Islamic ceremony, however, remained sufficient to legitimize a union socially, and Malians widely disregarded the law requiring that civil marriages come first (Ba Konaré 1993; I. Camara 2002). Indeed, since the government failed to enforce this provision of the 1962 code from the outset (Boye 1987), most Malians celebrated religious weddings first, holding customary and civil ceremonies later (Marcoux, Gueye, and Konaté 1995; Antoine and Marcoux 2014).[10] Moreover, twenty years after the 1962 code's enactment, nearly half of Malian girls married before reaching the legal age of fifteen (DHS 1987); even in the 2010s, the legal minimum age for brides was commonly flouted (Diarra 2018). The code's caps on bridewealth payments, like those attempted by customary and colonial authorities in the early 1900s (B. Camara 2011), were similarly ignored (Schulz 2010). Thus, key provisions of the code that had been hailed as progressive at their inception slipped into irrelevance.

Why did religious wedding ceremonies dominate in Bamako? City residents' increasing religiosity was one reason; practicality was another. Simple to organize, inexpensive, and without bureaucratic entanglement, an Islamic wedding could initiate a trial run for civil marriage, enabling "the future spouses to live conjugally without being legally married" (Boye 1987, 19). Many couples married through religious ceremonies with the intention to follow up shortly with a civil wedding but postponed the latter due to economic constraints (Antoine and Marcoux 2014), particularly as they sought to acquire their own dwellings and save up for the many expenses accompanying civil wedding ceremonies. The delay might last several years. In my civil records sample, men's median age at their first civil wedding ceremony was thirty-one years old—nearly three years older than the median age of Bamako grooms surveyed by the 2018 DHS. The probable reason for this age disparity was couples' tendency to put off their civil ceremonies until they were on firmer ground, economically or otherwise. Many couples tying the knot at the municipal office had been living together as husband and wife for years before their civil ceremony.

Bamakois manipulated the three marital categories for practical and strategic reasons, molding the institution of marriage to serve their needs (Brand 2001).[11] A young couple could seal a religious union as a provisional, easily ended marriage while assessing their compatibility. An unsuccessful union could be aborted under the rationale that it had never been fully enacted to begin with (de Jorio 2002; cf. Cooper 1997). "For me, it's better to do a religious wedding and wait ten years before doing the civil wedding, which will let you get to know your spouse better and avoid the penalties of divorce," said a wife in a focus group discussion.

In this environment of legal pluralism, what happened when a couple's needs were at odds? A woman might prefer to delay pregnancy until civil marriage, seeking greater commitment from her husband, whereas he might rather delay civil marriage until proof of his wife's fertility. A young man pressured into marriage by a pregnant girlfriend might agree to a quick religious wedding ceremony but delay a more costly civil wedding, thereby saving money and steering clear of binding legal commitments to exploit his dyadic power to seek a better partner (Broqua and Doquet 2013). A woman might agree to a religious union with an already-married man in hopes of later conferring legal status on their marriage with a civil ceremony, whereas he might prefer to placate his first wife by not registering his second union with the state, thereby denying the junior wife and her children any future legal claim to his property. A polygamous husband might even choose a different form of marriage for each of his wives depending on his circumstances at the time of union. Having withstood French colonial efforts to render marriage more administratively "legible" (Burrill 2015), the ambiguity generated by these multiple marital registers enabled individuals to pursue their own aims with flexibility (de Jorio 2002).

This ambiguity also produced risks, especially for women seeking greater clarity regarding their male partners' obligations toward them. Among the most widely acknowledged risks was that a husband who opted for a monogamous civil marriage (an act known in Bamako as "signing monogamy") could later take another wife through a customary or religious union. This was the tactic used by Oumar (profiled in the introduction); after Sira refused to renegotiate their monogamous contract, Oumar simply married Korotimi in an Islamic ceremony. Since the state did not recognize religious unions, this violated only the law requiring civil ceremonies to come first. Prosecutors ignored such infractions, allowing men like Oumar to circumvent their monogamous marriage contracts with impunity. In the early 1990s, Adame Ba Konaré (1993) estimated that half of Malian husbands who signed monogamous contracts eventually either renegotiated them or reneged on them in this manner. Many a wife agreed to switch her matrimonial option to polygamy when the request arose, seeing formal polygamy—which mandates equitable treatment of co-wives (chapter 3)—as preferable to sharing her husband with a mistress whose expenses he would pay secretly (Schulz 2003; A. Tounkara 2015).

Men's views on monogamy often evolved over the course of married life. Consider this dialogue from a focus group discussion with a group of married

males (some monogamous, some polygamous) in their late thirties and early forties in the Sabalibougou neighborhood:

PARTICIPANT 1: When you marry your first wife, at that time you might like her
    so much you're thinking, "This is the woman I've chosen, better than all
    other women." If someone asked you that day, "Are you going to take another
    wife?" you'll probably say no. Because at that time you really love her. But a
    time comes—a time comes when you're out there roaming around, your
    thinking starts to change. [*laughter from group*]

PARTICIPANT 2: Once he gets money, he changes his mind!

PARTICIPANT 3: [. . .] Let's say I have one wife. I go to the municipal office [for a
    civil wedding]. The mayor asks, "Will you take another wife?" I say, "No, this
    one is enough for me." I mean, you'll find that lots of men these days in
    Bamako [do this]. But after the marriage has lasted some time, if they're not
    careful, they start thinking "I'll take another." Many of those marriages end
    because the [first] wife refuses: once she refuses, it's over. But if she doesn't
    refuse and the man has means, he might say, "OK, we'll change [our mar-
    riage option] to polygamy."

A wife refusing her husband's request to convert their monogamous union to a
polygamous one could find herself divorced. Recall from chapter 1 that divorce
was a daunting prospect for women, whom it deprived of a dwelling and compelled either to move back into their fathers' houses or to find other husbands,
most likely polygamists themselves. Divorce jeopardized mothers' future access
to their children, who remained in their fathers' lineages and, usually, in their
homes, as well. If a wife initiated a divorce, she also forfeited her right to economic support from her ex-husband and she (or her parents) would have to
return his bridewealth payment.

    The environment of legal pluralism enabled Malians with power, notably
men, to maneuver between the most suitable registers of law and mediation in
any given circumstance. "Sometimes in making a certain argument, we will base
it on religious grounds, sometimes on culture, sometimes on the law," blogger
Sadya Touré lamented during our 2020 interview. "Whenever it suits us we go
to one side. Whenever the other side doesn't suit us we try to exchange it."
A man was far more likely to invoke religious authority to legitimize a union
through an Islamic ceremony than to demand the strict punishment of adultery
(chapter 4) or insist on providing economic support to an ex-wife. He might use
civil law to access state benefits for dependents linked to him through civil marriage, while using the lack of a civil ceremony to deny his responsibilities to
other dependents. As political scientist Susanna Wing (2012, 155) argued, "The
problem is not customary or religious law per se, but rather the ambiguous and
precarious position of individuals who might presume the continued protections

of religious or customary norms only to find that these norms are not legally binding and, therefore, can easily be ignored." Over many decades, Malians' legal mash-up widened the gulf between civil law and everyday practice and undermined state legitimacy (Schulz 2010). By exploiting this postcolonial polyphony of competing rules to pursue their individual goals in a widening legal gray zone, Bamakois diminished marriage's state-building capacity.

Bargaining with Polygamy (Redux)

Relatively few grooms at Bamako civil marriage ceremonies established monogamous contracts through the 1962 code's *option matrimoniale*. My sample of civil records shows that when marrying for the first time, about 20 percent opted for monogamy, a rate that scarcely fluctuated over twenty-five years (1991–2016). Given that most of their unions would never become polygamous (officially, at any rate), and given wives' clear preference for keeping their husbands to themselves (chapter 2), why didn't more couples exercise their legal right to take polygamy off the table?

In chapter 2, we saw that the possibility of polygamy hanging over a monogamous marriage provided leverage with which husbands could discourage wives from being willful or disobedient. Many men viewed this threat as key to a harmonious marriage, and some considered Malian women so inherently defiant that they would be reckless to sign this power away. As Fily, an unmarried thirty-year-old civil servant told me in 2011:

> Outside Mali, there are many women who, if you sign monogamy with them, they won't give you trouble [*te faire voir du feu*] every time. They won't be too disobedient or too demanding. But here in Mali, if you sign monogamy, it starts to set the wife against you. She'll think you'll never bring another woman, you'll never love another woman more than her, or you can never marry another woman without her consent, or she can get whatever she wants because you can never marry any woman besides her. . . . In my view, the risk of divorce isn't as serious when you sign polygamy to show the wife that, anytime you want, you can marry another girl. That way she'll have this idea in her head, you know—she'll hesitate before thinking of doing something foolish.

Fily claimed to oppose polygamy, yet he feared that ruling it out would spark marital trouble. Note that he also saw polygamy as a stronger threat than divorce for bringing a willful wife to heel. Like many Bamakois, Fily held that no wife should see her husband's commitment to her as absolute and exclusive—a stance undermining a core assumption of companionate marriage.

Male opposition to civil marriage's monogamy option also stemmed from a lack of faith in men's ability to maintain monogamous relationships, at least in

Bamako. "Monogamy isn't suited to this place," claimed Moctar (M, 39, engineer, one wife). "What I personally detest is monogamy, because it exacerbates infidelity. You know, it's not likely that a man can limit himself to one wife, things being what they are."

Paradoxically, women expressed many of the same reasons as men did for opposing the monogamy option. During focus groups and interviews, women's remarks on polygamy and monogamous contracts were equally scathing. Some echoed men's worries that a wife in a legally monogamous union would become arrogant and immune to her husband's attempts to discipline her (see Whitehouse 2017). More often, however, they echoed concerns that men could never respect the strictures of monogamous marriage. Consider these quotations from our interview sample:

> Monogamy is never respected in Mali, because Malian men have the idea that they have a right to more than one wife.
>
> —Nafissatou (F, 20, housewife, no co-wife)

> Polygamy isn't a good thing, but I'm also against signing monogamy with an African man because they can never respect it. Monogamy has destroyed the marriages of many couples in Bamako. I even know female cabinet ministers who couldn't save their marriages because of monogamy.
>
> —Djatta (F, 23, student, two co-wives)

> [Signing] monogamy is a thoughtless act—everyone knows that men cannot limit themselves to just one [wife].
>
> —Aminata (F, 21, housewife, no co-wife)

> Monogamy is worthwhile when the husband is a man of his word, which is rare these days.
>
> —Demba (F, 52, cloth dyer, one co-wife)

> I've never liked monogamy. This option is too reassuring to women, while men these days never keep their promises. Better to sign polygamy and prepare yourself psychologically for the arrival of a second wife.
>
> —Mamou (F, 30, secretary, one co-wife)

> Monogamy makes the wife too trusting, but with men you always have to be cautious. In my view, Malian men cannot respect this commitment. No Malian man can limit himself to one woman.
>
> —Nènè (F, 26, housewife, no co-wife)

> Monogamy as a marriage option isn't a good thing in the Malian context, for the simple reason that men will always end up regretting their decision

after their friends or family get involved to criticize it. The husband will ask his wife's permission to change the option, and if she refuses, she risks losing her home. I've personally seen several cases like that.

—Mariétou (F, 34, executive secretary, no co-wife)

In fact, wives in our interview sample voiced even more wariness toward civil marriage's monogamy option than husbands did. As the previous quotes suggest, wives also tended to cast monogamy as unsuitable for men, especially Malians. Their naturalizing discourses about men's inability to abide by monogamous commitments were sometimes grounded in cultural stereotypes (e.g., "No Malian man can limit himself to one woman") or beliefs about men's biologically determined sex drives. They feared that a monogamous civil marriage agreement could lull a wife into a false sense of security ("This option is too reassuring to women"; "Monogamy makes the wife too trusting") which, given the duplicitous nature of men "these days," would only lead to betrayal. As with women's views of polygamous husbands' unfairness (chapter 3), they often framed men's supposed unsuitability for monogamy within tropes of contemporary moral and social decay.

Yet the trouble with monogamy in Bamako never hinged entirely on the views of individual men and women entering marriage. This was because, as with so many other aspects of the city's marriage system, the choice of matrimonial option (i.e., a monogamous or polygamous civil marriage contract) was often not really up to the couple. As Mariétou suggested above, a groom's relatives might forbid him from signing monogamy for fear it would put him at a marital disadvantage. In fact, his female kin often led the charge for polygamy in the run-up to his civil wedding ceremony. "If a man wants to sign monogamy, the first people to protest in his family are his sisters and his mother," a family law specialist told me in 2020. A woman who would bridle at the prospect of being in a polygamous marriage herself might insist that her brother choose the polygamy option. I heard many accounts of grooms determined to make a monogamous commitment during their civil weddings who were dissuaded at the last minute, sometimes during the ceremony itself, especially by his sisters. By insisting on polygamy even against the groom's objections, these women defended the interests of their patrilineage. The irony was not lost on my interviewee: "On the one hand," he said, "we claim to need to protect wives through monogamy, and on the other hand, it's women who are fighting for other men to be able to practice polygamy!"

Grooms were even talked out of making monogamous declarations by their own brides. However much she might have hoped to keep her new husband to herself, she also knew that his selection of monogamy could reflect badly on her, spurring malicious gossip among neighbors and in-laws about who really "wore the pants" in their household. Such worries strongly discouraged women from seeking legal guarantees of monogamy.[12]

In sum, many women in Bamako lacked the bargaining power to convince fiancés to commit to monogamous unions, particularly when facing opposition from prospective in-laws. Even women who wanted no part of polygamous marriage rarely contested their husbands' decisions in this regard. "I accepted polygamy because I had no choice," said Barakissa (F, 25, student, one co-wife). "In the Malian context, no woman has a choice in her couple's option." Lallaicha (F, 30, birth attendant, no co-wife) used similar words: "In Mali no woman has a choice of [option]. It's all up to God."

Perhaps few first-time grooms envisioned actually practicing polygamy. The combination of beliefs, social norms, and family pressures outlined above, however, led most grooms to leave the door open to it. Brides hoped that by voluntarily surrendering their right to a monogamous union and acquiescing to familial expectations of normative polygamy, they would be permitted more tranquil marital lives, and they hoped their husbands would not actually exercise their legal right to polygamy. This aspect of the polygamous patriarchal bargain (chapter 4) reflected not women's *preference* for polygamy but their *inability to negotiate better marital terms* in Bamako's social, economic, and political landscape.

How the Malian State Gave Monogamy a Bad Name

Even when a woman in Bamako did decide that a legally monogamous union was in her interest, and even when she could convince her husband (and in-laws) to accept the monogamous civil marriage option, she might, nonetheless, be unable to hold him to that commitment when his resolve wavered. As veteran women's rights activist Assa Diallo Soumaré told me during a 2012 interview:

> After he reaches a certain age, a husband might say, "I'm a Muslim, I have the right to take another wife." . . . If [his wife] chooses not to accept, she goes to court—but, my God, what obstacles there are to justice! Very few men will apply the law for what it says; they apply it as a form of self-defense.

Weakened by decades of poor governance, the formal justice apparatus—from the police to the courts—was inadequate for protecting the legal rights of any Malian citizen, let alone its most vulnerable members. Mamadou Ismaïla Konaté, appointed Mali's minister of justice in 2016, later wrote of his shock at discovering the extent of the ministry's disarray. He described a pervasive "lack of rigor, absenteeism, accumulated delays in producing documents, far-fetched or unjustified rulings, disorderly record keeping, poor maintenance of court buildings, [and] carelessness in security procedures" (2018, 88). Laws were seldom enforced fairly or consistently, when they were enforced at all. In surveys, Malians described the national justice system and police force as their government's most corruption-plagued institutions and expressed high levels of distrust toward them, characterizing the courts as "expensive, slow, complex, distant and corrupt" (HiiL 2019, 177; see, also, Friedrich Ebert Foundation 2020 and Wing 2012). When adjudicating marital disputes in this setting "where institutional oversight was weak," wrote Schulz (2012b, 37), "many (male) officials were interested in maintaining a situation that was to their own advantage." And few judges were women.

Malians were more likely, in any case, to seek redress through customary or religious mediation structures such as neighborhood and village chiefs, imams, griots, or family councils, which they trusted much more than state courts, especially concerning marriage-related conflicts (Wambua and Logan 2017). Because Malian women distrusted the institutions responsible for upholding the principles of gender equality and equal rights enshrined in their country's constitution, the monogamous option meant little to them. When courts would not enforce monogamous marriage contracts, women could only submit to alternative local institutions animated by different principles that privileged collective over personal needs, respect for authority over individual rights, and preservation of existing customs and power structures over progressive change (chapter 4).

All this explains why, when speaking of la monogamie, Bamako residents framed it not as the marital form that most of them actually practiced but as a highly suspect, even culturally alien emanation of a dysfunctional postcolonial state. Men disliked the monogamous matrimonial option because they saw it as undercutting both their male prerogatives and their power over their wives. Women disliked it because they saw men as unable to abide by it and saw the state as unable to enforce it. Men used the gray area surrounding their society's multiple marital registers to bypass the 1962 code's few restrictions on taking additional wives. In this setting of patriarchy, legal pluralism, and weak state institutions, the legal option established to secure a couple's right to monogamous marriage—hailed by Decottignies (1965, 274) as "extraordinary" shortly after its passage—became hollow, if not unthinkable, to many Bamakois.

Legal Reform: Alternatives and Movement for Change

Unlike Mali, several Muslim-majority countries actively regulated polygamy during the twentieth century. Some even banned it altogether. Albania and Turkey did so by supplanting Islamic law with secular civil law modeled on Western European legal traditions, thereby avoiding the tensions arising from competing legal frameworks. The government of Tunisia, by contrast, justified its 1956 legal abolition of polygamy through an interpretation of the Qur'anic requirement that a husband treat his wives with perfect equitability. This requirement, Tunisian leaders claimed, set an impossible standard that justified suppressing polygamy altogether (Mashhour 2005).

More common were attempts to regulate the practice of polygamous marriage. Provisions like Mali's allowing a woman to stipulate a monogamous union with her husband were widespread, as were laws requiring a husband to inform or obtain the authorization of his existing wife or wives prior to taking a new one. Several countries enacted legal measures requiring the husband to win a judge's approval before taking another wife. The husband might have to prove his ability to provide for multiple wives, for example, or demonstrate that his first wife was unable to fulfill her wifely duties. And whereas Muslim societies had historically viewed a man's impartial treatment of his wives as a matter of individual conscience rather than law (K. Ali 2006), modern laws (e.g., in Algeria, Indonesia, Malaysia, Morocco, Pakistan, and Syria) allowed courts to prosecute polygamous husbands for failing to treat their wives fairly (Haider 2000; Kütük-Kuriş 2019; Tucker 2008). A 1976 law in Jordan required polygamous husbands not only to treat their wives equally but to house them separately, too (Tabet 2005). In Malaysia, a man seeking to marry a second wife had to appear before a judge who might require the first wife's consent, or have the husband prove that a second marriage would be just (avoiding adverse consequences for his first wife and other dependents) and that he would be able to treat his wives equally (Tucker 2008).

Men could still circumvent state measures meant to restrict their practice of polygamy, however. Malaysian husbands, fearing that local judges would deny their requests to marry additional wives, might contract secret, unregistered marriages; they might opt, instead, to cross into southern Thailand to perform polygamous weddings there (Mohd Razif 2021). Malaysian women, one anthropologist observed, widely regarded their country's sharia courts as unable or unwilling to enforce laws limiting men's access to polygamy (Koktvedgaard Zeitzen 2018). In nearby Indonesia, provisions of a 1974 marriage law intended to curb polygamy yielded similarly mixed results (Nurmila 2009).

African states' few attempts to restrict polygamy also frequently proved ineffective. For example, the revolutionary government in Guinea, Mali's neighbor, passed a 1962 law allowing a woman to forbid her husband from taking an additional wife whom he could not support economically; in 1966, Guinea fully prohibited polygamy. Yet despite the ban and the ruling party's strong support for women's equality, Guinea's rate of plural marriage remained among the world's highest, and in 2016 the prohibition was scrapped (Ammann 2020). Nearly a third of wives in Côte d'Ivoire were in polygamous unions during the 2010s, despite the fact that the government had refused to recognize polygamous marriages since 1964 (Tabutin and Schoumaker 2020). In Burkina Faso, policies intended to normalize and privilege monogamy made little headway (Paré 2018), attesting to the resilience of "the African family of yesteryear."

In Mali, polygamy faded from public debate following passage of the 1962 code. With the transition from military rule in the early 1990s, however, Mali's newly democratizing government came under growing domestic and international pressure to update and amend its laws governing marriage, women's rights, and the family. Domestically, political liberalization fostered the proliferation of nongovernmental organizations, including women's rights groups eager to reform these laws. Abroad, global discourses about human rights and gender issues were significantly reshaping African societies (Boyd and Burrill 2020).

The Malian state signed many laws and international treaties to safeguard women's rights. In 1985, well before its turn to pluralism, the government signed and ratified the United Nations Convention on the Elimination of All Forms of Discrimination against Women (CEDAW). Although this convention did not mention polygamy by name, its prohibitions against discrimination within marriage have been used to advocate the abolition of polygamy. After the advent of political pluralism in 1991, Malian voters approved a new constitution that prohibited sexual discrimination. In the early 2000s, the Malian state signed and ratified the Maputo Protocol, also known as the African Union's Protocol to the African Charter on Human and Peoples' Rights on the Rights of Women in Africa. This treaty included progressive provisions on marriage and women's rights, such as Article 6c explicitly upholding monogamy as the "preferred form of marriage" (see Jonas 2012, 144). In all these texts, egalitarian and pro-monogamy language led to legal interpretations describing polygamy as inherently discriminatory (Mwambene 2017).[13] In 1994, for example, a CEDAW follow-up session declared that polygamy "contravenes a woman's right to equality with men, and can have such serious emotional and financial consequences for her and her dependents that such marriages ought to be discouraged and prohibited" (CEDAW Committee 1994). With this, the UN system effectively deemed polygamy a harmful cultural practice and encouraged its eradication (Ickowitz and Mohanty 2015).

In the wake of Mali's democratic transition and the enactment of CEDAW, momentum gathered in Bamako during the 1990s and early 2000s to create new institutions and laws protecting women's rights within marriage. Under the presidency of Alpha Oumar Konaré (1992–2002), the government established the Ministry for the Promotion of Women, Children and the Family and a task force to propose revisions to national laws, including the 1962 code. Many Malian women's NGOs and Western donors were eager to see discriminatory provisions repealed and new protections added. Among the changes discussed were: putting Mali in line with international norms (embodied by CEDAW and the Maputo Protocol) by setting the minimum marriage age at eighteen for all; limiting bridewealth to make marriage more affordable; and ending wives' legal obligation to obey their husbands, a provision many women's rights advocates regarded as antiquated.

Throughout this early stage of multiparty politics, Mali's political rulers remained deeply invested in state secularism and were unwilling to alienate Western support on which their government's budget heavily depended. They, thus, rejected Muslim activists' repeated calls to accord legal status to religious marriages, an issue that had long divided women's groups (de Jorio 2009; Soares 2011; Wing 2012). But neither women's rights activists nor politicians in Mali contested men's right to multiple wives. So strong was normative polygamy that provisions to regulate or restrict polygamous practice never emerged onto the reform agenda.

Momentum for changing the 1962 code slowed after Mali's 2002 election, which saw the country's first (and, so far, only) changeover between two elected presidents. Facing opposition from Muslim organizations, President Konaré did not secure passage of the progressive family and marriage legislation he had sought. He passed the project on to his successor, President Amadou Toumani Touré, a retired army general who had overseen Mali's 1991–1992 transitional government. Reluctant to risk his political capital by pushing controversial marriage and family laws through parliament, Touré postponed reform until his second term (2007–2012), when he expected to enjoy greater leeway (Wing 2012). But Touré's government and women's rights NGOs discovered that Islamic civil society, once relatively passive regarding Mali's secular state and its laws, had become a political force to be reckoned with.

Rewriting the Law

In 2008, Malian Ministry of Justice officials convened a working group to write a *Code des personnes et de la famille* (hereafter, the "2009 code") to supersede various laws governing marriage, family, and legal guardianship. Alongside the ministry's own personnel, the working group included legal scholars, human rights advocates, representatives of women's NGOs, and representatives of Islamic associations and Christian churches. The group built on the work begun by the previous administration to replace Mali's 1962 code.

The working group's draft code contained significant proposed reforms with respect to Malian marriage. It included protections to prevent widows from being thrown out of their homes after their husbands died; equal rights for illegitimate and legitimate children; a minimum marriage age of eighteen for both sexes; and language stating that spouses owed each other "mutual respect" (replacing the requirement for wives to obey their husbands). It also maintained the status of civil marriage as Mali's only lawful nuptial type. It proposed no changes whatsoever regarding polygamy.

Muslim organizations in Bamako were disappointed that the new code did not recognize religious marriage, and they rejected several provisions as contravening Islamic law. Mali's justice minister, however, noting that these same organizations' representatives had participated in drafting the bill, declared that "the Muslim community's concerns have largely been taken into account" (Famanta 2012, 216). On August 3, 2009, the bill was approved by the National Assembly, Mali's parliament, winning by 117 votes to five, with four abstentions.

The bill's passage touched off an unprecedented public backlash, spearheaded by Mali's *Haut Conseil Islamique* (HCI) or High Islamic Council, a national umbrella organization of Islamic advocacy groups. HCI secretary Mohamed Kimbiri denounced the new code as "treason," adding: "We are not against the spirit of the code, but we want a code appropriate for Mali that is adapted to its societal values. We will fight with all our resources so that this code is not promulgated or enacted" (IRIN News 2009). Crowds of protestors surrounded the National Assembly for weeks after the vote, demanding the code be scrapped. Religiously oriented activists were joined in their opposition by traditionalists of all stripes, including leaders of the traditionalist N'ko writing movement and the brotherhood of hunters (both seen as custodians of Mande custom) and Bamako's traditional neighborhood chiefs (O. Koné 2018).

The protesters' grievances concerned a few of the code's 1,143 articles, many of which pertained to marriage. First and foremost, Islamic leaders sought legal recognition for religious marriage. Imams saw officiating Islamic marriage ceremonies as a vital part of their role in community life, and they wanted the state to shore up their influence by making those ceremonies legally binding (Wing 2012). They argued that recognizing religious marriage under the law, as many other secular states in the region (not to mention Europe and North America) had done, would close the gap between legal texts and everyday practice and extend protections to most Malian wives.

Another conservative grievance concerned the new code's elimination of the provision requiring wives' obedience to their husbands. To defenders of the 2009 code, this change was necessary to bring the law into the modern era. "The word 'obedience' or the obligation of obedience is somewhat outdated," female parliamentarian Aissata Cissé Haidara told a Malian journalist (Segbedji 2009). "It reminds one of slavery." Protest leaders countered that this change was incompatible with both Islam and Malian culture. "It's just the way our society is organized," claimed HCI President Mahmoud Dicko (BBC 2009). "The head of the family is the man, and everyone in the family has to obey him. It's like that to create harmony." Dicko also objected to raising girls' marriage age to eighteen, saying that it would lead to more unwed mothers. Other provisions branded as "contrary to Islam" concerned inheritance, adoption, and filiation (the legal relationship between parent and child).

In pressing the government to withdraw these reforms, protest leaders framed them as an imposition by Western governments rather than a product of inclusive deliberations among Malians. HCI secretary Kimbiri described the code as "imported from donors, notably the European Union, which conditions its aid on certain social reforms" (IRIN News 2009). One editorial in the Bamako press lambasted it as "dictated by the West to set the country ablaze" (*Liberté* 2010). Such critics, in the words of sociologist Assitan Diallo, "argued that external pressures from the international community were forcing the authorities and legislators to bow down to material interests, selling out Malian social and religious values" (2009, 121–122). The protestors also accused the code's supporters, most of whom considered themselves Muslims, of being anti-Islam. Rejecting the reforms became, to many Malians, a matter of anti-imperialist principle and patriotic duty as well as religious conviction. Tens of thousands of demonstrators, including thousands of women, marched in Bamako to denounce the new code. On two consecutive Saturdays that August, their rallies filled the country's biggest sports stadium (with 50,000 seats)—the most massive public protests the city had seen since those that toppled the military regime in 1991.

Anti-reform activists unleashed a flood of disinformation (see Interlude 3).[14] Online and in newspapers, on private radio stations and in mosque sermons, messages warned that the new code would turn traditional family structure upside down. Children, for example, would no longer have to obey their parents and could, henceforth, inherit their family names from their mothers; wives would replace husbands as heads of household; homosexual marriage would be legalized. While the code incorporated none of these changes, a cacophony of voices claimed that it would spell the death of Malian kinship and culture. The editor-in-chief of a leading (and normally restrained) Bamako newspaper labeled the bill's provisions Satanic heresies and warned, "Don't be surprised to see daughters slapping their fathers, wives walking out after the slightest marital spat, weddings becoming rare and divorces common, and infidelity being the rule on both sides" (Doumbia 2009). Rhetoric grew so heated that the bill's supporters no longer felt welcome at their neighborhood mosques, and several reported receiving death threats (O. Koné 2018).

Reform advocates were aghast at this torrent of falsehoods. "They misled an illiterate population, and they didn't even know what the code was about," fumed Fatoumata Siré Diakité, a leading women's rights activist and former ambassador to Germany, during our 2012 interview. "Those religious leaders were acting in bad faith." Several of her peers made similar observations. Why, they wondered, had there been no outcry throughout the two months prior to the vote, during which the draft code had been before the National Assembly? Muslim civil society groups had participated in the drafting process, and dissenters had been given ample opportunity to express their views and amend the bill's language. Yet protest ignited only after votes were cast—as though the anti-reform camp had planned to spring a trap on their unsuspecting opponents. Protest leaders managed to out-communicate would-be reformers at every turn, successfully framing the issue and preventing opposing messages from gaining traction in public discourse (O. Koné 2015).

Facing impassioned, well-coordinated opposition, the Malian government backpedaled. Before the month of August was out, President Touré sent the bill back to the National Assembly for revision, a step he described as "necessary to preserve tranquility and social peace" (*L'Essor* 2009). Many members of parliament now claimed they had lacked time to read the entire code before voting on it. The HCI and other Islamic civil society groups, sensing the political winds shifting in their favor, expanded fourfold their demands for changes to the bill. They received free rein from parliamentary leaders to amend the code to their liking in subsequent revision sessions, while women's rights organizations complained of being shut out of the process (Famanta 2012). Two years later, the National Assembly passed a revised bill without a single dissenting vote. President Touré signed Mali's new *Code des Personnes et de la Famille* (hereafter, the "2011 code") into law the following month.

For perhaps the first time in postcolonial Mali, political Islam carried the day. Unlike its predecessors, the 2011 code granted legal recognition of religious marriage, set females' minimum age at marriage to sixteen (versus eighteen for males), and required wives to obey their husbands. When Malians died without written or sworn testaments, articles inspired by Islamic jurisprudence would, henceforth, determine their inheritance, with daughters receiving only half their brothers' shares of their late fathers' estates. Many feared the legalization of religious marriage would make it impossible to enforce monogamous civil marriage contracts.

Reform advocates saw the clock turned back on years of efforts to eliminate discriminatory provisions from national law. "Not only were the areas of discrimination not lifted, but they added more," women's rights activist Batogoma told me a few weeks after the 2011 code was enacted; "It was a disaster, because the provisions of the [colonial-era] law were better than those of our own code." Fatoumata Siré Diakité characterized the new law's recognition of religious marriage to me as "a clever plan to put an end to civil marriage." Advocates also frequently bemoaned Muslim organizations' newfound power in Malian politics. Assa Diallo Soumaré, for example, described the Malian government as "a slave to Islam," adding: "These days an Islamist can do whatever he wants in Mali. I think these Islamists' war is more serious than the separatist rebels' war up north. One day there will be a confrontation. They exploit religion for a very material cause."

Yet while Mali's 2011 code was a clear political victory for Islamic activists, it failed to settle fundamental questions about women's rights in marriage. In 2017, two human rights organizations sued the Malian government in the African Court on Human and People's Rights, claiming the new code contained discriminatory clauses violating both the Malian constitution and the Maputo Protocol. The court decided in the plaintiffs' favor, ruling that Mali should again revise its family code (Burrill 2020). While the Malian state had no obligation to comply, the verdict highlighted enduring tensions between egalitarian and inegalitarian principles in Malian marriage law.[15]

Moreover, core provisions of the 2011 code had not been enacted a decade later and it was unclear whether they would be. Advocates had promised that legalized religious marriage would end the abuses endemic to Mali's multitiered legal environment, such as husbands' ability to practice de facto polygamy even after signing monogamous civil marriage contracts. But the government issued almost none of the decrees necessary to make religious marriage legal. Despite support from prominent Malian Islamic organizations, the administration of President Ibrahim Boubacar Keita (2013–2020) never attempted to translate the code into bureaucratic reality. Notably, it neither defined the officials eligible to perform religious wedding ceremonies nor established procedures to generate legal marriage certificates from those ceremonies. Some mosques were issuing to newlyweds their own marriage forms, which municipal authorities, lacking instructions from the central state, were unable to validate. "When a minister of worship officiates a wedding," Judge Mahamadou Diawara of the Bamako Appellate Court explained during our 2020 interview, "he's supposed to send the paper to the municipal official in charge of civil records, who is supposed to process it as a civil record. But today, none of these weddings is being entered in the civil records."

Many other thorny questions lingered. Would the state grant retroactive legal status to spouses in religious marriages that predated the new law's passage, as many Muslim activists had promised? How would the law regard husbands like Oumar who had formed monogamous civil marriages but later took additional wives through religious ceremonies? Would it respect their original monogamous contracts, thereby invalidating their subsequent unions, or would it legalize their subsequent unions, invalidating their monogamous contracts? Who would verify brides' and grooms' ages and consent to marry in ceremonies from which brides and grooms had customarily been absent?

The state offered no clarification. "On a purely structural, organizational level, nothing's changed—nothing," Judge Diawara stated flatly. "And men continue to exploit this situation—they keep celebrating monogamous marriages at the municipal office and then go celebrate other marriages before their religious leaders. They're still doing so because the situation is so confused." Instead of eliminating the gray areas and legal ambiguities surrounding Mali's multiple registers of marriage, the decades-long reform process had magnified them; despite the promises of Islamic leaders, many marriages would remain illegible to the Malian state.

And in the 2020s, as in the 1960s, Mali's rulers showed no desire to regulate polygamous marriage. Whereas abolishing polygamy had at least been a subject of public debate in 1960, it no longer was discussed in the twenty-first century, nor was increased regulation of plural marriage. I asked Judge Diawara, who had been consulted on the 2011 code's drafting, whether the parliamentary committee had considered any restrictions on polygamy, like requiring husbands to show sufficient means to support multiple wives, or mandating equal treatment of and separate housing for co-wives. "I made that proposition," the judge responded:

> But I'll acknowledge that it didn't go anywhere. They didn't even want to discuss it—"*Non non non,* that's not our place." So you see, often they mix up the principles of religious marriage and customary marriage. . . . They try to take whatever suits them from this or that, they mix them up, and make them into religious marriage.

Bamako women largely acquiesced to this situation even though they saw it was to their disadvantage. Khadidja, the Muslim public intellectual and co-host of a radio call-in show about marriage and family matters, strongly doubted polygamous husbands could be honest (chapter 4). Yet she also opposed any attempt by the state to regulate a man's ability to take additional wives. "I think it would be best to leave things to God's own formalities, rather than creating other formalities," she said. "But if it was up to the wife, no husband would ever be allowed to remarry."

Conclusion: Left in the Cold

In twenty-first-century Mali, the process of reforming marriage and family law highlighted the fact that Islam had "acquired a new symbolic function as an idiom of legitimacy" in Malian public life (Schulz 2003, 166; see, also, de Jorio 2009 and Soares 2011). Public officials and women's rights activists who had previously taken the secular character of Malian law for granted were outmaneuvered by those seeking to use the state and its laws to legitimize their particular interpretations of Islam regarding marriage, gender roles, and family relations. These interpretations often were more conservative and inflexible than those that guided ordinary Malians. Only three years later, the country was torn asunder by armed conflict as Mali's northern half was taken over by rebels, many of them mobilizing under the banner of militant jihad. Both the scuttling of the 2009 code and the 2012 rebel takeover stemmed from public disaffection with Mali's secular postcolonial state and its governance of everyday life. As the conflict intensified, clarifying and implementing new marriage and family laws vanished from the public agenda.

Mali's legal reform efforts might be likened to a tug-of-war pitting advocates of natural rights, Enlightenment values, and personal freedoms against defenders of identity, tradition, and social interdependence (see Boyd and Burrill 2020). By this interpretation, leaders of Mali's secular state had failed in their bid to modernize their country. Surveys showed that only 39 percent of Malians supported equal rights for women; 60 percent felt women should remain subject to "traditions and customs" (Afrobarometer 2013, 17). In backing egalitarian laws and international conventions out of step with Mali's more conservative populace, perhaps the reformers misjudged their opponents' strength (O. Koné 2015).

Perhaps, though, Mali's politicians wanted it both ways. By signing those laws and conventions, they satisfied powerful supporters abroad (donor governments and international organizations on which the Malian state budget depended). At the same time, by not implementing them effectively, they assuaged key constituencies at home (traditional authorities, Islamic groups, and elder males more generally), ensuring their continued political survival (Schulz 2010). By this interpretation, persistent ambiguity around core legal questions—who was married and who was not, which husbands could take additional wives and which could not—preserved the privileges of an elite that remained atop Mali's socioeconomic hierarchy by forestalling social change. Patriarchy was one of those privileges.[16]

I contend that confusion was *built into this system*. Maintaining legal gray areas around marriage and the rights that came with it protected the status quo and perpetuated men's dominance in a context where their economic power was declining relative to women's (chapter 1). By allowing men to keep their marital options open, those gray areas also helped preserve the institution of polygamy. My sense that legal ambiguity was a deliberate choice rather than a mere byproduct stems from a pattern among Malian leaders to favor uncertainty over predictability in many domains. Whether implementing peace agreements, organizing elections, establishing a system of land title, or allocating defense spending, authorities have repeatedly opted *against* order and clarity (Craven-Matthews and Englebert 2018; Neimark, Toulmin, and Batterbury 2018; Soumano 2020; Tull 2019). Perhaps meaningful state-led solutions to these problems, like meaningful marriage law reform with the trade-offs it imposes, were never actually in the cards.

Mali's family law controversy demonstrated the law's limits for promoting social change. A state implementing progressive laws opposed by much of its population undermines its own legitimacy. In the Malian case, donor funding, training workshops, and aid conditions intended to spur reform proved not only ineffective but counterproductive in the face of religious and neotraditionalist objections. West and North African precedent suggests that neither strict Islamic laws nor well-intentioned civil laws shaped by progressive readings of women's rights can, on their own, resolve politicized disputes over women's rights in marriage. And when these reform efforts fail, Barbara Cooper (2010, 17) writes, "it is women and children—who are so regularly invoked as the beneficiaries of interventions of all kinds—who are left in the cold."

Legal pluralism, with its attendant risks and opportunities, was integral to Bamako's marriage system. The vagueness of marital status, coupled with the weakness of state institutions and legal protections, encouraged men to leave the polygamy option open even when they did not aspire to have multiple wives. In this legal and social environment, most women lacked the bargaining power to demand better terms of marriage. This explains why, in 2020, defying the *New York Times* correspondent's prediction six decades earlier, polygamy in Bamako was by no means on its way out.

Conclusion

The Polygamy of the Future

Once Again: Why Polygamy?

At the start of this book, I asked why men and women in twenty-first-century Bamako entered plural marriage and how to account for polygamy's resilience in the face of significant social change. The next chapters offered a holistic overview of the city's marriage system, surveying a range of social, economic, demographic, legal, and political forces and their influence over marriage. Now, to knit together an answer to our question, let's group the elements of Bamako's marriage system into four categories: 1) an emphasis on universal marriage in which the interests of kin groups frequently overrode those of individuals and couples; 2) patriarchal and gerontocratic social hierarchies; 3) a marriage market structured to include more female than male participants; and 4) a legal environment privileging men's marital prerogatives over women's. These pillars of Bamako's marriage system upheld polygamy as a continuing institution even in the absence of strong economic justification.

The cultural norm of universal marriage (recall from chapter 1 the Manding proverb *furu ye waajibi ye*—"marriage is an obligation") made it difficult to remain single. The experiences of women like Halima and Fatou, who were single well past their mid-twenties, attest to this difficulty. The obligation to marry applied to both sexes, whose marital options remained subject to considerable control by their families, but females were expected to marry much younger than men; this pressure to find husbands flooded Bamako's marriage market with young women. We saw in chapter 2 that men had many justifications for forming polygamous unions, and that wives were both wary of and resigned to the prospect of their marriages becoming polygamous. Because marriage often was not really about the couple, and because women were socialized to sublimate their own needs to those of children, husbands, and in-laws, husbands were more likely to become polygamists and wives more likely to acquiesce to polygamy despite their misgivings. Chapter 3 showed how women, unable to avoid polygamy altogether, exercised agency within polygamous households to increase its benefits and mitigate its costs to them.

Entrenched social hierarchies in Bamako ensured that, while women could exercise some autonomy and resist male dominance in many areas of life, most had insufficient power to challenge male marital prerogatives, particularly regarding polygamy. Youths, likewise, lacked the power to challenge elders' marital prerogatives. While Bamakois frequently represented plural marriage as both an ancient cultural institution and an absolute right for men, I argued in chapter 4 that polygamous marriage in modern Mali had more to do with gender and age stratification than with cultural or religious norms. Polygamy endured in Bamako less because Bamakois were good Mande folk or good Muslims and more because of the subordinated position of women and youth in Bamako's social hierarchy.

Chapter 5 showed how demographic conditions—specifically, a significant age gap between husbands and wives plus a youth-heavy age structure—generated a surplus of women in Bamako's marriage market. This marriage squeeze meant there were 40 percent more women than men of "marrying age" in the city. This skewed marriage sex ratio fueled local perceptions of a *natural* surplus of females in the general population, a myth of female overpopulation that undervalued women and sapped their bargaining power in the marriage market. Bamakoises' collective perception of a "reserve army" of single women undermining their dyadic power compelled many to put aside their objections to polygamy. Single women did so in hope of acquiring married status, and married women did so in fear of losing that status—further illustrating the power of universal marriage in Bamako.

Finally, prevailing conditions of legal pluralism and frail Malian state institutions, described in chapter 6, allowed men to pursue polygamy even after signing monogamous civil marriage contracts. State dysfunction thoroughly undermined protections for monogamous marriage in Malian civil law, and this was probably no accident[1]; the male-dominated institutions applying civil and Islamic legal codes obscured alternative approaches that could curb abuses of polygamy and restrict men's ability to take additional wives. Polygamy's normative character in Malian society dampened opposition to plural marriage. Early twenty-first-century attempts to curtail legal discrimination against women, incentivized by donor governments but organized by Malian government officials and civil society activists, engendered a backlash that narrowed women's existing legal rights within marriage. If in 1960 it seemed possible that the men running Mali might act to limit their own freedom to practice polygamy, by 2020 that prospect was unthinkable, and Malian women still lacked the structural power necessary to win such concessions.

In this book's introduction, I discussed three explanations for polygamous marriage in modern urban societies. The first was the consumption hypothesis, the idea that polygamy was mainly due to inequality among men, and that women's tendency to select fitter (i.e., wealthier) husbands helped perpetuate polygamy. My findings challenge this hypothesis. Bamako's marriage system limited women's marital choices, making it difficult for them to satisfy their marital preferences. Moreover, polygamous marriage in Mali was negatively correlated with socioeconomic status.[2] The labor-sharing hypothesis, contending that co-wives pool their domestic labor, is similarly unconvincing. Women's growing opposition to coresidential polygamy relegated pooled labor to a consolation prize for wives unable to avoid this arrangement, if not a moot point (chapter 3).

The final explanation, the oppression hypothesis, attributes polygamy primarily to women's lack of power and agency relative to men. The evidence presented in this book would appear to support this hypothesis, since it shows that Bamako's marriage system restricted women's agency and diminished their bargaining power, not only in their selection of husbands but also in their abilities to delay marriage, manage their relationships with their spouses and in-laws, and (most importantly for this book) prevent their monogamous marriages from becoming polygamous. Women could resist and sometimes stymie men's efforts to control them, but in the marital domain, they too often were outmatched by patriarchal power.

Yet women's oppression cannot fully account for polygamy's durability in Bamako. We should recall that patriarchy was not the sole oppressive element of the city's marriage system, which also reduced the agency of youths of both sexes relative to their elders (chapter 5). This age-based power disparity further buttressed plural marriage by pressuring women to marry young, thereby shaping the marriage market in a way that limited the bargaining power of young men and women in general. In short, polygamy in Bamako has largely been a manifestation of social hierarchy.

Is Polygamy Inherently Harmful?

We have seen that most Bamakoises, and many Bamakois, too, criticized the prevailing practice of plural marriage as unfair to wives. Should we, then, understand polygamy as a harmful cultural practice?

My research team asked participants in our interview sample to discuss the advantages and disadvantages of polygamous marriage. Malik (M, 45, office worker, two wives) gave a response that characteristically challenged the question's premise:

> It is marriage itself that can have problems, not polygamy or monogamy. [It's] the people in a marriage, they're the ones who can have problems, not the format [of marriage]. It's not the format that can be blamed, it's the men who use it. . . . Polygamy and monogamy don't have problems,

they are formats which exist, which our culture has accepted, which the
legislature has accepted. This means that there aren't problems with it;
it's the way you *live* it that can create advantages or disadvantages.

For several years I disagreed with Malik's argument. I regarded it as his rationalization of one of his core masculine prerogatives. My egalitarian leanings
led me, like many in the Global North, to view polygamy as intrinsically harmful. Many scholars have linked polygamous marriage to women's lack of
agency. Some (e.g., McDermott 2018; McDermott and Cowden 2016; Tertilt 2005
and 2006) have portrayed polygamy as a causal agent of women's oppression,
contending that laws banning polygamy would be the best way to end this
oppression.

But my findings suggest that polygamy in Bamako was more an outcome
than a cause of women's lack of agency. The fact that women are not randomly
selected into polygamous marriages casts doubt on much analysis of polygamy's
effects on wives (Lawson and Gibson 2018). Women who married polygamously
were already disadvantaged upon entering Bamako's marriage market, lacking
the bargaining power to insist on certain types of suitors or conditions within
marriage. It would be more accurate to say that these women's diminished agency
led them to plural marriage than to say that plural marriage diminished their
agency.

Moreover, legal measures such as bans on polygamy are unrealistic in settings like Mali. Apart from the political and practical difficulties of implementing
one there, a ban would not increase women's agency or bargaining power, since
it would leave the pillars of the local marriage system and their attendant power
hierarchies untouched. Questions about whether polygamy is good or bad for
women, or for society, have too often overlooked the factors leading women
(and men, for that matter) into polygamous marriage in the first place.[3] Rather
than focus on polygamy's supposed role in generating violence, perpetuating
poverty, or harming children's health, let's focus on root causes: social inequality,
patriarchy, and other social forces that curb women's autonomy (Gleditsch et al.
2011; Lawson et al. 2015; Lawson and Gibson 2018). To understand how power
conditions West African marriage, let's also recall how social systems privilege
the needs of elders over those of youth.

What if the problem really lies with marriage rather than specifically with
polygamy, as Malik suggested? Women's marginalization in twenty-first-century
Bamako was determined in part by an array of social, cultural, demographic, and
legal forces—a marriage system—that pushed many women toward marital outcomes they did not desire but, nevertheless, felt obliged to accept. Polygamy was
only one of these outcomes in which a woman could find herself disadvantaged;
others included residing in her in-laws' household after marriage, losing the
right to work outside the home, being married to an inveterate philanderer or

abuser, or being stigmatized as unmarried. Bamakoises encountered multiple forms of gender discrimination, and not in their marriages alone.

As a uniquely male privilege, plural marriage (and specifically polygyny) is unequal by definition, for it violated principles of equal rights for men and women (Strauss 2012). In assessing whether harm is inherent or incidental to polygamy, then, one must ask whether an inegalitarian form of marriage can avoid doing harm. If power disparities are intrinsic to *all* forms of matrimony, however—as political philosopher Clare Chambers (2017) has contended— perhaps our true quarrel is not with polygamy but with marriage itself. If outlaw- ing polygamy were enough to advance women's rights, Lori Beaman (2016, 48) has argued, "there is sufficient evidence of women's continuing inequality (unequal division of labor, disadvantages women face in the paid labor force as a result of their inequality in the home, and violence against women in the domestic setting) within monogamous family forms to consider criminalizing [monogamy] as well."

Given recent queer and feminist critiques of the institutions of marriage (e.g., Brake 2012) and monogamy (Willey 2016) in the Global North, singling out any particular marital type as uniquely oppressive seems unwarranted. The argument that heterosexual marriage everywhere coerces women into unjust domestic arrangements, and that dysfunctional heterosexual culture requires intervention to remedy its misogyny problem, offers an unsettling parallel to criticism of supposedly "backward" polygamous cultures. "I think straight people's obsession with monogamy and the nuclear family unit makes people miserable," a queer American woman told Jane Ward (2020, 139).[4]

Most Bamakoises during the 2010s continued to desire marriage, seeing polygamy as preferable to remaining single and monogamous marriage as pref- erable to polygamy. Some opted for polygamy due to childlessness, the need for household labor, or the desire for more robust social networks within their mar- ital homes. They did not expect to enjoy the same rights as their husbands within marriage and did not value exclusive emotional bonds with their hus- bands over all other marital qualities. Women in Bamako can, theoretically, opt into polygamy, exercising moral agency both in making that choice and in liv- ing as wives within polygamous marriage (cf. Majeed 2015)—but this has too sel- dom been the case. Should the current constraints on women's marital choices be removed, I believe polygamy would become a much more marginal practice in the city.

This is because *women in Bamako have long had little choice* regarding matri- mony. Should they ever be able to exercise agency to a degree even close to their male peers (not to mention their male elders), polygamy rates in their city will plummet. Women preferring monogamous husbands would have more latitude to act on that preference. Absent the constraints of Bamako's marriage system, polygamous marriage also would be less prone to abuse. As Debra Mubashshir

Majeed (2015, 34) has observed, "Where female power and moral agency are acknowledged and embraced, misuses of polygyny are less frequent and less toxic." Women's agency is essential for minimizing misuses of *marriage*, period. In Bamako, women's primary problem resided not in any given form of marriage but in their lack of agency—specifically, their lack of bargaining power over the terms of marriage.

Polygamy in the Future Tense

Throughout the twentieth century and into the twenty-first, plural marriage in the Sahel withstood a barrage of social transformation, in large part thanks to the inertia of underlying demographic structures. A marriage system, demographer Gilles Pison declared, "cannot be brutally modified from one day to the next, as the marriage market would be disrupted. Demographic constraints work toward its maintenance, allowing only slow and gradual modifications" (1986, 120). This is how Bamako's marriage system has endured over time.

Having written most of this book in the past tense to situate my field observations in the second decade of the twenty-first century, I now switch to the present and future tenses to consider how marriage and polygamy are likely to evolve in the city, highlighting some of the most significant changes underway and anticipating their impact on generations to come.

Perhaps the most significant change is that *universal marriage is weakening and will continue to weaken*. Although universal marriage remains a solid component of Bamako's marriage system in the 2020s, as demonstrated in chapter 1, fissures have developed in its once invulnerable facade. Penda, a journalist last quoted in chapter 4, provided an early glimpse of this trend when I interviewed her shortly after beginning fieldwork in 2010:

> Many women now don't want to get married. Women used to accept marrying into an extended family, taking care of their husbands and in-laws, but now with the Western example, the young generation of women is saying, "No, I just want my husband and my children, and it stops there." . . . Some women who were working and financially autonomous thought it was normal to come home and contribute their salary to their husbands out of respect. They wouldn't make any decision without consulting their husbands, it was always the husband's opinion that mattered.
>
> But the new generation, with Western influence, says "No, we went to school, we have the same diplomas, we have the same abilities. There's equality—my opinion counts as much as yours." You can live without a man, you can have free relations now, which was perhaps unimaginable for the generation before ours, who couldn't manage without getting married. There's even a saying: "For a woman, marriage is what matters

most." Now the new generation says, "Your first husband is your job." This has come from schooling, TV, perhaps travel. It's a new vision of women, and now with marriage, some Malian men are afraid of intellectual women.

When that interview occurred, I didn't yet know professional, intellectual, single women in Bamako. Over the following decade, I met women like Halima and Fatou from well-off families that had invested heavily in their educations and who were delaying marriage into their thirties. (As of this writing, Halima remains single at age forty-two and continues to put her professional life ahead of marriage plans. Fatou emigrated to Canada, where she works, lives in a non-marital partnership, and is raising a son.) While cases like theirs remain unusual, they represent a growing possibility in Bamako—a pathway by which the previously unthinkable becomes thinkable to more people.

"I think there's a rationalization of status going on these days, such that it's not surprising at all to see 30-year-old women without husbands," sociologist Aly Tounkara told me in Bamako in early 2020. "There's a rationalization of life itself, which means that today it's not surprising at all to see 40-year-old men who've never married." He ascribed these rationalization processes to multiple factors: increased access to education; the circulation of youth-centric worldviews via social media; changing sexual norms; women's greater financial autonomy; and increasingly materialist values in urban society. These factors, Tounkara said, could explain:

> Why we see young women, very far along, who aren't living in [marital] households, and why we have young men who even think they can live without getting married. This would have been unimaginable 20 years ago—unimaginable that you could live outside of a family, or reach a certain age and still be admired by society [without marrying]. Because society is now more about the economic than about the social, that's important. . . . With these realities today, daughters can go without marrying and still be appreciated because they have financial power.

Consider the bureaucratization of Bamako's housing market. Until recently, the city's landlords—mostly older males—dealt directly with their tenants and refused to rent to anyone whose morality they deemed questionable; a building owner's reputation would suffer if it became known that his tenants defied dominant social norms, particularly with regard to gender and sexuality. Amid Bamako's rapid expansion, however, landlords (many of whom live abroad) have begun using property agencies to interact with tenants. "Now, these property agents have their own rationality," Tounkara explained. "They want to know about a potential tenant's income—can they pay? What motivates them at the

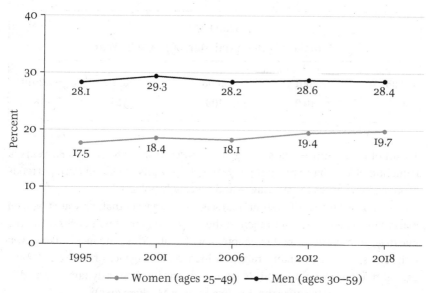

FIGURE C.1 Median age at first marriage in Bamako, by gender.
Source: Demographic and Health Surveys.

end of the day is money." A prospective tenant's marital status is irrelevant as long as she can afford the rent.

Transformations like these are creating spaces—still relatively few, but in growing numbers—in which younger Bamakoises can delay marriage, and older ones who leave marriage through divorce or widowhood can also remain effectively single, outside the direct gaze and control of parents and other kin. Even if they continue to pay lip service to the marital ideal (as in the takkoo marriages described in chapter 1), their example softens the obligation to marry and makes it easier for wives to leave bad marriages.

Marriage's status as a perceived "universal social good to which all should aspire" will likely endure in Bamako for the foreseeable future.[5] Yet even as new social norms and a redistribution of economic opportunity are altering gender relations and the experience of marriage for elite youths, rising costs of living are making marriage increasingly inaccessible to the urban poor. For many, marriage risks turning into a desirable but unattainable condition; this is already becoming the case in other fast-growing African cities like Nairobi (Pike, Mojola, and Kabiru 2018).

A second change to Bamako's marriage system is the *reduction of the differential marriage age*, the age gap between men and women entering marriage. As data in figure C.1 and table C.1 indicate, this decline has been very gradual: across

TABLE C.1

Bamako's Differential Marriage Age by Year

1995	2001	2006	2012	2018
10.6	10.9	10.1	9.2	8.7

a span of twenty-three years, the gap narrowed from 10.6 years to 8.7 years, a reduction of less than 1 percent per year. Yet even this modest change portends major consequences for marriage—and especially polygamy.

Bamako's falling differential marriage age suggests that, as young women marry later, the surplus of women in the marriage market will decline and the marriage squeeze described in chapter 5 will abate. This outcome is likely even if the city's birth rate remains relatively high. A convergence of male and female ages at marriage would certainly transform marital power dynamics and discourage polygamy (Lesthaeghe, Kaufmann, and Meekers 1989).

The age gap between Bamako's husbands and wives may never completely close (in the United States, the gap has fluctuated between one and a half and three years since the 1940s). Even reducing the differential marriage age from nine to five years by further delaying Bamakoises' entry to marriage, however, would dramatically reshape the city's marriage market. In a hypothetical scenario based on 2009 census data, such a change would raise Bamako's marriage sex ratio (in this example, the ratio of males aged twenty-five to thirty-nine to females aged twenty to thirty-four) from 0.70 to 0.85, halving the number of "surplus women" in the city's marriage market. Demographers are observing similar processes at work elsewhere on the continent as women's delayed marriage indirectly reduces polygamy rates by reshaping local marriage markets. According to Véronique Hertrich, "The decline of polygamy corresponds to a remodeling of the system. It is notably associated with the weakening of marital arrangements that shape inegalitarian relations between the sexes, namely women's early marriage and the large age gap between the sexes" (2006, 45). This weakening process is well underway in Bamako, and other shifts have similar potential to alter women's experiences with polygamy.

Changes in Malian Women's Agency

Bamako of the early 2020s is in dismal shape. Its schools are shuttered more than they are open. Its public services are shoddy or absent. Insecurity of all types (pertaining to climate, food, crime, and political violence) is rising. Politics is such a Machiavellian game that a former presidential adviser likened the scene at the executive mansion in the months preceding Mali's 2020 coup d'état to the Netflix drama *House of Cards*. Yet beneath the tumult and disarray, egalitarians can take heart from the incremental reconfiguration of gender relations playing out in Bamako and in Mali more generally. Two noteworthy trends, examined below, are women's improved access to education and greater political inclusion.

Education

For decades, education has been the linchpin of modern strategies to promote women's agency. In Mali, these strategies date to the era of French colonial rule. In 1920, Auguste Brunet, France's governor-general in West Africa (see epigraph to chapter 6), commented on a directive issued by a subordinate seeking to strengthen local women's rights. Brunet identified education policy as the colonial administration's best hope of promoting more supposedly enlightened, egalitarian values in its African possessions, particularly concerning women's rights. More direct intervention in local domestic affairs would, he warned, threaten colonial authority. While he was all in favor of "the progress of native customs toward a state where human beings would have better assurance against abuse of authority by the household head, the village chief, etc.," Brunet wrote in reply, "it is through education policy—determined, even over the long term— that we should work toward this goal. Outside of this path, we risk creating defiance around us" (quoted in Rodet 2007, 5).

More than a century later, Mali's postcolonial rulers show the same reluctance to confront patriarchal authority head-on. As we saw in the previous chapter, attempts to reshape marriage and gender dynamics directly, in the guise of progressive legal reform, caused a massive public outcry. Marriage- and family-related policies remain the "third rail" of Malian politics. Yet educating young girls has become a key priority for most Malians in the twenty-first century. Privately run madrasa schools, combining modern pedagogy with Islamic curricula, have become a widespread alternative to secular schools (Boyle 2019), and although girls made up 60 percent of the Malian children not enrolled in school (Bleck 2015), few voices now publicly oppose educating them. Malians in general, and Bamako residents in particular, have come to see their daughters' educations as investments in the country's future (Bertrand 2013). Malians overwhelmingly favor giving girls the same educational opportunities as boys (Afrobarometer 2013). By increasing women's literacy and allowing them greater access to information, education also can alter long-standing gendered power dynamics in Malian society.

Some scholars doubt that schooling is the best path to improving women's lives in poor countries, and have portrayed efforts to improve women's lives through education as misguided. For them, exposing girls to modern ideas is pointless in societies controlled by patriarchal value systems, where men exercise power over texts as well as marriage markets. "As long as male control of reading material is maintained, female literacy alone cannot begin to shift patterns of patriarchal control until women begin to possess the financial, economic, and social foundations of independence as well," Rose McDermott and Jonathon Cowden assert (2018, 92; see, also, McDermott 2018). These skeptics prescribe political measures, including the legal abolition of polygamy, as necessary first steps to strengthen women's civil liberties and political inclusion.

We would be mistaken, however, to see the impact of schooling on young women as limited to literacy and access to information. Sending more girls to school and keeping them in school longer also has powerful effects on the marriage market. Schooling postpones young women's entry into marriage, less by exposing them to modern values than by instilling in them the desire to complete their studies before marrying. By delaying marriage, education reduces a society's differential marriage age and balances its marriage sex ratio, giving women more options in the marriage market (see chapter 5). Should this process continue in Mali, it will enable women to enter marriage on a stronger footing, with more bargaining power before marrying and more dyadic power afterward. It also will lower the birth rate, diminishing population growth and weakening another demographic pillar of polygamous marriage (Antoine, Djiré, and Nanitelamio 1998). Moreover, evidence from many African countries (Bledsoe 1990; Courbage and Todd 2011; Diamouténé 2015; Fenske 2015; Tabutin and Schoumaker 2020; Ware 1979) suggests that raising a society's education rates gives women more agency, making them significantly less likely to enter polygamous marriage—if only over the long term and in tandem with other factors.[6]

Nor should we dismiss the power of knowledge to challenge male-dominated power dynamics. Bamako's gendered literacy gap has narrowed dramatically since the dawn of the twenty-first century. According to DHS surveys, 69 percent of male residents were literate in 2006 compared to just 43 percent of females (a 26-point gap); by 2018, the rates were 70 percent and 56 percent respectively (a 14-point gap). School strikes and closures notwithstanding, girls have benefited in various ways from more schooling. Girls who go to school, even in troubled education systems like Mali's, come to imagine alternative futures for themselves and gain leverage over professional and marital decisions. Malian fathers, including those who express strong opposition to expanding their female compatriots' legal rights, also love their daughters and want to see them succeed—as fathers do everywhere. Even in the absence of formal schools, community-oriented education programs like those carried out by the NGO Tostan can translate human rights discourse into local cultural contexts and boost women's inclusion in local decision-making processes (Cislaghi 2019).

Finally, we must consider education in its broadest sense, as exposure to new ideas and horizons independent of schooling, and consider how this exposure can improve women's lives. Those teenage female domestic workers coming from the countryside have benefited by experiencing Bamako and its shifting gender dynamics despite having little formal education. Their time in the city necessarily delays their entry into marriage. Their greater mobility helps them develop critical perspectives on age and gender hierarchies in their communities of origin, leading them to reject arranged marriages (Hertrich and Lesclingand 2012; Kassogué 2014; Lesclingand and Hertrich 2017). Under the influence of returned domestic laborers, village girls have begun to imagine different lives for themselves. As women's rights campaigner Assa Diallo Soumaré told me in 2012, "Many refuse to get married at 13 or 14. Even girls in conservative Muslim families, their parents agree for them to work during the day so long as they're home at night." These changes have a multiplier effect. Once those girls reach sixteen or eighteen, they refuse to marry significantly older or conservative men who would bar them from working outside the home. "After being too hemmed in for years," Soumaré asserted, "one day [women] just say 'That's enough of that. I'm a Muslim but I'm not a slave.'"

In sum, a lengthened period of youth—whether due to formal schooling, labor, migration, or some combination of the three—can considerably broaden women's opportunities. Not only does it lead young women to wait a few more years before marriage and childbearing, altering the relationship between them and their husbands, it also exposes them to new ideas that can increase their agency. The trend toward extended education, labor participation, and single living throughout Mali seems unlikely to be reversed—even if it will play out slowly over many years.

Political Participation

Another hopeful sign is that Malian women's inclusion in politics is rising. At the national level, women hold various cabinet posts and even have run (unsuccessfully, so far) for president. At the local level, women are winning seats in legislative and municipal elections throughout the country. They still are frequently treated as second-class citizens and face major barriers to political participation, especially in rural communities where patriarchal authority remains most firmly entrenched. Yet even in villages, signs point to women gaining political agency through heightened mobility. Whether through labor migration (for young unmarried females) or short-term, family-related visits (for wives), mobility promotes knowledge acquisition and opinion formation for these females, making them more likely to support women-friendly policies and laws at the national level. Identifying this trend in survey data from one set of rural Malian communities, political scientists Jaimie Bleck and Kristen Michelitch have identified what could be "the beginnings of a virtuous cycle of women's overall empowerment in both socioeconomic and political spheres" (2018, 310).

In 2015, Mali's National Assembly passed a gender quota law requiring Malian political parties to field women as at least 30 percent of their candidates for municipal councils and the National Assembly, and to feature women prominently on their lists of candidates. More than half of African countries have adopted such gender quotas for political parties. While we cannot yet judge the lasting impact of Mali's gender quota law, early evidence suggests that it has already boosted women's political participation. In the wake of the law's passage, political scientist Cathryn Evangeline Johnson found an eagerness among Malian women in one rural area to stand for local office, and described a "shared sentiment that now that women are on the local government council, more information and advice will be available to women" (2019, 9). Perhaps most remarkably, she noted that no male interviewees in the community described Mali's gender quota law as illegitimately imposed by the national government or foreign donors—in stark contrast to the 2009 family code reforms (chapter 6). Indeed, the law generated no controversy and surprisingly little notice, perhaps because Malians see electoral politics as less central to their culture and identity than family structure. Yet it has produced tangible effects on women's involvement in their communities' decision-making processes, notably by boosting their efficacy—that is, their perception of their own capacity to act. By Johnson's assessment (2019, 17), the gender quota "served to unlock new participatory opportunities for women that were not possible in the context of prevailing social structures. At least for the time being, the quota has broken the longstanding cycle of exclusion and abstention in women's participation in local government leadership. Now it is possible for women to apply the efficacy they gained through associational participation in the domain of local government."

The 2015 gender quota law's influence endured in the face of political upheaval. Following military coups in 2020 and 2021 that ousted civilian governments, interim authorities named women to over 20 percent of the seats on a transitional governing council and a similar portion to a transitional cabinet (spurring Malian women's groups to demand the full 30 percent). This outcome, if less than ideal, marked a significant improvement over Mali's transitional body in 1991, when women constituted only 5 percent of delegates. By boosting women's involvement in local politics, these changes can initiate a virtuous cycle in which female role models encourage further participation by younger women and girls. In other settings, such as India, this cycle has delayed women's entry into marriage (Castilla 2018).

A related development is also facilitating Malian women's exercise of public responsibility. In the community studied by Johnson (2019), women have come to be viewed as more impartial, better at adhering correctly to procedure, and more efficient in handling money than men. This is partly due to women's experience as members of local rotating savings and credit associations (ROSCAs), which, since the 1990s (through the concerted efforts of development agencies and NGOs), have helped women pool savings and access micro-loans. Research elsewhere in Mali has found ROSCAs to have similar positive outcomes for women (Deubel and Boyer 2020), and men have even begun setting up their own savings associations in some rural areas.

Taken together, these findings offer intriguing indications of change afoot in gendered power structures at the household and community level. Mobility, schooling, the gender quota law, and ROSCA membership seem to be generating new skills and agency for Malian women. If these trends continue, women stand to gain bargaining power in politics as well as in the marriage market. Perhaps, as geographer Monique Bertrand envisioned, "a feminine image of modernity could emerge" in Mali "without mounting a frontal attack on hegemonic masculinity" (2013, 338–339). The changes outlined above, by chipping away at men's authority over women without directly inciting their patriarchal anxieties, promise to facilitate that emergence.

The Death of Marriage and Family?

When I think about Bamako's marriage system, I often remember the words of Hassan, the representative of Mali's High Islamic Council, from our 2012 interview (see Interlude 3): "The family has disappeared in Europe, and Europe wants it to disappear here too."

Hassan's alarmist assessment reflects something quite real. Marriage and family structure in Europe and North America has changed dramatically in recent decades. Greater individual autonomy and self-expression have ushered in various nonmarital living arrangements and more symmetrical gender relations. By the early twenty-first century, this so-called "second demographic transition" had transformed life in the Global North and was well underway in East Asia (Lesthaeghe 2010). Marriage rates have fallen even in parts of Africa.

But Hassan's assessment also deploys a polarized frame commonly used by defenders of the social status quo to misrepresent the options available. These defenders tell opponents of women's sexual repression, "You want to make all women into prostitutes." They tell defenders of gay and lesbian rights, "You want to make everyone a homosexual." And they tell anyone speaking out against wives' subjugation to their husbands, "You want to destroy marriage."[7]

Such frames always pose a grim choice: either the institutions of society remain unchanged and the prerogatives of those atop the social hierarchy remain unchallenged or society falls into ruin. "If we make these changes our opponents demand," defenders of the status quo tell their followers, "the world will be turned on its head. Women will dominate men; children will disrespect their parents; the family will disappear." The disingenuous stoking of fear to mobilize resistance to change was the primary strategy used to defeat Mali's 2009 family code.

The polarized options presented above, however, seem far-fetched in Bamako. Families will not disappear from the city, despite the many changes to the marriage system and the wider society wrought by urbanization, economic stress, and women's increasing agency. Mali, unlike European countries, has no welfare state to replace the family in providing for the needy and vulnerable. As marriage becomes less universal, family units will certainly be redefined and domestic hierarchies altered. Senior males will continue to lose power in their households relative to women and youths, but this means neither that women or youths will dominate nor that households will lose all cohesion. Women may increasingly pursue sexual liaisons outside of marriage, as they have elsewhere in Africa (Archambault 2017; Hannaford and Foley 2015), but this foreshadows the breakdown not of marriage but of the sexual double standard within it (see chapter 4). Marriage and family in Bamako will be transformed, certainly, but they will endure.

As for Bamako's polygamous unions, they will continue adapting to urban life, especially through decohabitation (see chapter 3), gradually becoming less like the polygamous unions of previous generations. Polygamy rates will continue their decades-long decline, but plural marriage is in no danger of vanishing. It might even gain popularity among educated urban women to whom it provides greater personal autonomy within marriage. A slow transition to serial monogamy may occur, with divorces and remarriages supplanting many polygamous unions; this transition will depend on the pace of poverty alleviation and on the redistribution of wealth within society (de la Croix and Mariani 2015). And amid continuing government instability and weak law enforcement, the ambiguous status of many marriages will probably persist well into the future.

Politically, Malians are unlikely to press for the abolition of plural marriage. Enforcement even of existing marriage laws seems remote as long as Mali's postcolonial state remains ineffective, internally contested, and widely perceived as illegitimate by the Malian people (see Schulz 2021). Not until Malians can reinvent their state as a set of public institutions worthy of their aspirations will a more active government approach toward marriage and the family become imaginable.

By continuing to ramp up their political participation and by mobilizing transnational discourses to strengthen their rights, Malian women may finally become full citizens of the nation. Those discourses might not share the assumptions of secular liberalism, however. The liberal creed has suffered badly in Mali, where the secular state's slide into chaos exposed the hollow promises of supposedly democratic politicians and of foreign donors underwriting them. Fears of moral decay, of a corrupt elite insulated by impunity, and of youths reduced to idleness and petty crime have further delegitimized Mali's secular state. Where universalist conceptions of human rights have failed to gain traction, more pluralist conceptions might succeed (Goodale 2022). Islamic modernity, for example, might manage to "vernacularize" human rights discourse (cf. Cislaghi 2019) and promote women's autonomy. Islamic piety movements in the region even could become a force for fairer, more companionate marriage (cf. Janson 2016). The best-case scenario I can envision is that through the gradual shifting of social norms, Malian women will gain much of the power and agency legal reform has failed to deliver. This scenario depends, however, on a return to political stability and a peaceful resolution of the insurgencies afflicting the country since 2012, a scenario that appears distant as of this writing.

Dealing with Difference: Marrying Relativism with Rights

Far from finding polygamy or monogamy to be biologically "natural," this study of marriage in Bamako has underscored the power of social, political, and economic forces to shape individual marital and sexual behaviors. What people value most in marriage varies significantly between, and even within, cultural groups. We must understand these differences, as Lila Abu-Lughod has put it (2002, 787), as "products of different histories, as expressions of different circumstances, and as manifestations of differently structured desires." Understandings of justice are similarly context dependent. Inhabitants of the Global North who seek to strengthen the autonomy of women in the Global South must accept the possibility that these women will value collective responsibility over individual freedom, pious reserve over personal expression, social legitimation in the eyes of their elders over emotional intimacy with their husbands, or their children's destinies over their own marital satisfaction. Malians will continue organizing their relationships and aspirations along principles that do not necessarily reflect the assumptions and priorities of secular modernity. In true Afropolitan fashion, the people of Bamako will continue to balance African, Islamic, and Western styles and values in their everyday lives.

Beyond its focus on polygamy, this book has highlighted broader issues of women's rights within marriage, and I want to conclude by considering these rights more directly. Cultural relativism, taken to the extreme, suggests that because different communities use different moral standards there can be no universal rights. Few anthropologists adopt this absolute stance, however. Most of us, I suspect, keep the approach of cultural relativism in productive tension— one might say married—with the concept of universal rights. We move forward not by choosing between these two contradictory imperatives but by converting the tension between them into insight. Our relativism cannot be absolute; there are offenses to which we believe no human being should ever be subjected, such as murder, torture, and enslavement. Moreover, social hierarchies complicate the relativistic ideal of studying a culture "on its own terms." In Bamako, where men and women viewed polygamy and marriage from such disparate perspectives, I could not sustain the illusion of a people speaking with one voice about women's rights. Yet I found important areas of agreement between the city's men and women, its youth and its elders.

First, as previously discussed, Bamako residents largely agree that boys and girls should be able to go to school and experience a period of youth before marriage. Disagreement remains over what *kind* of school children should attend. Some parents fear the influence of state-run, French-language schools, and prefer to send their offspring to Islamically oriented schools (Bleck 2015; Boyle 2019). There also is disagreement over how long children should stay in school. Boys are much likelier than girls to continue through secondary school, as families tend to curtail their daughters' education sooner. But this gap is narrowing, and as more girls attend school, Bamakoises will gain autonomy and agency.

The second area of agreement in Bamako concerns the necessity for marital consent. A scene in the 1990 film *Finzan* by Cheick Oumar Sissoko, perhaps Mali's most renowned filmmaker, depicts young widow Nanyuma being bound by her hands and feet at her father's behest; this is to subdue her into marrying her late husband's feckless younger brother, who beats her mercilessly. A tyrannical government official even orders men to manhandle the illiterate Nanyuma into affixing her ink-smeared fingerprint on a civil marriage certificate, registering her legal "consent." Sissoko's film is an indictment of authoritarian rule at many levels in Malian politics during the late twentieth century.

In twenty-first-century Bamako, it has become unimaginable that a recalcitrant daughter would be tied up and beaten into accepting a husband she despises.[8] The consent of both bride and groom has been a formal requirement of civil marriage since the colonial era, and even if social structures often have overshadowed this legal requirement, broad agreement has emerged in Bamako that consent is a rightful and necessary precondition of a strong marriage. The fact that Islamic law also mandates both parties' explicit consent has only strengthened this consensus. Subtle forms of coercion survive, of course, but as women gain autonomy in Malian society, these forms of coercion will hold diminishing sway.

Discord persists over other rights pertaining to gender and marriage. We saw in chapter 6 that a wife's duty to obey her husband was a potent symbol. Adherents of Mande neotraditionalism and Islamic conservatism alike framed this duty as integral to the ordering of a just society. When the 1962 law enshrining that duty was to be replaced in 2009, these adherents mobilized en masse to reinstate husbands' legal supremacy over their wives. This backlash was predictable given the economic precarity in which most Bamakois lived, as well as senior males' anxiety over their perceived loss of domestic authority—and with it, part of their honor.

As of this writing, Mali's national sovereignty remains tenuous. Much of the country's territory lies outside central government control, and the state's security and everyday operations depend on considerable foreign support. This arrangement's foundations are not new, having been laid during the droughts of the 1970s (Mann 2015). As long as economic and political insecurity persist, marriage and polygamy will be sensitive issues in Malian society, liable to stoke protest by men afraid of losing their remaining gendered prerogatives. Fueled by similar patriarchal anxieties, opposition to liberal projects (like CEDAW and the UN's Sustainable Development Goals) intended to promote gender equality has risen all over the world, from the western Sahel (Cooper 2010 and 2019) to Southeast Asia (Koktvedgaard Zeitzen 2018; Mutaqin 2018).

Supporting Women's Agency and Autonomy

People in the United States are enamored of "win-win" scenarios. The notion that difficult issues can be resolved without sacrifice, without taking anything away from anyone, is another of our beloved myths—like that of "the economy" and its need for endless growth—that we have exported around the world. Win-win scenarios are fixtures of campaign speeches, TED talks, and community development pitches. "We can settle all these problems," the experts promise, "and everyone will come out ahead!"

Anthropology has taught me to be wary of such promises. Resolving difficult issues usually requires that at least one of the parties involved make trade-offs and sacrifices; we cannot pretend these parties' interests are always aligned. The problem of women's rights defies win-win solutions because it is a fundamentally political problem. It is, using sociologist Harold Lasswell's (1950) definition of politics, a matter of who gets what, when, and how. For women in Bamako to gain control over their bodies and their lives, men in Bamako must give up the control they have exercised over women's bodies and lives. These men's social and domestic authority has been diminishing for many years. Events in the early twenty-first century revealed men's determination to arrest or reverse this decline, and women's bodies and lives were the frontline in that contest.

I end this book, therefore, with a few suggestions for readers who aspire to be allies in women's struggles for agency around the world. These suggestions are informed by my professional commitment to cultural relativism and egalitarianism and by my findings from Bamako. I intend them mainly for readers in the Global North wishing to help improve the lives of women in the Global South, particularly in societies like Mali.

The first suggestion: don't dictate to people in other societies how they should live their lives. My own conviction is that I have no business, as an outsider, telling Malians how to organize their communities, their government, or their households. This conviction stems from a large body of research (much of it by anthropologists) showing the harm from decades of outsiders' efforts to reshape impoverished economies, states, and societies. Disastrous U.S. interventions in the Muslim world, most notably in Iraq and Afghanistan, demonstrate that even when a superpower decides to undertake nation-building projects abroad, it lacks the knowledge, political will, cultural awareness, and patience to succeed. Advocates of intervention by the "international community" in the Global South must recognize that attempts to reshape other societies according to supposedly universal norms have been ineffective at best and harmful at worst.

Wealthy governments and individuals, if they wish to play constructive roles in the long process of strengthening women's agency, must envision humbler approaches in which they do not presume to have all the answers. They must remember that their own societies are rife with gender-based violence, pay disparities, and other forms of discrimination. Facilitating emancipatory social change in impoverished societies is a very long game. Cultural relativism can help them maintain their humility during this process.

The second suggestion is to approach the inhabitants of impoverished societies as cultural equals. This suggestion, too, is informed by cultural relativism, and, specifically, its tenet that no culture is superior to any other. Malians are justifiably proud of their culture and heritage. Like Hassan, many think of their country as not poor but rich—in history, in artistic expression, in human diversity, in ideas for living together harmoniously amid that diversity. Outsiders seeking to facilitate what they see as positive change in Mali must first learn to overcome their impulse to understand Malian society in terms of what it lacks (technology, infrastructure, or modern institutions) and deal with Malian society on its own terms. Too many talk down to Malians while urging them to change their ways with respect to politics, marriage, gender relations, or a host of other issues. Judge Mahamadou Diawara, featured in chapters 5 and 6, spoke passionately on this point when we met in 2020:

> If you call my culture barbaric, you won't see what's positive in that culture anymore—you won't see it, and I won't tell you about it. And that's what they've done to us: they've called us barbaric, archaic, and they offered us money to renounce our ways. Some countries have abolished [polygamy] after taking money to agree to do that. Despite that funding, people keep marrying up to four wives! . . .
>
> Culture is stronger than you, you see? It's true that certain things must be banned, but you must provide reasons for banning them. When you say, "Other people must do things the way we do," it won't work.

As Judge Diawara observed, the act of casting moral judgment—which is what we do whenever we consider people of a different culture to be barbaric, backward, uncivilized, or lesser in some way—forecloses the possibility of further understanding or dialogue, leading to a hardening of positions.

Twelve years into this research, I find I have become somewhat more relativist and less egalitarian. I have recognized that many in Mali—even many women and members of other ostensibly marginalized groups—do not share my desire for equality to prevail among humans everywhere. And because equality is not a universal aspiration, I will refrain from moral judgments about the cross-cultural *institution* of polygamy. In this book, I have tried, instead, to highlight diverging views about the *practice* of polygamy and its abuse, such as a husband's unfair treatment of his wives. To criticize polygamy as an institution within Malian society, however, would be to impose my own set of standards about what people in Mali should value most in marriage. Malians must decide that for themselves. But, in my scholarly role, I can point out false public narratives (both in Mali and the Global North) about polygamy, like the ones concerning marriage squeezes and sex ratios discussed in chapter 5. Insofar as possible, decisions about marriage should be based on accurate information rather than myths.

My last suggestion is to concentrate on areas of accord rather than discord. Egalitarians might disagree with conservative Muslims about gender equality while agreeing with them about other issues. Education for girls and spousal choice are two such issues regarding women's agency in Bamako. While both were problematic or controversial for many Bamakois a generation or two ago, they are no longer controversial in the twenty-first century. Allies can help Malians build on these gains to continue strengthening women's agency and undermining the norms, ideologies, and attitudes that devalue women and girls (Meekers and Gage 2017). Allies can help Mali to strengthen its abysmal public school system so that it has something to offer to boys and girls (especially in rural areas). Allies also can allow Malians the space in which to reimagine their state in such a way that it protects its citizens and applies its laws fairly.

Frontal assaults on the redoubts of male dominance in Mali will continue to fail, as they did in 2009. Raising girls' minimum marriage age from sixteen to eighteen, a change that Mali's secular politicians failed to win, might be a noble goal. But girls' interests are not served when even the current legal minimum marriageable age of sixteen is routinely flouted; the successful enforcement of this and other existing laws would constitute a huge step forward. The promotion of inclusive economic opportunity to help young Malians establish themselves and set up their own households, particularly in fast-growing cities, would be another intervention that Malians would welcome. It also would significantly reshape Malian marriage markets by balancing marriage sex ratios and increasing young men's agency within marriage markets—to the detriment of their elders.

Over time, women in Bamako can gain agency and contribute more fully to their society by sometimes negotiating *with* patriarchal authority and sometimes negotiating *around* it—sidestepping male anxieties to pursue goals that men and women broadly agree upon (cf. Nnaemeka 2004). In this scenario, Bamakois would experience the changes wrought by such an indirect approach (cf. Cislaghi 2019) less as an abrupt revolution than an imperceptible realignment of their society's power and opportunity structures. Men would gradually adjust to having less control over women's bodies and lives. Elders, both male and female, would gradually adjust to having less control over their juniors. There most likely would be no declarations of victory and, for that matter, no embittered losers.

Would this be a win-win scenario for Mali? Perhaps not, from the perspective of those accustomed to the benefits of entrenched elder and patriarchal authority. Moreover, Mali faces many alternative scenarios that are far less promising for gender equity. I view the above scenario, however, as the best path to a future in which Malians can continue to honor their collective heritage, their Afropolitan ideals, and their religious convictions while adapting their marriage practices and gender roles to new realities. Bamako residents, in this promising future, will continue to marry. Some will marry polygamously.

Despite their marginalized status in society, women and young people have always played a vital part in Bamako's public life. As they gain bargaining power and agency in important life decisions—particularly but not only pertaining to marriage—they stand to play a more important and valued role in writing their city's story and in shaping its future.

ACKNOWLEDGMENTS

While I cannot name everyone who contributed time and insights during fieldwork in Bamako, I am particularly indebted to Djénéba Dembélé and Yaya Bamba for arranging and conducting focus group discussions in 2010 and 2011, and to Nana Touré and Noumouké Keita for arranging and conducting structured interviews in 2012. Houryata Diarra introduced me to many key informants. The Commune V municipal office generously allowed me to pore over their marriage records.

Several American undergraduate students helped carry out fieldwork. Lehigh University's Sofia Covarrubias and Sarah Steinberg (2010), Jordan Rejaud and Lucy Xia (2011–2012), and Carleton College's Julian Wyss (2012) conducted interviews and shared observations during the early data gathering stage. On the Lehigh campus, Gael Boucka assisted with data processing and analysis (2014).

I am grateful to my research funders: Lehigh University's Office of International Affairs (for preliminary research in 2010), the Fulbright US Scholar Program (for 2011–2012 fieldwork), Lehigh University's College of Arts and Sciences Dean's Associate Professor Advancement grant (for 2019–2020 fieldwork), and Lehigh University's Global Studies program (for additional research support).

The Lehigh library staff, particularly in the interlibrary loan office, connected me to essential publications. I also relied on resources from the Bethlehem Area Public Library and the Free Library of Philadelphia, both of which are priceless assets to their communities. And the Bethlehem Martial Arts Academy provided a good setting to read all this material while my son was taking classes there (2014–2018).

Beth Wright helped me refine a promising proposal. Faculty writing retreats organized by Kate Bullard at Lehigh University's Office of Research and by the Lehigh University Humanities Center (2018–2019) got my writing process underway. Musical inspiration from Jacob Moon powered me through the final chapters. Rokia Whitehouse's cover art gave the project visual form.

Nothing about writing this book was easy, but a vibrant transnational community of scholars and readers provided inspiration and wisdom while I was conceiving and revising it. Special thanks in this regard to Jaimie Bleck,

Joanna Davidson, Rosa de Jorio, Isaie Dougnon, Amadou Guissé, Sten Hagberg, Dinah Hannaford, Sten Hagberg, Joseph Hellweg, Barbara Hoffman, Chérif Keïta, Julie Kleinman, and Daniel Jordan Smith. I received feedback while presenting my work during conference panels at the African Studies Association (2016, 2017, 2018, and 2020) and the Mande Studies Association (2021). Hugo Ceròn-Anaya, Coleman Donaldson, A'ame Joslin, Judy Lasker, and Gregory Mann offered precious suggestions on chapter drafts. Carl and Barbara Whitehouse also read and helped me improve the manuscript (thanks, mom and dad!). Cody Benkoski, Emma Burke, Rakene Chowdhury, Scott Grenestedt, Zachary Lubart, Alyssa Morales, Marisol Nugent, and Megan Reimer, all students in five successive Cultural Diversity and Human Nature classes at Lehigh University (2021–2022), read chapter drafts, posed questions, and wrote comments that helped me refine the final product. Kathi Anderson spotted many mistakes and omissions during the copy-editing process. Development editor Katherine Wiley provided the best ideas I have ever received for restructuring and strengthening my argument; her contributions were absolutely priceless. Feedback from three anonymous peer reviewers was also helpful.

Thanks to those named here and others left unnamed, this is a better book. The only part for which I can claim full credit is its errors and imperfections.

NOTES

INTRODUCTION

1. Political scientist Valerie Hudson (2018, 149), for instance, characterized social tolerance of polygamy as "nuts."

2. Not all anthropologists find the concepts of culture and cultural relativism useful. See, for example, critiques by Lila Abu-Lughod (1991 and 2002).

3. Scriptural interpretations by figures from Saint Augustine to Martin Luther found polygamy permissible (at least under certain circumstances) until the sixteenth century, while pro-polygamy arguments circulated throughout the English-speaking world into the nineteenth century (Kilbride 1994; Pearsall 2022).

4. Even in societies where polygamy is widespread, it always exists in tandem with monogamy, which remains the numerically dominant form of marriage in terms of the number of unions (Schacht and Kramer 2019).

5. See, for example, David de la Croix and Fabio Mariani (2015); Eric Gould, Omer Moav, and Avi Simhon (2008); and Satoshi Kanazawa and Mary C. Still (1999).

6. The concept of marriage systems is deeply rooted in cultural anthropology, going back at least to A. R. Radcliffe-Brown and Daryll Forde's landmark *African Systems of Kinship and Marriage* (1950).

7. Bamako's annual growth rate between the 1998 and 2009 Malian censuses was 6.1 percent (Mesple-Somps et al. 2014). A 2006 ranking of estimated urban growth rates appears on the website of the City Mayors Foundation, www.citymayors.com /statistics/urban_growth1.html.

8. Throughout the 1990s and early 2000s, over one in five men in their early twenties was unemployed in Bamako (Marcoux and Piché 1998; INSTAT 2019).

9. "Mande" is not a widely used ethnonym in Mali, and scholars disagree on its applicability to local cultural categories. My use of "Mande" applies mainly to speakers of Bamanan, Maninka, and Soninke—a much narrower group of people than the Mande category used by linguists, for whom it designates a West African language family.

10. Slavery was abolished under French rule in 1905, but its legacy survived in the form of inherited inferior status for generations of descendants of enslaved people.

11. Additionally, while Bamakois of all backgrounds used the seven-day week, some Malian villages followed local calendars with five- or six-day weeks.

12. See, for example, https://youtu.be/4NhZs38YKio. Some of hip hop's appeal in Bamako stemmed, I suspect, from the fact that it defied this tripartite cultural schema and, thus, could easily integrate Mande, Muslim, and Western inputs.

13. Bamako is composed of six administrative units known as *communes*. Of these, only the Commune V records staff offered access to their marriage registers. Staff in the remaining five communes claimed that registers had not been preserved.

14. In an earlier article (Whitehouse 2017), I analyzed a sample drawn from a twenty-year span of civil marriage records (1991–2010). My sample here includes records from an additional five years (2012–2016).

CHAPTER 1 "MARRIAGE IS AN OBLIGATION"

1. According to the same survey, another 52 percent were married, 43.5 percent single, 3.2 percent widowed, and 0.8 percent divorced (INSTAT 2019). While unwed young mothers had become more common (Brand 2001; Lardoux 2004), there remained no socially legitimate way for a Bamako couple to live together outside of marriage. As one woman in our interview sample said, entering such a relationship "devalues the woman in the man's eyes, but also in society. A woman who does it is unlikely to marry the man, for he will lose respect for her."

2. At 7.3 years, West Africa's average spousal gap was the widest of any world region (Hertrich 2017), with spousal age gaps correlated positively with rates of polygamous marriage.

3. These figures come from UN data analyzed by Jean-François Mignot (2010), who reported that the average husband was older than the average wife in 202 of 203 countries surveyed. The lone exception was the Italian microstate of San Marino, where wives averaged 0.1 year older than their husbands.

4. This one-way taboo was observed in communities from Mali (Hoffman 2002) to Senegal (Dial 2008). Bamanan husbands could reciprocate the taboo if they wished (K. Koné 2002). In our sample of fifty Bamako wives, only four reported calling their husbands by their first names. Twenty-one used husbands' last names, fourteen referred to them as *Tonton* (French for "uncle"), and eleven used nicknames such as "Papa" or "Chéri." Compare this taboo, which has been described as an expression of wives' inferior status vis-a-vis their husbands (A. Tounkara 2015), to the rule in many cultures against calling senior kin (especially one's parents) by their first names. In Jane Austen's novel *Emma* (1815), the titular heroine resolves to call her fiancé by his Christian name only once, at their wedding, and otherwise to call him "Mr. Knightley."

5. In the early years of Mali's neoliberal transition, men's mean age at first marriage increased among urban residents (who bore the brunt of economic austerity) while holding steady in rural areas (Antoine 2006). In 2018, the median age at first marriage for Bamako men (aged thirty to fifty-nine at the time of the survey) was 28.7, 2.7 years older than for rural Malian men (DHS 2019).

6. Islamist militants who took over northern Mali in 2012 enacted a popular ban on expensive wedding ceremonies and large bridewealth payments (Schulz and Diallo 2016).

7. Anthropologist Anne Doquet (2014, 396) observed that among young women in and near Bamako, age twenty-five was an important milestone: "not to marry before this fateful age is to risk being called '*vieille*'" [old] (cf. Ammann 2017, 115). In Saudi Arabia, legal scholar Maha Yamani (2008) found a common assumption that spinsterhood began at age twenty-four. Compare to young Lydia Bennet's declaration in Jane Austen's *Pride and Prejudice*: "How ashamed I should be of not being married before three-and-twenty!"

8. Instead of patrilocality, newlyweds in northern Mali often practiced *neolocality*; that is, moving into a new household of their own.

9. "A woman who shows an interest in being on her own raises deep suspicion," wrote Schulz (2012a, 115–116). "As expectations are strong and generally accepted that a decent woman should spend as little time as possible outside the family, it is relatively easy for a husband or mother-in-law to reprimand a woman for freely wandering around . . . a reproach that implies the charge of promiscuity." See also Chantal Rondeau (1996) on the stigmatization of women living independently in Bamako.

10. Bamakois put little stigma on premarital pregnancy in Bamako as long as it culminated in marriage; many described it as a matter of destiny, not a reflection on the mother's character (see Miseli 1998).

11. A *jeli* (or "griot") is a member of a caste responsible for maintaining the oral histories and public relations of noble families (see introduction).

12. A more literal translation would read, "Household power is broken."

13. "All societies recognize that there are occasional violent emotional attachments between persons of opposite sex," wrote anthropologist Ralph Linton in the 1930s, "but our present American culture is practically the only one which has attempted to capitalize these and make them the basis of marriage" (1936, 175). By the late twentieth century, people in many cultures around the world similarly judged a couple's marital suitability using romantic love.

14. The Mande philosophy of duality is expressed in the Bamanan saying *kelenya ka di Allah dɔrɔn de la* [Oneness is fitting only for God]. A male interviewee conveyed his disapproval of monogamous marriage through this expression (see chapter 4).

15. Members of polygamous Mormon communities in the United States were similarly wary of romantic attachment when arranging their children's marriages (Jankowiak 2023).

16. The two strongest taboos regarding sexual relations and marriage between members of specific ethnic and caste groups in Malian society forbade pairings: 1) between persons of Dogon and Bozo ethnicity; and 2) between members of the Fulani ethnic group and the *numu* (blacksmith) caste. Such pairings were believed to violate an ancient pact between these groups. Tales recounted the sad fates of couples who transgressed these taboos: the roof collapses on a mixed Dogon/Bozo couple's nuptial chamber, killing them in their bed; a numu/Fulani pair cannot uncouple themselves after sexual intercourse, resulting in their hospitalization and public shaming. See Brand's analysis of such marital taboos (2001, 69–70).

17. In neighboring Niger, wrote Barbara Cooper (2019, 246), young girls are "often as much the 'bride' of their mothers-in-law as they are of their husbands."

18. "My wife shouldn't be sad to know that I love my mother more than her," a Malian man tweeted in 2022, "because I'll teach her sons to love her more than their wives."

19. This comes from a refrain in her song "Bi Fourou," released in 1993.

20. Already in Abidjan of the 1970s, sociologist Claudine Vidal noted that "men willingly ascribe to women the blame for the sex-money equation, as if they themselves were barely implicated by it" (1977, 138). The same held true in twenty-first-century Mali.

21. "Couple" is always a problematic label (Willey 2016) but particularly so in Bamako, where the word connotes a false primacy to the husband-wife relationship. Unable to avoid this word completely in writing about marriage, I use it sparingly. Note that "couple" has a ready analogue in French (*le couple*) but none in Manding.

22. On homosocial group dynamics among urban Malian youth, see Julien Bondaz (2013), Charlotte Joy (2011), and Dorothea Schulz (2002).

23. Seydou Badian's 1957 novel *Sous l'Orage*, in which a Bamako teen resists her father's attempt to marry her to a polygamous husband, was required reading for generations of Malian students. By the time my fieldwork began, the generation of the novel's protagonists (who had come of age in the 1950s and 1960s) were the elders imposing their will on romantic youths.

24. Adame Ba Konaré (1993, 26n3) documented the belief that "the more a wife suffers and withstands in her marriage, the more chance she has to bring fortunate children into the world." See Carole Ammann (2017 and 2020) and Emily Lynn Osborn (2011) on similar views in neighboring Guinea.

25. Rural Bamana women, according to Sarah Brett-Smith (2014, 146), often "viewed their marriages as a kind of indentureship or 'slavery' from which they would be partially redeemed by their children."

26. Ironically, Aisha also opined that the children of a woman who withheld sex from her husband would not succeed in life.

27. Of the fifty wives in our interview sample, twenty-six listed themselves as housewives; there were also nine traders, seven office workers, three unemployed, two students, one *jeli*, one cloth dyer, and one midwife.

28. Female-headed households tended to be poorer than male-headed households in Mali (D. van de Walle 2013).

29. Note that Malian women defined independence substantially as "financial independence from men," though not from their children (Heywood and Ivey 2021, 7).

30. As with all co-wives who do not live under the same roof, demographers have debated whether to count each wife's home as a separate household (Antoine 2018; Gning 2011; Gning and Antoine 2015).

31. In Senegal, nine of ten widows and divorcees remarried within five years (Antoine and Nanitelamio 1996).

32. Marriage scholars have noted a strong positive correlation between marriage universality and gender inequality: the higher a society's marriage rate, the wider the gap between men's and women's rights (Cohen 2018a).

CHAPTER 2 POLYGAMOUS MARRIAGE FORMATION

1. Census data from 2009 analyzed by Aminata Coulibaly Diamouténé (2015) show that, among Mali's Christians, 22.5 percent of married women and 14.3 percent of married men were in polygamous unions.

2. Mothers' need to breastfeed infants once led to long periods of postpartum abstinence for women in the Sahel (Cooper 2019). Yet none of our interviewees mentioned this factor. By the 2010s, postpartum abstinence was commonly limited to forty days in Bamako, in line with Islamic laws.

3. Many wives' rotation intervals depended on the geographic distance to be traversed. The wives of a Malian trader I knew in Brazzaville, Congo (more than 3,000 kilometers from Bamako by air), switched places every couple of years. The wives of his cousin, who lived in Bamako (160 kilometers from their village), switched at least twice annually.

4. In any case, Ngolo knew that his wives, not he, would bear many of the costs of his acquiescence.

5. From her fieldwork in The Gambia, Inge Wittrup (1990, 123–124) reported a Mandinka saying: "With the first marriage one satisfies the family, whereas the second one is to satisfy oneself."

6. Issa's case is unusual in that his second wife was older than his first. Most polygamous husbands' second wives were several years younger than their first wives.

7. Some Malian husbands, typically civil servants who traveled regularly between two or more households in different communities, had secret marriages (cf. Koktvedgaard Zeitzen 2018).

8. While Muslim figures such as Egyptian Islamist leader Hassan Al Banna used men's supposedly higher sex drive as a justification for polygamy (Mashhour 2005), few Malians referred openly to this factor.

9. In the Malaysian context, Mohd Razif describes a perception of husbands using polygamy to "halalize" (i.e., render Islamically licit) their extramarital affairs (2021, 9).

10. Writing about gender and power relations in urban Uganda, Wyrod characterized compensatory sexuality as men's "privilege of starting another sexual partnership if their relationship with their wife or girlfriend had become contentious" (2016, 174).

11. An Egyptian Islamic scholar made a similar argument, paraphrased by Maha Yamani (2008, 23): "Polygamy in Islam can cure the illness of Westernised, masculine behaviour in the first wife, thus improving her haughty attitude towards her husband."

12. In the Nigeria of the mid-1970s, demographer Helen Ware (1979) found women in monogamous marriages less likely than those in polygamous marriages to refuse sex with their husbands during periods of postpartum recovery.

13. About Malaysia, Miriam Koktvedgaard Zeitzen (2018, 201) writes that "second wives tend to be the most reviled part of any polygamous union by women inside and outside the immediate family."

CHAPTER 3   POLYGAMOUS HOUSEHOLD DYNAMICS

1. Some listed fadenya among polygamy's benefits, seeing rivalry as a productive dynamic among children, bringing advantage to them and to their households. As Karim (M, 52, trader, two wives) said, "Polygamy is beneficial because it creates competition among children and co-wives, whereas it's hard for children of a lone wife to compete."

2. This custom resembled widespread practices of child-sharing between West African households. Research in Mali found nearly one-third of weaned children under the age of five living away from their biological mothers (Adams and Castle 1994; Porcelli 2016). Patterns of inter-household and inter-village sharing existed throughout the region (Bledsoe 1993; Tabutin and Schoumaker 2020).

3. William Jankowiak (2023) found similar practices among Mormon polygamous families in the United States.

4. This verse, appearing here in Ahmed Ali's English translation, has been subject to divergent interpretations (Hasan 2019; Wadud 1999). A related saying of the Prophet Muhammad holds: "A man who has two wives and favors one over the other will be resurrected at the final judgment with one side of his body drooping" (K. Ali 2006, 503–504).

5. Malik chose to do his interview in French. The Manding version of this question asked interviewees if they felt that a polygamous husband could *musow bɛɛ mara bolo kelen kan*—literally, "to keep all [his] wives on one arm," an idiom designating equal treatment.

6. Issa had two adjoining houses built, one for each wife, with a doorway connecting their front courtyards. He divided his home life between these houses.

7. The words for "co-wife" in Hausa, Luo, and Yoruba all evoke jealousy or rivalry (Meekers and Franklin 1995); the Ronga name for the space between co-wives' huts means "the quarreling place" (Sheldon 2002); among the Maroons of Suriname, one phrasing of the verb "to fight" literally means "to make [act like a] co-wife" (Price 1984, 53).

8. Quoting singer Hawa Kasse Mady Diabaté, Lucy Durán (2017, 173) translates this saying as "No matter how much co-wives seem to get on, underneath there is darkness in their relations."

9. According to men in Senegal, "cowives were known to engage in occult practices to harm their rivals or their children," and polygamy took "at least ten years off" husbands' lives (Kringelbach 2016b, 152). A medical study in Saudi Arabia and the United Arab Emirates found risks of heart disease were significantly higher among polygamous husbands than monogamous ones (Daoulah et al. 2017).

10. This term derives from "cohabitation" in its generic sense of living together, rather than its more specific sociological connotation of living together outside of marriage.

11. Note that polygamy also was less common in northern Mali than elsewhere in the country. According to 2009 census data analyzed by Aminata Coulibaly Diamouténé (2015), the polygamy rate among wives in Timbuktu and Gao was about 23 percent, compared to 52 percent in the southern Sikasso region and the western Kayes region. In the northern Kidal region, it was only 4 percent.

12. This aspiration concerned more than co-wives. Tenants renting rooms in crowded Bamako compounds also yearned to escape the everyday indignities and squabbles that came with living in close proximity to others (Dougnon 2020).

13. In neighboring Senegal, Sadio Ba Gning and Philippe Antoine (2015) estimated that over 30 percent of polygamous households were non-coresidential.

14. Social support among co-wives also seems to be the exception to the rule. A study of Bamako wives (Bove, Vala-Haynes, and Valeggia 2012) found women in polygamous marriages unlikely to be supported by their co-wives during illness.

CHAPTER 4 WHAT'S CULTURE GOT TO DO WITH IT?

1. Cases of "transcontinental" plural marriage are not uncommon among West African migrants; see Brzezińska (2021).

2. Makan's notion that women aged faster than men recalls the notion of "depreciation through use" of the female body, critiqued by philosopher Raphaël Liogier (2020, 73).

3. Rates are taken from these countries' most recent DHS reports. In cases where reports did not list the percentage of Muslims in the population (Egypt, Jordan, Yemen), I used the percentage from the CIA World Factbook's entry for that country.

4. This permissive stance toward gender-based violence was intimately linked with polygamy. Survey data from seventeen African countries reveal a positive correlation between tolerance for wife-beating and the polygamy rate. They also show women to be far more likely than men to justify wife-beating (Uthman, Lawoko, and Moradi

2010); the share of Bamako men expressing agreement with the wife-beating statement was only 6.6 percent (DHS 2019).

5. Of a rural Bamanan village she studied in the early 1980s, Camilla Toulmin (1992, 236) wrote, "Women, half-jokingly, call their position akin to that of slaves as they are bought and sold by men who take and give them in marriage. They play no official role in village politics, having no forum for regular meetings." Women were only slightly less excluded from national politics. Of the 1,086 participants in the national conference establishing Mali's democratic institutions in 1991, for example, only fifty-two were women (Ba Konaré 1993).

6. Malian law allowed judges considerable discretion in their rulings, which tended to reflect dominant patriarchal norms (D. Tounkara 2012). Moreover, Mali's 1962 code construed a wife's adultery very differently from a husband's (Kombo 2021).

7. The term *deuxième bureau* or "second office" is a common euphemism for a mistress in francophone Africa.

8. Islamic law theoretically held men and women to equal account for adultery, even if many Muslim militants and vigilantes punished only women (Cooper 2010). In the Western world, by contrast, the sexual double standard was written into laws from ancient Rome to modern France punishing only women's infidelity (Liogier 2020).

9. Schulz (2010) notes that through the early 2000s, Mali's political Islamists were too pragmatic to push for full implementation of religious law. In any case, since Muslim jurists traditionally set a near-impossible evidentiary standard—four male eyewitnesses—for convicting accused fornicators under Islamic law (Lydon 2018), it is unclear how frequently hudud punishment could be used against adulterers or how effectively it might deter marital infidelity under this precedent.

10. "Gendered symbolic capital" is not a term used by Pierre Bourdieu, who rarely factored gender into his analysis. I thank my colleague Hugo Ceròn-Anaya for suggesting this term.

11. This apparent paradox existed elsewhere. Researchers studying the Kaguru of Tanzania, for example, found that women generally opposed polygamy but were unable to challenge it, hence "institutionalized support for it . . . remained strong" (Meekers and Franklin 1995, 326).

12. Khadidja's remarks echo the views of Oumou Sangaré, perhaps Mali's best-known female singer: "Polygamy is false, ultra-false, it is sheer hypocrisy. The man who practices it will never be happy, he's obliged to be a hypocrite all the time. . . . There are maybe only two out of one hundred polygamous families for whom it works, the rest are utterly miserable" (quoted in Durán 2017, 185). Recall also Kani's comment in Interlude 2: "Polygamy is difficult because the man is never sincere."

13. Whereas Western feminists and academics tend to emphasize challenge, disruption, deconstruction, and tensions, writes Obioma Nnaemeka (2004, 378), African feminism "challenges through negotiations and compromise. It knows when, where, and how to detonate patriarchal landmines; it also knows when, where, and how to go around patriarchal landmines. In other words, it knows when, where, and how to negotiate with or negotiate around patriarchy in different contexts."

14. See, respectively, abamako.com (2021) and *Le Pays* (2021).

15. Recall from the previous chapter that Malik was reluctant even to speak of a woman's sterility. He added the phrase "if I can say that" after evoking this sensitive subject to acknowledge the difficulty of addressing it openly.

16. Similar observations have been made about women in other ostensibly male-dominated African societies (Falen 2011; Sudarkasa 1986).

17. Edward Baptist (2014, 90 and 113) distinguishes between "right-handed power" ("the strength to force an outcome") and "left-handed power" ("the secret way of seemingly passive resistance").

CHAPTER 5   MARRIAGE MARKETS AND MARRIAGE SQUEEZES

1. This definition is based on one by sociologist Philip Cohen: "the social space in which people search for potential marriage partners" (2018b, 291).

2. For related arguments about the harmful effects of polygamy's production of "excess men" and aggravated sexual competition, see, among others: Eric D. Gould, Omer Moav, and Avi Simhon (2008); Joseph Henrich, Robert Boyd, and Peter Richerson (2012); Valerie M Hudson (2018); Satishi Kanazawa (1999); Stephen Macedo (2015); Rose McDermott and Jonathan Cowden (2016).

3. Scholars disagree over whether prevalent conflict in a society is correlated with the institution of bridewealth, widely associated with polygamy (Cook and Thies 2019; Hudson and Matfess 2017).

4. For anthropological views of the demography of multiple marriage, see Monica Wilson's (1950) discussion of Nyakyusa marriage, or Vernon Dorjahn's (1959) analysis based on his research in Liberia. Demographer Etienne van de Walle (1968, 217) acknowledged speculation about a surplus of females in polygynous societies while pointing out that the problem "is quite simply resolved by taking account of the age structure of populations and differences by sex in age at marriage." For subsequent demographic analysis of the relationship between polygyny and marriage markets, see Philippe Antoine (2006), Venkataraman Bhaskar (2015), Véronique Hertrich (2017), Ron Lesthaeghe, Georgia Kaufmann, and Dominique Meekers (1989), Gilles Pison (1986 and 1988), or Dominique Tabutin (1988).

5. Note that these ratios reflect not the relative numbers of males and females at birth, but in each country's total population; data are from the UN World Population Prospects, https://population.un.org/wpp/DataQuery/.

6. In the Kingdom of Saudi Arabia, religious and political authorities have similarly framed the maintenance of polygamous marriage as "an issue for the general public good" (Yamani 2008, 183).

7. This interpretation, while common in Bamako and conforming to "traditional literalism" in Islamic jurisprudence (Majeed 2015, 69 ff.), contradicts many Muslim jurists' readings of the Qur'an (K. Ali 2006 and 2016; Mashhour 2005); see discussion in chapter 4.

8. Another male interviewee who had described the population as 51 percent female expressed an identical view: "Since women are more numerous than men, without this polygamy, there would be plenty of unmarried women."

9. I am reminded of a cynical line from comedian Chris Rock: "A man is only as faithful as his options."

10. The effect of this marriage squeeze on women's status was undercut in the early twenty-first century, according to Leta Hong Fincher (2014), by Chinese Communist Party propaganda inciting public alarm over a supposed crisis of "leftover women" unable to find husbands.

11. To reflect the general exclusion of female migrant domestic workers from the Bamako marriage market, I reduced the size of the city's fifteen- to nineteen-year-old female cohort by 14 percent in these calculations.

12. Polygamy tends to be closely correlated with social structures in which elders command a great deal of power in everyday life. Writing from his research on pastoral groups in East Africa, Paul Spencer (1998, 53) wrote that polygamy served as a broad measure of gerontocracy, "both in terms of the younger men who have to wait and more poignantly in terms of the extent to which women are subordinated to husbands much older than themselves."

INTERLUDE THREE   FAMILY LAW, IDENTITY, AND POLITICAL ISLAM

1. At the time of our interview, Sarkozy and Hollande were campaigning against each other in the French presidential election.

CHAPTER 6   MARRIAGE LAW, POLYGAMY, AND THE MALIAN STATE

1. The original term used by Brunet, *indigènes*, was a paternalistic label with which the French often designated their colonial subjects.

2. "If 'ignorant women' are generally favorable toward polygamy that allows them to leave their conjugal homes regularly to visit their own families [i.e., their parents]," a representative of the *Union des Femmes Maliennes* declared around 1960, "'educated women' consider monogamy alone as compatible with their dignity" (quoted in Decheix 1967, 125).

3. Only Keita's first wife, Mariam Travélé, whom he married in 1939, was recognized as Mali's first lady during his presidency. After being unable to have children with her, Keita remarried in 1952 and again in 1962; his third wife was twenty-eight years his junior (Rillon 2021).

4. A groom could not wed multiple brides simultaneously in Bamako; by custom and by law, a polygamous man had to hold a different wedding ceremony for each wife. The term "couple" is, therefore, appropriate here.

5. Labels like "traditional" or "customary" were meaningless in Mali before the advent of Islam and French colonization; see discussion in this book's introduction.

6. See Sarah Brett-Smith (2014, chapter 1) for a description of konyo in a Beledugu Bamanan village.

7. On monogamy agreements in twenty-first-century Mauritania and Saudi Arabia, see Corinne Fortier (2011) and Maha Yamani (2008).

8. Of the fifty-one husbands in our interview sample who indicated where their marriage ceremonies were celebrated, forty (78 percent) specified both mairie and mosque, eight (16 percent) mosque only, and three (6 percent) mairie only. Interestingly, none mentioned the home, where customary weddings usually took place; some may simply have taken this type of ceremony for granted. Every male interviewee who had not done a civil ceremony worked as a market vendor and had little or no formal schooling. Those having performed a civil ceremony included twenty-five office workers, eight teachers, seven traders, and two students. Of the sample's fifty wives, thirty (60 percent) celebrated both religious and civil ceremonies, while twenty (40 percent) celebrated religious ceremonies only. Women in the latter group were less educated, with only three of the twenty having some secondary schooling, compared to eighteen of the thirty women

who did both ceremonies. Among the thirty women with civil and religious ceremonies were twelve housewives, seven office workers, four traders, three unemployed graduates, a jeli, a cloth dyer, a midwife, and one woman who described herself as jobless. The remaining twenty included fourteen housewives, five traders, and a student.

9. An English translation of the 1962 code's Article 6 reads: "Any worship minister who conducts religious ceremonies for a marriage not validated by a certificate from a civil wedding ceremony, delivered by a state official, will be punished by a fine of 2500 to 15000 francs. In case of recidivism, he will be punished with imprisonment of not less than two months" (Boye 1987, 19).

10. By contrast, some in the rural Wasulu area looked askance at a couple having multiple wedding celebrations. According to Ibrahima Camara (2002, 212), elders would comment ironically, "marriages celebrated three times are more brittle than those celebrated just once."

11. Such manipulation was already common by the early 1900s in French West Africa, where military officers used legal ambiguities to legitimize African recruits' polygamous unions and allocate spousal benefits (Zimmerman 2020).

12. A similar situation prevailed in neighboring Senegal, where women feared that pursuing the monogamy option under civil law would "mark them as 'troublesome' women and undesirable wives" (Cooper 2010, 11).

13. CEDAW's Article 16 pledged "to eliminate discrimination against women in all matters relating to marriage and family relations." The United States signed CEDAW in 1980 but left it unratified, in part because many U.S. states were unwilling to prohibit marriage to persons under the age of eighteen. As for Mali's 1992 constitution, Article 2 reads, "All Malians are born and live free and equal in their rights and duties. Any discrimination based on social origin, color, language, race, sex, religion, or political opinion is prohibited." In the United States, by contrast, the Equal Rights Amendment banning sexual discrimination, passed by both houses of Congress in the 1970s, was not ratified by enough states to become law.

14. This aspect of the campaign against Mali's 2009 code recalled tactics used to defeat women's rights measures in neighboring Niger (Kang 2015), as well as the Equal Rights Amendment (ERA) in the United States. Like Mali's 2009 code, the ERA had broad political support until conservative activists mounted concerted counterefforts (Perlstein 2020).

15. Marriage laws in many other African states were rife with similar contradictions (Mwambene 2017).

16. This interpretation draws on concepts such as "the instrumentalization of disorder" (Chabal and Daloz 1999) and "strategies of extraversion" (Bayart 2000).

CONCLUSION

1. While the word "dysfunction" suggests problems that defied the state's mission, I have argued that we should not interpret the legal uncertainties surrounding marriage in Mali as unintended (see chapter 6).

2. Analysis of cross-national data from dozens of African countries has also challenged the supposed link between male inequality and polygamy (Fenske 2015).

3. I am grateful for insights by Julia Behrman (2019) and David Lawson and Mhairi Gibson (2018) in this regard.

4. Reading Jane Ward's *The Tragedy of Heterosexuality* (2020) made me wonder whether queer scholars might describe social tolerance of traditional heterosexual marriage as "nuts" (cf. Hudson 2018).

5. "It is inconceivable that society will continue to deny adult status to large numbers of mature females," Saskia Brand once wrote about Bamako, adding that she expected single women's status to "become normalized in the near future" (2001, 306). Two decades later, that future has not yet arrived, but seems somewhat nearer.

6. Demographers do not expect Mali's youth-heavy age structure to change significantly until after 2050; until then, the proportion of sixteen- to twenty-five-year-olds is predicted to hold steady at 20 percent of the population, and Malians' median age will rise only from 16.3 to 20 years (UNFPA 2020).

7. Such messages, used to great effect in the United States during the late 1970s (Perlstein 2020), have become globally widespread among conservatives of all faiths.

8. Rural Malian communities, where forced marriage and physical coercion have been more persistent (WILDAF 2018), are a different story. Moreover, even many Bamakois view physical coercion and force as permissible *within* the bonds of marriage (see chapter 1).

REFERENCES

abamako.com. 2021. "Poignardé pour avoir voulu prendre une deuxième femme." December 31. http://news.abamako.com/h/264151.html.

Abu-Lughod, Lila. 1991. "Writing against Culture." In *Recapturing Anthropology: Working in the Present*, edited by Richard G. Fox, 137–162. Santa Fe: School of American Research Press.

———. 1999. [1986.] *Veiled Sentiments: Honor and Poetry in a Bedouin Society.* Berkeley: University of California Press.

———. 2002. "Do Muslim Women Really Need Saving? Reflections on Cultural Relativism and Its Others." *American Anthropologist* 104 (3): 783–790.

Adams, Alayne, and Sarah Castle. 1994. "Gender Relations and Household Dynamics." In *Population Policies Reconsidered: Health, Empowerment, and Rights*, edited by Gita Sen, Adrienne Germain, and Lincoln C. Chen, 161–173. Cambridge: Harvard University Press.

Afrobarometer. 2013. "Sommaire des résultats round 5 Afrobarometer Enquête au Mali, 2012." https://afrobarometer.org/sites/default/files/publications/Summary%20of%20results/mli_r5_sor.pdf.

Akhtar, Ayad. 2020. *Homeland Elegies.* New York: Little, Brown and Company.

Ali, Kecia. 2006. "Polygamy." In *The Qur'an: An Encyclopedia*, edited by Oliver Leaman, 503–505. London: Routledge.

———. 2008. "Marriage, Family, and Sexual Ethics." In *The Islamic World*, edited by Andrew Rippin, 615–627. London: Routledge.

———. 2016. *Sexual Ethics and Islam: Feminist Reflections on Qur'an, Hadith, and Jurisprudence*, 2nd edition. London: OneWorld.

Ali, Kecia, and Oliver Leaman. 2007. *Islam: The Key Concepts.* New York: Routledge.

Ammann, Carole. 2017. "Looking for Better Opportunities: An Analysis of Guinean Graduates' Agency." In *Dealing with Elusive Futures: University Graduates in Urban Africa*, edited by Noemi Steuer, Michelle Engeler, and Elísio Macamo, 93–122. Bielefeld: Transcript.

———. 2020. *Women, Agency, and the State in Guinea: Silent Politics.* New York: Routledge.

Amone, Charles. 2019. "Polygamy as a Dominant Pattern of Sexual Pairing among the Acholi of Uganda." *Sexuality & Culture* 24: 733–748.

Anderson, Connie M. 2000. "The Persistence of Polygyny as an Adaptive Response to Poverty and Oppression in Apartheid South Africa." *Cross-Cultural Research* 34 (2): 99–112.

Antoine, Philippe. 2006. "The Complexities of Nuptiality: From Early Female Unions to Male Polygamy in Africa." In *Demography: Analysis and Synthesis*, edited by Graziela Casseli, Jacques Vallin, and Guillaume Wunsch, 355–371. Boston: Elsevier.

———. 2018. "La polygamie urbaine et la polygamie rural au Sénégal: Configurations à partir des données de recensement." In *Nouvelles Dynamiques Familiales en Afrique*, edited by Anne-Emmanuèle Calvès, Fatou Binetou Dial, and Richard Marcoux, 17–53. Québec: Presses de l'Université de Québec.

Antoine, Philippe, and Mamadou Djiré. 1998. "Un célibat de crise?" In *Trois générations de citadins au Sahel: Trente ans d'histoire sociale à Dakar et à Bamako*, edited by Antoine Philippe, Dieudonné Ouédraogo, and Victor Piché, 117–146. Paris: L'Harmattan.

Antoine, Philippe, Mamadou Djiré, and Jeanne Nanitelamio. 1998. "Au cœur des relations hommes-femmes: Polygamie et divorce." In *Trois générations de citadins au Sahel: Trente ans d'histoire sociale à Dakar et à Bamako*, edited by Antoine Philippe, Dieudonné Ouédraogo, and Victor Piché, 147–180. Paris: L'Harmattan.

Antoine, Philippe, and Richard Marcoux. 2014. "Pluralité des formes et des modèles matrimoniaux en Afrique: Un état des lieux." In *Le Mariage en Afrique: Pluralité des formes et des modèles*, edited by Richard Marcoux and Philippe Antoine, 1–18. Québec: Presses de l'Université de Québec.

Antoine, Philippe, and Jeanne Nanitelamio. 1996. "Can Polygyny be Avoided in Dakar?" In *Courtyards, Markets, City Streets: Urban Women in Africa*, edited by Kathleen Sheldon, 129–152. Boulder: Westview.

Appel, Hannah. 2017. "Toward an Ethnography of the National Economy." *Cultural Anthropology* 32 (2): 294–322.

Archambault, Julie Soleil. 2017. *Mobile Secrets: Youth, Intimacy, and the Politics of Pretense in Mozambique*. Chicago: University of Chicago Press.

Austen, Ralph A. 1999. *In Search of Sunjata: The Mande Oral Epic as History, Literature, and Performance*. Bloomington: Indiana University Press.

Ba Konaré, Adame. 1993. *Dictionnaire des Femmes Célèbres du Mali*. Bamako: Editions Jamana.

Bagayogo, Shaka, and Tiéman Coulibaly. 2014. "Les jeunes et l'ailleurs du pouvoir au Mali." In *Le Mali Contemporain*, edited by Joseph Brunet-Jailly, Jacques Charmes, and Doulaye Konaté, 511–541. Bamako: Editions Tombouctou.

Bao, Jiemin. 2006. *Marital Acts: Gender, Sexuality, and Identity among the Chinese Thai Diaspora*. Honolulu: University of Hawai'i Press.

Bao, Jiemin, and William Jankowiak. 2008. "Introduction: Privilege Disguises Torment." *Ethnology* 47 (3): 137–144.

Baptist, Edward E. 2014. *The Half Has Never Been Told: Slavery and the Making of American Capitalism*. New York: Basic Books.

Barash, David P. 2016. *Out of Eden: The Surprising Consequences of Polygamy*. New York: Oxford University Press.

Barr, Abigail, Marleen Dekker, Wendy Janssens, Bereket Kebede, and Berber Kramer. 2019. "Cooperation in Polygynous Households." *American Economic Journal: Applied Economics* 11 (2): 266–283.

Baugh, Carolyn G. 2021. "Sex and Marriage in Early Islamic Law." In *The Routledge Handbook of Islam and Gender*, edited by Justine Howe, 43–56. New York: Routledge.

Bayart, Jean-François. 2000. "Africa in the World: A History of Extraversion." *African Affairs* 99: 217–267.

BBC. 2009. "To Love, Honour, and Obey in Mali." 27 August. http://news.bbc.co.uk/go/pr/fr/-/2/hi/africa/8223966.stm.

Beaman, Lori G. 2014. "Introduction: Is Polygamy Inherently Harmful?" In *Polygamy's Rights and Wrongs: Perspectives on Harm, Family, and Law*, edited by Gillian Calder and Lori G. Beaman, 1–20. Vancouver: UBC Press.

———. 2016. "Opposing Polygamy: A Matter of Equality or Patriarchy?" In *The Polygamy Question*, edited by Janet Bennion and Lisa Fishbayn Joffe, 42–61. Boulder: University of Colorado Press.

Becker, Gary S. 1974. "A Theory of Marriage: Part II." *Journal of Political Economy* 82: 511–26.

Beckwith, Carol, and Angela Fisher. 1999. *African Ceremonies*. New York: Harry N. Abrams.

Behrman, Julia A. 2019. "Polygynous Unions and Intimate Partner Violence in Nigeria: An Examination of the Role of Selection." *Journal of Marriage and Family* 81 (4): 905–919.

Bennion, Janet. 2016. "The Variable Impact of Mormon Polygyny on Women and Children." In *The Polygamy Question*, edited by Janet Bennion and Lisa Fishbayn Joffe, 62–84. Boulder: University of Colorado Press.

Bergmann, Barbara R. 1995. "Becker's Theory of the Family: Preposterous Conclusions." *Feminist Economics* 1 (1): 141–150.

Bertrand, Monique. 2004. "Femmes et modernité citadine au Mali." In *Femmes et Villes*, edited by Sylvette Denefle, 283–304. Tours: Presses Universitaires François-Rabelais.

———. 2013. "Fils, frères, pères: Masculinités sous contrats, du nord à la capitale du Mali." *Cahiers d'Études Africaines* 53 (1–2): 209–210, 323–344.

———. 2021. *Bamako: De la ville à l'agglomération*: Marseille: IRD Editions.

Bhaskar, Venkataraman. 2015. "The Demographic Transition and the Position of Women: A Marriage Market Perspective." Centre for Economic Policy Research Discussion Paper no. DP10619.

Bird, Charles S., and Martha B. Kendall. 1980. "The Mande Hero: Text and Context." In *Explorations in African Systems of Thought*, edited by Ivan Karp and Charles S. Bird, 13–26. Bloomington: Indiana University Press.

Blanc, Ann K., and Anastasia J. Gage. 2000. "Men, Polygyny, and Fertility over the Life-Course in Sub-Saharan Africa." In *Fertility and the Male Life Cycle in the Era of Fertility Decline*, edited by Caroline Bledsoe, Susana Lerner, and Jane Guyer, 163–187. New York: Oxford University Press.

Bleck, Jaimie. 2015. *Education and Empowered Citizenship in Mali*. Baltimore: Johns Hopkins University Press.

Bleck, Jaimie, and Alison Lodermeier. 2020. "Migration Aspirations from a Youth Perspective: Focus Groups with Returnees and Youth in Mali." *Journal of Modern African Studies* 58 (4): 551–577.

Bleck, Jaimie, and Kristin Michelitch. 2018. "Is Women's Empowerment Associated with Political Knowledge and Opinions? Evidence from Rural Mali." *World Development* 106: 299–323.

Bledsoe, Caroline H. 1980. *Women and Marriage in Kpelle Society*. Stanford: Stanford University Press.

———. 1990. "Transformations in Sub-Saharan African Marriage and Fertility." *Annals of the American Academy of Political and Social Science* 510: 115–125.

———. 1993. "The Politics of Polygyny in Mende Education and Child Fosterage Transactions." In *Sex and Gender Hierarchies*, edited by Barbara Diane Miller, 170–192. New York: Cambridge University Press.

Bohannan, Paul, and Philip Curtin. 1971. *Africa and Africans*. Garden City: Natural History Press.

Boileau, Catherine, Bilkis Vissandjee, Vinh-Kim Nguyen, Sélim Rashed, Mohamed Sylla, and Maria Victoria Zunzunegui. 2008. "Gender Dynamics and Sexual Norms among Youth in Mali in the Context of HIV/AIDS Prevention." *African Journal of Reproductive Health* 12 (3): 173–184.

Boltz, Marie, and Isabelle Chort. 2016. "The Risk of Polygamy and Wives' Saving Behavior." *The World Bank Economic Review* 33 (1): 209–230.

Bondaz, Julien. 2013. "Le thé des hommes: Sociabilités masculines et culture de la rue au Mali." *Cahiers d'Études Africaines* 53 (1–2): 209–210, 61–85.

Boserup, Ester. 1970. *Woman's Role in Economic Development.* London: Allen & Unwin.

Bourdarias, Françoise. 1999. "La ville mange la terre: Désordres fonciers aux confins de Bamako." *Journal des Anthropologues* 77–78: 141–160.

———. 2009. "Mobilités chinoises et dynamiques sociales locales au Mali." *Politique Africaine* 113: 28–54.

Bourdieu, Pierre. 1986. "The Forms of Capital." In *Handbook of Theory and Research for the Sociology of Education,* edited by John Richardson, 241–258. Westport, CT: Greenwood Press.

———. 2002. *Masculine Domination.* Translated by Richard Nice. Stanford: Stanford University Press.

Bove, Riley M., Emily Vala-Haynes, and Claudia Valeggia. 2012. "Women's Health in Urban Mali: Social Predictors and Health Itineraries." *Social Science & Medicine* 75 (8): 1392–1399.

Bowles, Nellie. 2018. "Jordan Peterson, Custodian of the Patriarchy." *New York Times,* May 18. www.nytimes.com/2018/05/18/style/jordan-peterson-12-rules-for-life.html.

Boyd, Lydia, and Emily Burrill, eds. 2020. *Legislating Gender and Sexuality in Africa: Human Rights, Society, and the State.* Madison: University of Wisconsin Press.

Boye, Abd-el Kader. 1987. *Synthèse des Études Nationales et Observations Complémentaires sur la Condition Juridique et Sociale de la Femme dans Quatre Pays du Sahel: Burkina Faso, Mali, Niger, Sénégal.* Bamako: Institut du Sahel.

Boyle, Helen. 2019. "Registered Medersas in Mali: Effectively Integrating Islamic and Western Educational Epistemologies in Practice." *Comparative Education Review* 63 (2): 145–165.

Brake, Elizabeth. 2012. *Minimizing Marriage: Marriage, Morality, and the Law.* New York: Oxford University Press.

Brand, Saskia. 2001. *Mediating Means and Fate: A Socio-Political Analysis of Fertility and Demographic Change in Bamako, Mali.* Boston: Brill.

Brett-Smith, Sarah C. 2014. *The Silence of the Women: Bamana Mud Cloths in Mali.* Milan: 5 Continents Editions.

Broqua, Christophe. 2009. "Sur Les Rétributions Des Pratiques Homosexuelles à Bamako." *Canadian Journal of African Studies / Revue Canadienne des Études Africaines* 43 (1): 60–82.

Broqua, Christophe, and Anne Doquet. 2013. "Les normes dominantes de la masculinité contre la domination masculine? Batailles conjugales au Mali." *Cahiers d'Études Africaines* 53 (1–2): 209–210, 293–321.

Brzezińska, Magdalena. 2021. "Transcontinental Polygyny, Migration, and Hegemonic Masculinity in Guinea-Bissau and the Gambia." *The Australian Journal of Anthropology* 32: 257–271.

Buggenhagen, Beth. 2012. *Muslim Families in Global Senegal: Money Takes Care of Shame.* Bloomington: Indiana University Press.

Burrill, Emily. 2015. *States of Marriage: Gender, Justice, and Rights in Colonial Mali.* Athens: Ohio University Press.

———. 2020. "Legislating Marriage in Postcolonial Mali: A History of the Present." In *Legislating Gender and Sexuality in Africa: Human Rights, Society, and the State,* edited by Lydia Boyd and Emily Burrill, 25–41. Madison: University of Wisconsin Press.

Buss, David M. 2016. *The Evolution of Desire: Strategies of Human Mating.* New York: Basic Books.

Calvès, Anne-Emmanuèle. 2016. "First Union Formation in Urban Burkina Faso: Competing Relationship Transitions to Marriage or Cohabitation." *Demographic Research* 34: 421–449.

Camara, Bakary. 2011. "Fondements juridiques du mariage dans le pays bamanan malinke: Du système coutumier au code malien du mariage et de la tutelle de 1962—l'évolution dans la continuité." *Université, Recherche et Développement* 21: 207–240.

Camara, Ibrahima. 2002. *Le Cadre Rituel de l'Education au Mali: L'exemple du Wassoulou.* Paris: L'Harmattan.

Camara, Sory. 1978. "Femmes africaines, polygamie et autorité masculine." *Ethnopsychologie* 33 (1): 43–53.

Carmichael, Sarah. 2011. "Marriage and Power: Age at First Marriage and Spousal Age Gap in Lesser Developed Countries." CGEH Working Paper Series no. 15. www.cgeh.nl /working-paper-series/.

Castilla, Carolina. 2018. "Political Role Models and Child Marriage in India." *Review of Development Economics* 22: 1409–1431. https://doi.org/10.1111/rode.12513.

Castle, Sarah. 2003. "Factors Influencing Young Malians' Reluctance to Use Hormonal Contraceptives." *Studies in Family Planning* 34 (3): 186–199.

Castro, Julie. 2012. "'Les filles sont trop matérialistes!' Tensions et soupçons dans les transactions sexuelles au Mali." In *Economies Morales Contemporaines*, edited by Didier Fassin and Jean-Sébastien Eideliman, 309–330. Paris: La Découverte.

———. 2014. "L'épaisseur des transactions: Regard croisé sur la sexualité prémaritale et la 'prostitution' au Mali." In *L'échange économico-sexuel*, edited by Christophe Broqua and Catherine Deschamps, 89–123. Paris: EHESS.

CEDAW Committee. 1994. "General Recommendation no. 21—Thirteenth Session, 1994: Equality in Marriage and Family Relations." www.ohchr.org/en/hrbodies/cedaw/pages /recommendations.aspx.

Chabal, Patrick, and Jean-Pascal Daloz. 1999. *Africa Works: Disorder as Political Instrument.* Bloomington: Indiana University Press.

Chambers, Clare. 2017. *Against Marriage: An Egalitarian Defense of the Marriage-Free State.* New York: Oxford University Press.

Chappatte, André. 2018. "Crowd, Sensationalism, and Power: The Yearly Ansar Dine 'Pilgrimage' of Maouloud in Bamako." *Journal of Religion in Africa* 48 (1–2): 3–34.

Charsley, Katharine, and Anika Liversage. 2013. "Transforming Polygamy: Migration, Transnationalism and Multiple Marriage among Muslim Minorities." *Global Networks* 13 (1): 60–78.

Chisholm, James S., and Victoria K. Burbank. 1991. "Monogamy and Polygyny in Southeast Arnhem Land: Male Coercion and Female Choice." *Ethology and Sociobiology* 12: 291–313.

Cislaghi, Ben. 2019. *Human Rights and Community-Led Development: Lessons from Tostan.* Edinburgh: Edinburgh University Press.

Clignet, Remi. 1970. *Many Wives, Many Powers: Authority and Power in Polygynous Families.* Evanston: Northwestern University Press.

———. 1987. "On dit que la polygamie est morte: Vive la polygamie!" In *Transformations of African Marriage*, edited by David Parkin and David Nyamwaya, 199–209. Manchester: Manchester University Press.

Cohen, Philip N. 2018a. *Enduring Bonds: Inequality, Marriage, Parenting, and Everything Else that Makes Families Great and Terrible.* Berkeley: University of California Press.

———. 2018b. *The Family: Diversity, Inequality, and Social Change*, 2nd edition. New York: W. W. Norton & Company.

Cole, Jennifer, and Lynn M. Thomas, eds. 2009. *Love in Africa.* Chicago: University of Chicago Press.

Conrad, David C. 1999. "Mooning Armies and Mothering Heroes: Female Power in Mande Epic Tradition." In *In Search of Sunjata: The Mande Oral Epic as History, Literature, and*

Performance, edited by Ralph A. Austen, 189–229. Bloomington: Indiana University Press.

Cook, Cynthia T. 2007. "Polygyny: Did the Africans Get It Right?" *Journal of Black Studies* 38 (2): 232–250.

Cook, Scott J., and Cameron G. Thies. 2019. "In Plain Sight? Reconsidering the Linkage between Brideprice and Violent Conflict." *Conflict Management and Peace Science* 38 (2): 129–146.

Cooper, Barbara M. 1997. *Marriage in Maradi: Gender and Culture in a Hausa Society in Niger, 1900–1989*. Portsmouth: Heinemann.

——. 2010. "Secular States, Muslim Law, and Islamic Religious Culture: Gender Implications of Legal Struggles in Hybrid Legal Systems in Contemporary West Africa." *Droit et Cultures* 59 (2010–1): 1–21.

——. 2019. *Countless Blessings: A History of Childbirth and Reproduction in the Sahel*. Bloomington: Indiana University Press.

Coulibaly, Abdourahmane. 2014. "'Ah bon! C'est ça donc ton secret!' Pratique contraceptive, émergence de nouveaux rapports au corps et à la sexualité au Mali." *Cahiers d'Études Africaines* 54 (3): 665–684.

Courbage, Youssef, and Emmanuel Todd. 2011. *Convergence of Civilizations: The Transformation of Muslim Societies Around the World*. New York: Columbia University Press.

Craven-Matthews, Catriona, and Pierre Englebert. 2018. "A Potemkin State in the Sahel? The Empirical and the Fictional in Malian State Reconstruction." *African Security* 11 (1): 1–31.

Cunningham, Jerimy J. 2014. "Pots and Political Economy: Enamel-Wealth, Gender, and Patriarchy in Mali." *Journal of the Royal Anthropological Institute* 15: 276–294.

Dalton, John T., and Tin Cheuk Leung. 2014. "Why Is Polygyny More Prevalent in Western Africa? An African Slave Trade Perspective." *Economic Development and Cultural Change* 62 (4): 599–632.

Daoulah, Amin, Amir Lotfi, Mushabab Al-Murayeh, et al. 2017. "Polygamy and Risk of Coronary Artery Disease in Men Undergoing Angiography: An Observational Study." *International Journal of Vascular Medicine*, Article ID 1925176, 6.

de Jorio, Rosa. 1997. "Female Elites, Women's Formal Associations, and Political Practices in Urban Mali (West Africa)." PhD dissertation, Department of Anthropology, University of Illinois Urbana-Champaign. http://hdl.handle.net/2142/8530.

——. 2002. "When Is 'Married' Married? Multiple Marriage Avenues in Urban Mali." *Mande Studies* 4: 31–44.

——. 2009. "Between Dialogue and Contestation: Gender, Islam, and the Challenges of a Malian Public Sphere." *Journal of the Royal Anthropological Institute* 15 (S1): 95–111.

——. 2020. "Of Rumors and Transfers: The Short Life of Western-Educated Women's Associations in French Sudan (1955–1960)." *Kritisk etnografi—Swedish Journal of Anthropology* 3 (1): 63–82.

de la Croix, David, and Fabio Mariani. 2015. "From Polygamy to Serial Monogamy: A Unified Theory of Marriage Institutions." *Review of Economic Studies* 82 (2): 565–607.

de Suremain, Charles-Edouard, and Elodie Razy. 2011. "'Tu manges aujourd'hui, tu ne manges pas le lendemain, ça, c'est la pauvreté.' L'incertitude alimentaire à Bamako." In *La Lutte Contre l'Insécurité Alimentaire au Mali: Réalités et Faux-Semblants*, edited by Claude Arditi, Pierre Janin, and Alain Marie, 249–278. Paris: Karthala.

Decheix, Pierre. 1967. "L'engagement de monogamie dans le code malien du mariage." *Revue juridique et politique : Indépendance et coopération* 21 (1): 118–129.

Decottignies, Roger. 1965. "Requiem pour la Famille Africaine." *Annales Africaines* 1965: 251–286.

Den Otter, Ronald C. 2015. *In Defense of Plural Marriage*. New York: Cambridge University Press.

Dery, Isaac, and Sylvia Bawa. 2019. "Agency, Social Status, and Performing Marriage in Postcolonial Societies." *Journal of Asian and African Studies* 54 (7): 980–994.

Deubel, Tara F., and Micah Boyer. 2020. "Building *Benkadi*: The Role of Trust in Malian Women's Community Savings Groups." *Mande Studies* 22: 23–40.

DHS (Demographic and Health Survey). 1987. Enquête Démographique et de Santé au Mali 1987. https://dhsprogram.com/pubs/pdf/FR23/FR23.pdf.

———. 2013. Mali 2012–2013 DHS Final Report. https://dhsprogram.com/pubs/pdf/FR286/FR286.pdf.

———. 2019. Mali 2018 DHS Final Report. https://dhsprogram.com/pubs/pdf/FR358/FR358.pdf.

Dial, Fatou Binetou. 2008. *Mariage et divorce à Dakar: Itinéraires féminins*. Paris: Karthala.

———. 2014. "Divorce, remariage et polygamie à Dakar." In *Le Mariage en Afrique: Pluralité des formes et des modèles*, edited by Richard Marcoux and Philippe Antoine, 250–265. Québec: Presses de l'Université de Québec.

Diallo, Assitan. 2004. "Paradoxes of Female Sexuality in Mali: On the Practices of *Magnonmaka* and *Bolokoli-kela*." In *Re-Thinking Sexualities in Africa*, edited by Signe Arnfred, 173–189. Uppsala: Nordiska Afrikainstitutet.

———. 2009. "Women in the Back Seat in Malian Citizenship." In *Body Politics and Women Citizens: African Experiences*, edited by Ann Schlyter, 115–126. Stockholm: SIDA.

Diallo, Mahmoud, and Oumar S. Diarra. 2009. "La Polygamie au Mali." *Études Maliennes* 71: 57–68.

Diamouténé, Aminata Coulibaly. 2015. "La Polygamie au Mali à Partir des Données du Recensement de 2009." Research Report, Observatoire Démographique et Statistique de l'Espace Francophone, Université Laval. www.odsef.fss.ulaval.ca/sites/odsef.fss.ulaval.ca/files/odsef_rr_mali_polygamie.pdf.

Diarra, Aïssa. 2018. "Mariages d'enfants au Mali et au Niger, comment les comprendre?" *The Conversation*, November 27, https://theconversation.com/mariages-denfants-au-mali-et-au-niger-comment-les-comprendre-105877.

Dierickx, Susan, Gily Coene, Bintou Jarju, and Chia Longman. 2019. "Women with Infertility Complying with and Resisting Polygyny: An Explorative and Qualitative Study in Urban Gambia." *Reproductive Health* 16: 103.

Dissa, Yaya. 2016. "Polygamy in Mali: Social and Economic Implications on Families." *International Journal of African and Asian Studies* 27: 99–108.

Dixon-Spear, Patricia. 2009. *We Want for Our Sisters What We Want for Ourselves: African-Americans Who Practice Polygyny by Consent*. Baltimore: Black Classic Press.

Djiré, Kadidjatou. 2012. "Histoire de femmes: La magie noire ou l'arme de guerre des femmes." *L'Indicateur du Renouveau*, July 11. http://news.abamako.com/h/3330.html.

Donaldson, Coleman. 2019. "Linguistic and Civil Refinement in the N'ko Movement of Manding-Speaking West Africa." *Signs and Society* 7 (2): 156–185.

Doquet, Anne. 2014. "Les stratégies conjugales des jeunes Maliennes: De nouvelles formes d'autonomie?" In *Le Mali Contemporain*, edited by Joseph Brunet-Jailly, Jacques Charmes, and Doulaye Konaté, 387–415. Bamako: Editions Tombouctou.

Dorjahn, Vernon R. 1959. "The Factor of Polygyny in African Demography." In *Continuity and Change in African Societies*, edited by William Bascom and Melville Herskovits, 87–112. Chicago: University of Chicago Press.

Dougnon, Isaie. 2020. "'Être chez-soi' à Bamako ou la vie après la mort." *Cahiers d'Études Africaines* 60 (1) : 237, 115–140.

Doumbia, Mamadou Lamine. 2009. "Roue libre: Le Code du diable." *L'Indépendant*, August 12. http://malijet.com/a_la_une_du_mali/16613-le_code_du_diable.html.

Douyon, Denis. 2006. "Le Discours Diplomatique Et Démagogique Du Cousin Plaisant Au Mali [The Joking Cousin's Diplomatic and Demagogic Discourse in Mali]." *Cahiers d'Études Africaines* 46 (184): 883–906.

Durán, Lucy. 2017. "*An Jera Cεla* [We Share a Husband]: Song as Social Comment on Polygamy in Southern Mali." *Mande Studies* 17: 169–202.

The Economist. 2017. "The Perils of Polygamy: The Link between Polygamy and War." December 19. www.economist.com/news/christmas-specials/21732695-plural-marriage-bred -inequality-begets-violence-link-between-polygamy-and-war.

Edwards, Ian. 2012. "The Social Life of Wild-Things: Negotiated Wildlife in Mali, West Africa." PhD dissertation, Department of Anthropology, University of Oregon.

Ember, Melvin. 1974. "Warfare, Sex Ratio, and Polygyny." *Ethnology* 13 (2): 197–206.

Ember, Melvin, Carol R. Ember, and Bobbi S. Low. 2007. "Comparing Explanations of Polygyny." *Cross-Cultural Research* 41 (4): 428–440.

Engebretsen, Sarah, Mouhamadou Gueye, Andrea J. Melnikas, Sekou Fofana, Bourama Fane, and Sajeda Amin. 2020. "Adolescent Girls' Migration and Its Impact on Early Marriage: Qualitative Findings in Mali." *PLoSONE* 15 (3): e0230370.

L'Essor. 2009. "Intervention du chef de l'Etat sur le Code des personnes et de la famille: Le texte est renvoyé à une deuxième lecture."August 27. https://malijet.com/a_la_une_du _mali/17045-intervantion_du_chef_de_l_etat_sur_la_code.html.

Ezeh, Alex Chika. 1997. "Polygyny and Reproductive Behavior in Sub-Saharan Africa: A Contextual Analysis." *Demography* 34 (3): 355–368.

Fabian, Johannes. 2014 [1983]. *Time and the Other: How Anthropology Makes Its Object*. New York: Columbia University Press.

Fainzang, Sylvie, and Odile Journet. 1988. *La Femme de mon mari: Anthropologie du mariage polygamique en Afrique et en France*. Paris: L'Harmattan.

Falen, Douglas J. 2011. *Power and Paradox: Authority, Insecurity, and Creativity in Fon Gender Relations*. Trenton: Africa World Press.

Famanta, Ismaël. 2012. "Le code des personnes et de la famille au Mali: Un conflit de normes." In *Fécondité et contraception en Afrique de l'Ouest: Une contribution anthropologique*, edited by Yannick Jaffré, 211–224. Claunay: Éditions Faustroll.

Fenske, James. 2015. "African Polygamy: Past and Present." *Journal of Development Economics* 117 (C): 58–73.

Ferguson, James. 1999. *Expectations of Modernity: Myth and Meanings of Urban Life on the Zambian Copperbelt*. Berkeley: University of California Press.

Fincher, Leta Hong. 2014. *Leftover Women: The Resurgence of Gender Inequality in China*. London: Zed Books.

Fortes, Meyer. 1949. *The Web of Kinship among the Tallensi*. New York: Oxford University Press.

Fortier, Corinne. 2011. "Women and Men Put Islamic Law to Their Own Use: Monogamy versus Secret Marriage in Mauritania." In *Gender and Islam in Africa: Rights, Sexuality, and Law*, edited by Margot Badran, 213–231. Stanford, CA: Stanford University Press.

Foster, Andrew. 2008. "Marriage Markets." In *The New Palgrave Dictionary of Economics*, edited by Matias Vernengo, Esteban Perez Caldentey, and Barkley J. Rosser Jr., 8340–8343. London: Palgrave Macmillan.

Friedrich Ebert Foundation. 2020. "Mali Mètre 11: Enquête d'opinion politique: Qu'en pensent les Malien(ne)s?" www.fes-mali.org/images/Rapport_Final_Malimetre_N11_Site.pdf.

Fuentes, Agustín. 2012. *Race, Monogamy, and Other Lies They Told You: Busting Myths about Human Nature*. Berkeley: University of California Press.

Gaibazzi, Paolo. 2019. "Moving-with-Others: Restoring Viable Relations in Emigrant Gambia." *Migration & Society* 2: 26–39.

Gilbert, Véronique. 2018. "'A Slut, a Saint, and Everything in Between': Senegalese Women's *Mokk Pooj*, Interpretive Labor, and Agency." *Signs: Journal of Women in Culture and Society* 44 (2): 379–401.

Gleditsch, Kristian Skrede, Julian Wucherpfennig, Simon Hug, and Karina Garnes Reigstad. 2011. "Polygyny or Misogyny? Reexamining the 'First Law of Intergroup Conflict.'" *Journal of Politics* 73 (1): 265–270.

Gluckman, Max. 1950. "Kinship and Marriage among the Lozi of Northern Rhodesia and the Zulu of Natal." In *African Systems of Kinship and Marriage*, edited by A. R. Radcliffe-Brown and Daryll Forde, 166–206. New York: Columbia University Press.

Gnimadi, Destin. 2009. "Quand le portable privatise les relations." *Le Républicain*, March 16. http://malijet.com/les_faits_divers_au_mali/11497-vie_de_couple_quand_le_portable_privatise.html.

Gning, Sadio Ba. 2011. "La polygamie: Ménage unique, pluriel ou complexe." 6th African Population Conference, Ouagadougou, December 5-9. www.uaps2011.princeton.edu/papers/110647.

Gning, Sadio Ba, and Philippe Antoine. 2015. "Polygamie et personnes âgées au Sénégal." *Mondes en développement* 2015/3 (171): 31–50.

Golaszewski, Devon. 2020. "Last Acts of Mothering: Nuptial Counseling in Late Colonial Soudan (Mali)." *Past and Present* 246, Supplement 15: 239–262.

Goldberg, Jonah. 2018. *Suicide of the West: How the Rebirth of Tribalism, Populism, Nationalism, and Identity Politics is Destroying American Democracy*. New York: Crown Publishing Group.

Gomez, Michael A. 2018. *African Dominion: A New History of Empire in Early and Medieval West Africa*. Princeton: Princeton University Press.

Goodale, Mark. 2022. *Reinventing Human Rights*. Stanford: Stanford University Press.

Goode, William J. 1963. *World Revolution and Family Patterns*. New York: Free Press.

Goody, Jack. 1973. "Polygyny, Economy and the Role of Women." In *The Character of Kinship*, edited by Jack Goody, 175–190. New York: Cambridge University Press.

———. 1976. *Production and Reproduction: A Comparative Study of the Domestic Domain*. New York: Cambridge University Press.

Gould, Eric D., Omer Moav, and Avi Simhon. 2008. "The Mystery of Monogamy." *American Economic Review* 98 (1): 333–357.

Grange Omokaro, Françoise. 2009. "Féminités et masculinités bamakoises en temps de globalisation." *Autrepart* 49: 189–204.

Grossbard, Shoshana Amyra. 1980. "The Economics of Polygamy." *Research in Population Economics* 2: 321–350.

———. 2016. "An Economist's Perspective on Polygyny." In *The Polygamy Question*, edited by Janet Bennion and Lisa Fishbayn Joffe, 103–114. Boulder: University of Colorado Press.

Grillo, Laura S. 2018. *An Intimate Rebuke: Female Genital Power in Ritual and Politics in West Africa*. Durham: Duke University Press.

Grosz-Ngaté, Maria. 1988. "Monetization of Bridewealth and the Abandonment of 'Kin Roads' to Marriage in Sana, Mali." *American Ethnologist* 15 (3): 501–514.

———. 1989. "Hidden Meanings: Explorations into a Bamanan Construction of Gender." *Ethnology* 28 (2): 167–183.

Guengant, Jean-Pierre. 2017. "Africa's Population: History, Current Status, and Projections." In *Africa's Population: In Search of a Demographic Dividend*, edited by H. Groth and J. F. May, 11–31. Cham: Springer.

Gueye, Mouhamadou, Sarah Castle, and Mamadou Kani Konaté. 2001. "Timing of First Intercourse among Malian Adolescents: Implications for Contraceptive Use." *International Family Planning Perspectives* 27 (2): 56–62.

Guttentag, Marcia, and Paul Secord. 1983. *Too Many Women?* London: Sage.

Hafstein, Valdimar. 2000. "The Elves' Point of View: Cultural Identity in Contemporary Icelandic Elf-Tradition." *Fabula* 41 (1–2): 87–104.

Hagberg, Sten, and Bintou Koné. 2020. "Diaspora-Driven Development and Dispute: Home-Area Associations and Municipal Politics in Mali." *Kritisk Etnografi* 2 (1–2): 81–93.

Haider, Nadya. 2000. "Islamic Legal Reform: The Case of Pakistan and Family Law." *Yale Journal of Law and Feminism* 12 (2): 287–341.

Hannaford, Dinah. 2015. "Technologies of the Spouse: Intimate Surveillance in Senegalese Transnational Marriages." *Global Networks* 15 (1): 43–59.

———. 2017. *Marriage without Borders: Transnational Spouses in Neoliberal Senegal.* Philadelphia: University of Pennsylvania Press.

Hannaford, Dinah, and Ellen E. Foley. 2015. "Negotiating Love and Marriage in Contemporary Senegal: A Good Man is Hard to Find." *African Studies Review* 58 (2): 205–225.

Harrington, Brooke. 2016. *Capital without Borders: Wealth Managers and the One Percent.* New York: Cambridge: Harvard University Press.

Hasan, Abla. 2019. *Decoding the Egalitarianism of the Qur'an: Retrieving Lost Voices on Gender.* Lanham: Lexington Books.

Henrich, Joseph, Robert Boyd, and Peter J. Richerson. 2012. "The Puzzle of Monogamous Marriage." *Philosophical Transactions of the Royal Society* 367: 657–669.

Hertrich, Véronique. 2006. "La polygamie: Persistance ou recomposition? Le cas d'une population rurale du Mali." *Cahiers Québécois de démographie* 35 (2): 39–70.

———. 2007. "Le mariage, quelle affaire!" *Sociologie et sociétés* 39 (2): 119–150.

———. 2013. "Freer Unions, More Complex Itineraries? Male Premarital Life in Rural Mali." *Journal of Comparative Family Studies* 44 (3): 361–385.

———. 2017. "Trends in Age at Marriage and the Onset of Fertility Transition in Sub-Saharan Africa." *Population and Development Review* 43 (S1): 112–137.

Hertrich, Véronique, and Marie Lesclingand. 2012. "Adolescent Migration and the 1990s Nuptiality Transition in Mali." *Population Studies* 66 (2): 147–166.

———. 2013. "Adolescent Migration in Rural Africa as a Challenge to Gender and Intergenerational Relationships: Evidence from Mali." *Annals*, AAPSS 648: 175–188.

Hess, Rosanna F., Ratchneewan Ross, and John L. Gilliland Jr. 2018. "Infertility, Psychological Distress, and Coping Strategies among Women in Mali, West Africa: A Mixed-Methods Study." *African Journal of Reproductive Health* 22 (1): 60–72.

Heywood, Emma, and Beatrice Ivey. 2021. "Radio as an Empowering Environment: How Does Radio Broadcasting in Mali Represent Women's 'Web of Relations'?" *Feminist Media Studies*, https://doi.org/10.1080/14680777.2021.1877768.

Hidrobo, Melissa, Jessica B. Hoel, and Katie Wilson. 2020. "Efficiency and Status in Polygynous Pastoralist Households." *Journal of Development Studies* 57 (2): 326–342.

HiiL (Hague Institute for Innovation of Law). 2019. "Justice Needs and Satisfaction in Mali, 2018: Legal Problems in Daily Life." www.hiil.org/wp-content/uploads/2018/07/HiiL-Mali-JNS-report-EN-web.pdf.

Hillman, Eugene. 1970. "Polygyny Reconsidered." *Practical Anthropology* 17 (2): 60–74.

Hoffman, Barbara. 2002. "Gender Ideology and Practice in Mande Societies and in Mande Studies." *Mande Studies* 4: 1–20.

———. 2012. "Out on Malian Television: Media and Culture Change in an Emerging Cosmopolitan Metropolitan Center." *Mande Studies* 14: 127–148.

Hoornweg, Daniel, and Kevin Pope. 2017. "Population Predictions for the World's Largest Cities in the 21st Century." *Environment & Urbanization* 29 (1): 195–216.

Hudson, Valerie M. 2018. "The Deep Structure of Collective Security: Thoughts on McDermott, Smuts, and Sanday." In Rose McDermott, *The Evils of Polygyny: Evidence of Its Harm to Women, Men, and Society*, edited by Kristen Renwick Monroe, 147–163. Ithaca: Cornell University Press.

Hudson, Valerie M., and Hilary Matfess. 2017. "In Plain Sight: The Neglected Linkage between Brideprice and Violent Conflict." *International Security* 42 (1): 7–40.

Ickowitz, Amy, and Lisa Mohanty. 2015. "Why Would She? Polygyny and Women's Welfare in Ghana." *Feminist Economics* 21(2): 77–104.

INSTAT (Institut National de la Statistique). 2017. "Femmes et Hommes au Mali." http://instat-mali.org/contenu/eq/livret-instat-homme-femme_eq.pdf.

———. 2018. "Enquête Modulaire et Permanente auprès des Ménages (EMOP). Rapport d'analyse: Passages 1–4." http://instat-mali.org/contenu/eq/rana18pas1_eq.pdf.

———. 2019. "Enquête Modulaire et Permanente auprès des Ménages (EMOP). Rapport d'analyse: Premier passage." http://instat-mali.org/contenu/eq/rana19pas1_eq.pdf.

Inter de Bamako. 2009. "ATT-Bougou: Des quartiers habités par des femmes?" July 20. http://malijet.com/la_societe_malienne_aujourdhui/15878-att-bougou_des_quartiers_habit_s_par_des_femmes.html.

IRIN News. 2009. "Threats of Violence Greet New Family Code." August 11. www.thenewhumanitarian.org/report/85676/mali-threats-violence-greet-new-family-code.

Jankowiak, William. 2023. *Illicit Monogamy: How Romantic Love Undermines Polygamy inside a Mormon Fundamentalist Community*. New York: Columbia University Press.

Jankowiak, William, and Edward F. Fischer. 1992. "A Cross-Cultural Perspective on Romantic Love." *Ethnology* 31 (2): 149–155.

Jankowiak, William, Monika Sudakov, and Benjamin C. Wilreker. 2005. "Co-Wife Conflict and Co-Operation." *Ethnology* 44 (1): 81–98.

Janson, Marloes. 2016. "Male Wives and Female Husbands: Reconfiguring Gender in the *Tablighi Jama'at* in The Gambia." *Journal of Religion in Africa* 46: 187–218.

Jennaway, Megan. 2013. "Bitter Honey: Female Agency and the Polygynous Household, North Bali." In *Women and Households in Indonesia: Cultural Notions and Social Practices*, edited by Juliette Konig, Marleen Nolten, Janet Rodenberg, and Ratna Saptari, 142–162. New York: Routledge.

Johnson, Cathryn Evangeline. 2019. "Why Rural Malian Women Want to be Candidates for Local Office: Changes in Social and Political Life and the Arrival of a Gender Quota." *Journal of Modern African Studies* 57 (3): 1–21.

Jonas, Obonye. 2012. "The Practice of Polygamy under the Scheme of the Protocol to the African Charter on Human and Peoples' Rights on the Rights of Women in Africa: A Critical Appraisal." *Journal of African Studies and Development* 4 (5): 142–149.

Joy, Charlotte. 2011. "Negotiating Material Identities: Young Men and Modernity in Djenné." *Journal of Material Culture* 16 (4): 389–400.

Kai, Nubia. 2014. *Kuma Malinke Historiography: Sundiata Keita to Almamy Samori Touré*. Lanham: Lexington Books.

Kanazawa, Satoshi. 1999. "Evolutionary Psychological Foundations of Civil Wars." *Journal of Politics* 71 (1): 25–34.

Kanazawa, Satoshi, and Mary C. Still. 1999. "Why Monogamy?" *Social Forces* 78 (1): 25–50.

Kandiyoti, Deniz. 1988. "Bargaining with Patriarchy." *Gender & Society* 2 (3): 274–290.

Kang, Alice. 2015. *Bargaining for Women's Rights: Activism in an Aspiring Muslim Democracy.* Minneapolis: University of Minnesota Press.

Kassogué, Yada. 2014. "La restriction de la migration féminine au pays dogon et ses enjeux sociaux." In *Le Mali Contemporain*, edited by Joseph Brunet-Jailly, Jacques Charmes, and Doulaye Konaté, 417–440. Bamako: Editions Tombouctou.

Kaufmann, Georgia, Ron Lesthaeghe, and Dominique Meekers. 1988. "Les caractéristiques et tendances du mariage." In *Population et Sociétés en Afrique au Sud du Sahara*, edited by Dominique Tabutin, 217–247. Paris: L'Harmattan.

Keller, Candace M. 2021. *Imaging Culture: Photography in Mali, West Africa.* Bloomington: Indiana University Press.

Kilbride, Philip L. 1994. *Plural Marriage for our Times: A Reinvented Option?* Westport: Bergin & Garvey.

Kilbride, Philip L., and Janet C. Kilbride. 1990. *Changing Family Life in East Africa: Women and Children at Risk.* University Park: Pennsylvania State University Press.

Koktvedgaard Zeitzen, Miriam. 2008. *Polygamy: A Cross-Cultural Analysis.* New York: Berg.

———. 2018. *Elite Malay Polygamy: Wives, Wealth, and Woes in Malaysia.* New York: Berghahn.

Kombo, Brenda K. 2021. "Napoleonic Legacies, Postcolonial State Legitimation, and the Perpetual Myth of Non-Intervention: Family Code Reform and Gender Equality in Mali." *Social & Legal Studies* 30 (5): 704–725.

Konaté, Mamadou Ismaïla. 2018. *Justice en Afrique—Ce grand corps malade: Le cas du Mali (Un ancien ministre témoigne).* Bamako: Éditions La Sahélienne.

Konaté, Moussa. 2010. *L'Afrique Noir Est-Elle Maudite?* Paris: Fayard.

Koné, Kassim. 2002. "When Male becomes Female and Female becomes Male in Mandé." *Mande Studies* 4: 21–29.

Koné, Ousmane. 2015. "La controverse autour du code des personnes et de la famille au Mali: enjeux et stratégies des acteurs." PhD dissertation, Department of Sociology, Université de Montréal. https://papyrus.bib.umontreal.ca/xmlui/handle/1866/13576.

———. 2018. "L'influence des organisations islamiques dans le processus de l'élaboration du Code des personnes et de la famille au Mali: Autopsie d'une victoire." In *Nouvelles Dynamiques Familiales en Afrique*, edited by Anne-Emmanuèle Calvès, Fatou Binetou Dial, and Richard Marcoux, 329–347. Québec: Presses de l'Université de Québec.

Kringelbach, Hélène Neveu. 2016a. "'Marrying Out' for Love: Women's Narratives of Polygyny and Alternative Marriage Choices in Contemporary Senegal." *African Studies Review* 59 (1): 155–174.

———. 2016b. "The Paradox of Parallel Lives: Immigration Policy and Transnational Polygyny between Senegal and France." In *Affective Circuits: African Migrations to Europe and the Pursuit of Social Regeneration*, edited by Jennifer Cole and Christian Groes, 146–168. Chicago: University of Chicago Press.

Krulfeld, Ruth. 1986. "Sasak Attitudes towards Polygyny and the Changing Position of Women in Sasak Peasant Villages." In *Visibility and Power: Essays on Women in Society and Development*, edited by Leela Dube, Eleanor Leacock, and Shirley Ardener, 194–208. New York: Oxford University Press.

Kulick, Don. 2019. *A Death in the Rainforest: How a Language and a Way of Life Came to an End in Papua New Guinea.* Chapel Hill: Algonquin Books.

Kütük-Kuriş, Merve. 2019. "Muslim Feminism: Contemporary Debates." In *Handbook of Contemporary Islam and Muslim Lives*, edited by M. Woodward and R. Lukens-Bull. Cham: Springer Nature.

Lambert, Blake. 2006. "In West Africa, Chinese Motorcycles Find a Market." October 4. www
.worldpoliticsreview.com/articles/232/in-west-africa-chinese-motorcycles-find-a
-market.

Lardoux, Solène. 2004. "Marital Changes and Fertility Differences among Women and Men
in Urban and Rural Mali." *African Population Studies* 19 (2): 89–123.

Lasswell, Harold D. 1950. *Politics: Who Gets What, When, How.* New York: McGraw-Hill.

Launay, Robert. 1990. "Pedigrees and Paradigms: Scholarly Credentials among the Dyula of
the Northern Ivory Coast." In *Muslim Travelers: Pilgrimage, Migration, and the Religious
Imagination*, edited by Dale F. Eickelman and James Piscatori, 175–199. Berkeley: University of California Press.

Lawson, David W., Susan James, Esther Ngadaya, Bernard Ngowi, Sayoki G. M. Mfinanga,
and Monique Borderhoff Mulder. 2015. "No Evidence that Polygynous Marriage is a
Harmful Cultural Practice in Northern Tanzania." *PNAS* 112 (45): 13827–13832.

Lawson, David W., and Mhairi A. Gibson. 2018. "Polygynous Marriage and Child Health in
Sub-Saharan Africa: What is the Evidence for Harm?" *Demographic Research* 39 (6):
177–208.

Leach, Edmund. 1991. "The Social Anthropology of Mating and Marriage." In *Mating and
Marriage*, edited by Vernon Reynolds and John Kellett, 91–110. New York: Oxford University Press.

LeBlanc, Marie Nathalie. 2007. "*Imaniya* and Young Muslim Women in Côte d'Ivoire."
Anthropologica 49: 35–50.

Le Cour Grandmaison, Colette. 1971. "Stratégies matrimoniales des femmes dakaroises."
Cahiers ORSTOM 8 (2): 201–220.

Lengyel, Emil. 1960. "About: Polygamy." *New York Times*, April 24, p. SM 114, 116.

Le Pays. 2021. "Bamako: Une femme tue sa coépouse et son garçon à Kanadjiguila." March 11.
https://malijet.co/societe/faits-divers/bamako-une-femme-tue-sa-coepouse-et-son
-garcon-a-kanadjiguila.

Lesclingand, Marie, and Véronique Hertrich. 2017. "When Girls Take the Lead: Adolescent
Girls' Migration in Mali." *Population* 72 (1): 63–92.

Lesthaeghe, Ron J. 2010. "The Unfolding Story of the Second Demographic Transition." *Population & Development Review* 36 (2): 211–251.

Lesthaeghe, Ron J., Georgia L. Kaufmann, and Dominique Meekers. 1989. "The Nuptiality
Regimes in Sub-Saharan Africa." In *Reproduction and Social Organization in Sub-Saharan
Africa*, edited by Ron J. Lesthaeghe, 238–337. Berkeley: University of California Press.

Liberté. 2010. "22 Août 2010: Un coup d'Etat manqué contre ATT." September 29. www
.maliweb.net/societe/22-aout-2010-un-coup-d%E2%80%99etat-manque-contre-att
-2107.html.

Lindemann, Danielle. 2019. *Commuter Couples: New Families in a Changing World.* Ithaca: Cornell University Press.

Linton, Ralph. 1936. *The Study of Man: An Introduction.* New York: D. Appleton-Century Co.,
Inc.

Liogier, Raphaël. 2020. *Heart of Maleness: An Exploration.* New York: Other Press.

Locoh, Thérèse. 1988. "Structures familiales et changements sociaux." In *Population et Sociétés
en Afrique au Sud du Sahara*, edited by Dominique Tabutin, 441–478. Paris: L'Harmattan.

Luneau, Réné. 2010. *Chants de femmes au Mali.* Paris: Karthala.

Lydon, Ghislaine. 2018. "Inventions and Reinventions of Sharia in African History and the
Recent Experiences of Nigeria, Somalia and Mali." *Ufuhamu* 40 (1): 67–107.

Macedo, Stephen. 2015. *Just Married: Same-Sex Couples, Monogamy, and the Future of Marriage.*
Princeton University Press.

Madhavan, Sangeetha. 2002. "Best of Friends and Worst of Enemies: Competition and Collaboration in Polygyny." *Ethnology* 41 (1): 69–84.

Majeed, Debra Mubashshir. 2015. *Polygyny: What It Means When African American Muslim Women Share Their Husbands.* Gainesville: University Press of Florida.

Mann, Gregory. 2015. *From Empires to NGOs in the West African Sahel: The Road to Nongovernmentality.* New York: Cambridge University Press.

Marcoux, Richard. 1997. "Nuptialité et maintien de la polygamie en milieu urbain au Mali." *Cahiers Québécois de Démographie* 26 (2): 191–214.

Marcoux, Richard, and Victor Piché. 1998. "Crise, Pauvreté et Nuptialité à Bamako (Mali)." In *Crise, pauvreté et changements démographiques dans les pays du sud*, edited by Francis Gendreau, 219–235. Paris: Éditions ESTEM.

Marcoux, Richard, M. Gueye, and M. K. Konaté. 1995. "La nuptialité: Entrée en union et types de célébration à Bamako." In *L'insertion urbaine à Bamako*, edited by Dieudonné Ouédraogo and Victor Piché, 117–144. Paris: Karthala.

Marie, Alain. 2011. "'Il n'y a rien. Nous avons honte. Nous ne mangeons rien.' Anthropologie de la pauvreté à Bamako." In *La Lutte Contre l'Insécurité Alimentaire au Mali: Réalités et Faux-Semblants*, edited by Claude Arditi, Pierre Janin, and Alain Marie, 279–373. Paris: Karthala.

Mashhour, Amira. 2005. "Islamic Law and Gender Equity—Could There be a Common Ground? A Study of Divorce and Polygamy in Sharia Law and Contemporary Legislation in Tunisia and Egypt." *Human Rights Quarterly* 27 (2): 562–596.

Masquelier, Adeline. 2005. "The Scorpion's Sting: Marriage and the Struggle for Social Maturity in Niger." *Journal of the Royal Anthropological Institute* 11: 59–83.

McDermott, Rose. 2018. "The Meaning and Meanness of Polygyny." In Rose McDermott, *The Evils of Polygyny: Evidence of Its Harm to Women, Men, and Society*, edited by Kristen Renwick Monroe, 8–32. Ithaca: Cornell University Press.

McDermott, Rose, Michael Dickerson, Steve Fish, Danielle Lussier, and Jonathan Cowden. 2018. "Attitudes toward Polygyny: Experimental Evidence from Six Countries." In Rose McDermott, *The Evils of Polygyny: Evidence of Its Harm to Women, Men, and Society* edited by Kristen Renwick Monroe, 97–122. Ithaca: Cornell University Press.

McDermott, Rose, and Jonathan Cowden. 2016. "The Effect of Polygyny on Women, Children, and the State." In *The Polygamy Question*, edited by Janet Bennion and Lisa Fishbayn Joffe, 115–154. Boulder: University of Colorado Press.

McDermott, Rose, and Jonathan Cowden. 2018. "Polygyny and Violence against Women." In Rose McDermott, *The Evils of Polygyny: Evidence of Its Harm to Women, Men, and Society*, edited by Kristen Renwick Monroe, 52–96. Ithaca: Cornell University Press.

Meekers, Dominique, and Nadra Franklin. 1995. "Women's Perceptions of Polygyny among the Kaguru of Tanzania." *Ethnology* 3 (4): 315–329.

Meekers, Dominique, and Anastasia J. Gage. 2017. "Marriage Patterns and the Demographic Dividend." In *Africa's Population: In Search of a Demographic Dividend*, edited by H. Groth and J. F. May, 251–265. New York: Springer.

Meillassoux, Claude. 1981. *Maidens, Meal, and Money: Capitalism and the Domestic Community.* New York: Cambridge University Press.

Mernissi, Fatima. 1987. *Beyond the Veil: Male–Female Dynamics in Modern Muslim Society.* Bloomington: Indiana University Press.

Mesple-Somps, Sandrine, Harris Selod, Gilles Spielvogel, and Brian Blankespoor. 2014. "Urbanisation et croissance dans les villes du Mali." In *Le Mali Contemporain*, edited by Joseph Brunet-Jailly, Jacques Charmes, and Doulaye Konaté, 545–580. Bamako: Editions Tombouctou.

Mignot, Jean-François. 2010. "L'écart d'âge entre conjoints." *Revue Française de Sociologie* 51(2): 281–320.

Miseli. 1998. *Citadines: Vies et regards de femmes de Bamako.* Bamako: Miseli.

Muhd Razif, Nurul Huda. 2021. "*Nikah* Express: Malay Polygyny and Marriage-Making at the Malaysian–Thai Border." *Asian Studies Review*, https://doi.org/10.1080/10357823.2020.1870931.

Mohlabane, Neo, Ntombizonke Gumede, and Zitha Mokomane. 2019. "Attitudes towards Marriage in Postapartheid South Africa." In *South African Social Attitudes: Family Matters: Family Cohesion, Values and Strengthening to Promote Wellbeing,* edited by Zitha Mokomane, Jare Struwig, Benjamin Roberts, and Steven Gordon, 156–181. Cape Town: HSRC Press.

Mubangizi, John C. 2016. "An African Perspective on Some Gender-Related Cultural Practices that Violate Human Rights and Perpetuate Poverty." *Journal of Social Science* 47 (1): 68–78.

Mutaqin, Zezen Zaenal. 2018. "Culture, Islamic Feminism, and the Quest for Legal Reform in Indonesia." *Asian Journal of Women's Studies* 24 (4): 423–445.

Mwambene, Lea M. 2017. "What Is the Future of Polygyny (Polygamy) in Africa?" *PER / PELJ* 2017 (20): 1–33.

Neelakantan, Urvi, and Michèle Tertilt. 2008. "A Note on Marriage Market Clearing." *Economics Letters* 101: 103–105.

Neimark, Benjamin, Camilla Toulmin, and Simon Batterbury. 2018. "Peri-Urban Land Grabbing? Dilemmas of Formalising Tenure and Land Acquisitions around the Cities of Bamako and Ségou, Mali." *Journal of Land Use Science* 13 (3): 319–324.

Neubauer, Inès. 2016. "'I Took My Life in My Own Hands': The Clandestine Business of Prostitution in Bamako." In *Cultural Entrepreneurship in Africa,* edited by Ute Röschenthaler and Dorothea Schulz, 161–180. New York: Routledge.

Ngom, Fallou. 2016. *Muslims beyond the Arab World: The Odyssey of Ajami and the Muridiyya.* New York: Oxford University Press.

Nnaemeka, Obioma. 1997. "Urban Spaces, Women's Places: Polygamy as Sign in Mariama Bâ's Novels." In *The Politics of (M)Othering: Womanhood, Identity, and Resistance in African Literature,* edited by Obioma Nnaemeka, 163–192. New York: Routledge.

———. 2004. "Nego-Feminism: Theorizing, Practicing, and Pruning Africa's Way." *Signs* 29 (2): 357–385.

Nurmila, Nina. 2009. *Women, Islam and Everyday Life: Renegotiating Polygamy in Indonesia.* New York: Routledge.

Nwoye, Augustine. 2007. "The Practice of Interventive Polygamy in Two Regions of Africa: Background, Theory, and Techniques." *Dialectical Anthropology* 31: 383–421.

Olaore, Augusta, and Prince Agwu. 2020. "Women in African Marriages: Voice, Visibility, and Value." In *The Palgrave Handbook of African Women's Studies,* edited by Olajumoke Yacob-Haliso and Toyin Falola, 1–16. Cham: Springer International.

Orubuloye, I. O., John C. Caldwell, and Pat Caldwell. 1991. "Sexual Networking in the Ekiti District of Nigeria." *Studies in Family Planning* 22 (2): 61–73.

Osborn, Emily Lynn. 2011. *Our New Husbands Are Here: Households, Gender, and Politics in a West African State from the Slave Trade to Colonial Rule.* Athens: Ohio University Press.

Paré, Marie-Eve. 2018. "La polygynie et l'effectivité de la législation au Burkina Faso." In *Nouvelles Dynamiques Familiales en Afrique,* edited by Anne-Emmanuèle Calvès, Fatou Binetou Dial, and Richard Marcoux, 371–394. Québec: Presses de l'Université de Québec.

Pearsall, Sarah M. S. 2022. *Polygamy: A Very Short Introduction*. New York: Oxford University Press.

Perlstein, Rick. 2020. *Reaganland: America's Right Turn, 1976–1980*. New York: Simon & Schuster.

Peterson, Brian J. 2011. *Islamization from Below: The Making of Muslim Communities in Rural French Sudan, 1880–1960*. New Haven: Yale University Press.

Philips, S. U. 2001. "Gender Ideology: Cross-Cultural Aspects." In *International Encyclopedia of the Social & Behavioral Sciences*, edited by Neil J. Smelser and Paul B. Baltes, 6016–6020. Oxford: Pergamon.

Pike, Isabel, Sanyu A. Mojola, and Caroline W. Kabiru. 2018. "Making Sense of Marriage: Gender and the Transition to Adulthood in Nairobi, Kenya." *Journal of Marriage and the Family* 80 (5): 1298–1313.

Pilon, Marc, Valérie Delaunay, Richard Marcoux, Aminata Coulibaly, and Binta Dieme. 2019. "Essai de mesure et d'analyse de la présence de domestiques dans les ménages en Afrique subsaharienne." *Politique Africaine* 2 (154): 121–143.

Pison, Gilles. 1986. "La démographie de la polygamie." *Population* 41 (1): 93–122.

———. 1988. "Polygamie, Fécondité et Structures Familiales." In *Population et Sociétés en Afrique au Sud du Sahara*, edited by Dominique Tabutin, 249–278. Paris: L'Harmattan.

Porcelli, Paola. 2016. "'I Will Never Become a Crocodile but I Am Happy If I Eat Enough': A Psychological Analysis of Child Fosterage and Resilience in Contemporary Mali." In *Children on the Move in Africa: Past & Present Experiences of Migration*, edited by Elodie Razy and Marie Rodet, 85–103. London: James Currey.

Price, Sally. 1984. *Co-Wives and Calabashes*. Ann Arbor: University of Michigan Press.

Radcliffe-Brown, A. R., and Daryll Forde, eds. 1950. *African Systems of Kinship and Marriage*. New York: Columbia University Press.

Reniers, Georges, and Rania Tfaily. 2012. "Polygyny, Partnership Concurrency, and HIV Transmission in Sub-Saharan Africa." *Demography* 49 (2): 1075–1101.

Renner, Laura, and Tim Krieger. 2022. "Polygyny, Conflict, and Gender Inequality: A Cautionary Tale." *Global Society*. https://doi.org/10.1080/13600826.2022.2040444.

RGPH (Recensement Général de la Population et de l'Habitat). 2011. "Analyse des résultats définitifs. Thème 2: Etat et structure de la population, 2009." Institut national de la statistique, Bamako.

Rillon, Ophélie. 2021. "Le politique par l'intime. Histoires d'amour, de masculinités et d'engagements au Mali." *Politique Africaine* 161–162: 99–118.

Rodet, Marie. 2007. "Genre, coutumes et droit colonial au Soudan français (1918–1939)." *Cahiers d'Études Africaines* 187–188: 1–17.

———. 2019. "'Bigamy', 'Marriage Fraud' and Colonial Patriarchy in Kayes, French Sudan (1905–1925)." In *Courtship, Marriage and Marriage Breakdown: Approaches from the History of Emotions*, edited by K. Barclay, J. Meek, and A. Thomson, 96–110. New York: Routledge.

Rogers, Susan Carol. 1975. "Female Forms of Power and the Myth of Male Dominance: A Model of Female/Male Interaction in Peasant Society." *American Ethnologist* 2 (4): 727–756.

Rondeau, Chantal. 1996. "Femmes chefs de famille à Bamako." In *Femmes du Sud, Chefs de Famille*, edited by Jeanne Bisilliat, 151–170. Paris: Karthala.

Rosaldo, Michelle Z., Louise Lamphere, and Joan Bamberger, eds. 1974. *Woman, Culture, and Society*. Stanford: Stanford University Press.

Roth, Molly, and Jan Jansen. 2000. "Introduction: The Secret Life of Knowledge." *Mande Studies* 2: 1–5.

Sanday, Peggy Reeves. 1981. *Female Power and Male Dominance: On the Origins of Sexual Inequality*. New York: Cambridge University Press.

Sauvain-Dugerdil, Claudine. 2013. "Youth Mobility in an Isolated Sahelian Population of Mali." *Annals of the American Academy of Political and Social Science* 648: 160–174.

Sauvain-Dugerdil, Claudine, with Gilbert Ritschard. 2009. "Un samedi à Bamako: L'émergence d'une nouvelle culture-jeunes à travers l'utilisation du temps non structuré." In *Du Genre et de l'Afrique: Hommage à Thérèse Locoh*, edited by Jacques Vallin, 113–134. Paris: INED.

Schacht, Ryan, and Karen L. Kramer. 2019. "Are We Monogamous? A Review of the Evolution of Pair-Bonding in Humans and Its Contemporary Variation Cross-Culturally." *Frontiers in Ecology and Evolution* 7: 230.

Schacht, Ryan, Kristin Liv Rauch, and Monique Borgerhoff Mulder. 2014. "Too Many Men: The Violence Problem?" *Trends in Ecology and Evolution* 29 (4): 214–222.

Schulz, Dorothea E. 1999. "Pricey Publicity, Refutable Reputations: *Jeliw* and the Economics of Honour in Mali." *Paideuma* 45: 275–292.

———. 2002. "'The World Is Made by Talk': Female Fans, Popular Music, and New Forms of Public Sociality in Urban Mali." *Cahiers d'Études Africaines* 42 (4): 797–829.

———. 2003. "Political Factions, Ideological Fictions: The Controversy over Family Law Reform in Democratic Mali." *Islamic Law and Society* 10 (1): 132–164.

———. 2007. "Drama, Desire, and Debate: Mass-Mediated Subjectivities in Urban Mali." *Visual Anthropology* 20: 19–39.

———. 2010. "Sharia and National Law in Mali." In *Sharia Incorporated: A Comparative Overview of the Legal Systems in Twelve Muslim Countries in Past and Present*, edited by Jan Michiel Otto, 529–552. Leiden: Leiden University Press.

———. 2012a. *Culture and Customs of Mali*. Santa Barbara: Greenwood Press.

———. 2012b. *Muslims and New Media in West Africa: Pathways to God*. Bloomington: Indiana University Press.

———. 2021. *Political Legitimacy in Postcolonial Mali*. London: James Currey.

Schulz, Dorothea E., and Souleymane Diallo. 2016. "Competing Assertions of Muslim Masculinity in Contemporary Mali." *Journal of Religion in Africa* 46: 219–250.

Segbedji, Bruno Djito. 2009. "L'honorable Haidara Aissata Cissé à propos du nouveau code: 'Le devoir d'obéissance est dépassé et rappelle l'esclavage.'" *L'Indépendant*, August 19. http://malijet.com/a_la_une_du_mali/16721-l_honorable_haidara_aissata_ciss_dite _chato_propos_du_nouveau_co.html.

Selby, Jennifer A. 2014. "Polygamy in the Parisian Banlieues: Debate and Discourse on the 2005 French Suburban Riots." In *Polygamy's Rights and Wrongs: Perspectives on Harm, Family, and Law*, edited by Gillian Calder and Lori G. Beaman, 120–141. Vancouver: UBC Press.

Sembène, Ousmane. 1976. *Xala*. Chicago: Lawrence Hill Books.

Sheldon, Kathleen E. 2002. *Pounders of Grain: A History of Women, Work, and Politics in Mozambique*. Portsmouth: Heinemann.

Shi, Lihong. 2011. "'The Wife Is the Boss': Sex Ratio Imbalance and Young Women's Empowerment in Rural Northeastern China." In *Women and Gender in Contemporary Chinese Societies: Beyond Han Patriarchy*, edited by Shanshan Du and Ya-chen Chen, 89–108. Lanham: Lexington Books.

———. 2017. *Choosing Daughters: Family Change in Rural China*. Stanford: Stanford University Press.

Skinner, Ryan. 2015. *Bamako Sounds: The Afropolitan Ethics of Malian Music*. Minneapolis: University of Minnesota Press.

Slonim-Nevo, Vered, and Alean al-Krenawi. 2006. "Success and Failure among Polygamous Families: The Experience of Wives, Husbands, and Children." *Family Process* 45 (3): 311–330.

Smith, Daniel Jordan. 2017. *To Be a Man Is Not a One-Day Job: Masculinity, Money, and Intimacy in Nigeria.* Chicago: University of Chicago Press.

Soares, Benjamin F. 1999. "Muslim Proselytization as Purification: Religious Pluralism and Conflict in Contemporary Mali." In *Proselytization and Communal Self-Determination in Africa*, edited by Abdullahi Ahmed An-Na'im, 228–245. Maryknoll: Orbis Books.

———. 2006. "Islam in Mali in the Neoliberal Era." *African Affairs* 105: 77–95.

———. 2011. "Family Law Reform in Mali: Contentious Debates and Elusive Outcomes." In *Gender and Islam in Africa: Rights, Sexuality, and Law*, edited by Margot Badran, 263–290. Stanford: Stanford University Press.

Sølbeck, Ditte Enemark. 2010. "'Love of the Heart': Romantic Love among Young Mothers in Mali." *Culture, Health & Sexuality* 12 (4): 415–427.

Solway, Jacqueline S. 1990. "Affines and Spouses, Friends and Lovers: The Passing of Polygyny in Botswana." *Journal of Anthropological Research* 46: 41–66.

Song, Sarah. 2016. "Polygamy in Nineteenth-Century America." In *The Polygamy Question*, edited by Janet Bennion and Lisa Fishbayn Joffe, 25–41. Boulder: University of Colorado Press.

Soumano, Moumouni. 2020. "Stress-Testing Democratic Institutions in Mali: The Political Elite and the Breakdown of the State." In *Democratic Struggle, Institutional Reform, and State Resilience*, edited by Leonardo A. Villalón and Abdourahmane Idrissa, 79–103. Lanham: Lexington Books.

Spencer, Paul. 1998. *The Pastoral Continuum: The Marginalization of Tradition in East Africa.* Oxford: Clarendon Press.

Steady, Filomina Chioma. 1987. "Polygamy and the Household Economy in a Fishing Village in Sierra Leone." In *Transformations of African Marriage*, edited by David Parkin and David Nyammaya, 211–230. London: International Africa Institute.

Stowasser, Barbara. 1994. *Women in the Qur'an, Traditions, and Interpretation.* New York: Oxford University Press.

Strauss, Gregg. 2012. "Is Polygamy Inherently Unequal?" *Ethics* 122 (3): 516–544.

Sudarkasa, Niara. 1973. *Where Women Work: A Study of Yoruba Women in the Marketplace and in the Home.* Ann Arbor: University of Michigan Press.

———. 1982. "African and Afro-American Family Structure." In *Anthropology for the Eighties*, edited by Johnetta B. Cole, 132–161. New York: Free Press.

———. 1986. "'The Status of Women' in Indigenous African Societies." *Feminist Studies* 21 (1): 91–103.

Tabet, Gihane. 2005. "Women in Personal Status Laws: Iraq, Jordan, Lebanon, Palestine, Syria." SHS Papers in Women's Studies/Gender Research no. 4, https://unesdoc.unesco.org/ark:/482223/pf0000223760.

Tabutin, Dominique. 1988. "Réalités démographiques et sociales de l'Afrique d'aujourd'hui et demain, une synthèse." In *Population et Sociétés en Afrique au Sud du Sahara*, edited by Dominique Tabutin, 17–50. Paris: L'Harmattan.

Tabutin, Dominique, and Bruno Schoumaker. 2020. "La démographie de l'Afrique subsaharienne au 21e siècle: Bilan des changements de 2000 à 2020, perspectives et défis d'ici 2050." Working Paper 10, Centre de Recherche en Démographie, Université Catholique de Louvain.

Taiwo, Olufemi. 2010. *How Colonialism Preempted Modernity in Africa.* Bloomington: Indiana University Press.

Tatlow, Didi Kirsten. 2015. "Not Enough Women in China? Let Men Share a Wife, an Econo-mist Suggests." *New York Times*, October 26. https://sinosphere.blogs.nytimes.com/2015/10/26/china-polyandry-gender-ratio-bachelors/.

Tembely, Dieudonne. 2017. "Bars 'chinois' à Bamako: Une 'industrie' lucrative, mais nécessité de réglementer davantage." *InfoSept*, August 4. https://maliactu.net/mali-bars-chinois-a-bamako-une-industrie-lucrative-mais-necessite-de-reglementer-davantage/.

Temudo, Marina Padrão. 2019. "Between 'Forced Marriage' and 'Free Choice': Social Trans-formations and Perceptions of Gender and Sexuality among the Balanta in Guinea-Bissau." *Africa* 89 (1): 1–20.

Tertilt, Michèle. 2005. "Polygyny, Fertility, and Savings." *Journal of Political Economy* 113 (6): 1341–1371.

———. 2006. "Polygyny, Women's Rights, and Development." *Journal of the European Economic Association* 4 (2–3): 523–530.

Thiam, Madina. 2020. "Women in Mali." *Oxford Research Encyclopedias: African History.* https://doi.org/10.1093/acrefore/9780190277734.013.530.

Thoré, Luc. 1964. "Polygamie et monogamie en Afrique noire." *Revue de l'Action Populaire* 180: 807–821.

Tiger, Lionel, and Robin Fox. 1998 [1971]. *The Imperial Animal.* New Brunswick: Transaction Publishers.

Timaeus, Ian M., and Angela Reynar. 1998. "Polygynists and Their Wives in Sub-Saharan Africa: An Analysis of Five Demographic and Health Surveys." *Population Studies* 52 (2): 145–162.

Toulmin, Camilla. 1992. *Cattle, Women, and Wells: Managing Household Survival in the Sahel.* Oxford: Clarendon Press.

———. 2020. *Land, Investment, and Migration: Thirty-Five Years of Village Life in Mali.* New York: Oxford University Press.

Tounkara, Aly. 2015. *Femmes et discriminations au Mali.* Paris: L'Harmattan.

Tounkara, Dianguina. 2012. *L'émancipation de la femme malienne: La famille, les normes, l'État.* Paris : L'Harmattan.

Touré, Sadya. 2018. *"Un homme infidèle ne vaut pas mieux qu'une femme infidèle."* August 26. https://benbere.org/au-grin/infidele-homme-femme-societe/.

Traoré, Oumou Touré. 2016. "Préface." In Ladji Siaka Doumbia, *Un polygame à Paris: Les aven-tures de Titi*, 5–7. Bamako: Innov Éditions.

Trouillot, Michel-Rolphe. 2003. *Global Transformations: Anthropology and the Modern World.* New York: Palgrave Macmillan.

Tucker, Judith. 2008. *Women, Family, and Gender in Islamic Law.* New York: Cambridge University Press.

Tull, Denis M. 2019. "Rebuilding Mali's Army: The Dissonant Relationship between Mali and its International Partners." *International Affairs* 95 (2): 405–422.

Uecker, Jeremy E., and Mark D. Regnerus. 2010. "Bare Market: Campus Sex Ratios, Roman-tic Relationships, and Sexual Behavior." *Sociological Quarterly* 51 (3): 408–435.

UNFPA (United Nations Fund for Population Activities). 2020. *Monographic Study on Demog-raphy, Peace, and Security in the Sahel: Case of Mali.* http://wcaro.unfpa.org.

Uthman, Olalekan A., Stephen Lawoko, and Tahereh Moradi. 2010. "Sex Disparities in Atti-tudes towards Intimate Partner Violence against Women in Sub-Saharan Africa: A Socio-Ecological Analysis." *BMC Public Health* 10: 223.

Vallin, Jacques. 1999. "La polygamie est-elle une nécessité en Afrique?" *Jeune Afrique* 1986: 36–37.

van Beek, Walter. 1987. *The Kapsiki of the Mandara Hills*. Prospect Heights: Waveland.

van de Walle, Dominique. 2013. "Lasting Welfare Effects of Widowhood in Mali." *World Development* 51: 1–19.

van de Walle, Etienne. 1968. "Marriage in African Censuses and Inquiries." In *The Demography of Tropical Africa*, edited by William Brass, Ansley Coale, Paul Demeny, Don Heisel, Frank Lorimer, Anatole Romaniuk, and Etienne van de Walle, 183–238. Princeton: Princeton University Press.

Vidal, Claudine. 1977. "Guerre des sexes à Abidjan: Masculin, féminin, CFA." *Cahiers d'Études Africaines* 65/17 (1): 121–153.

Wadud, Amina. 1999. *Qur'an and Woman: Rereading the Sacred Text from a Woman's Perspective*. New York: Oxford University Press.

Waines, David. 1982. "Through a Veil Darkly: The Study of Women in Muslim Societies." *Comparative Studies of Society & History* 24 (4): 642–659.

Wa Karanja, Wambui. 1994. "The Phenomenon of 'Outside Wives': Some Reflections on its Possible Influence on Fertility." In *Nuptiality in Sub-Saharan Africa: Contemporary Anthropological and Demographic Perspectives*, edited by Caroline Bledsoe and Gilles Pison, 194–214. Oxford: Clarendon Press.

Wambua, Pauline M., and Carolyn Logan. 2017. "In Mali, Citizens' Access to Justice Compromised by Perceived Bias, Corruption, Complexity." Afrobarometer Dispatch no. 166. https://afrobarometer.org/publications/ad166-mali-citizens-access-justice-com promised-perceived-bias-corruption-complexity.

Ward, Jane. 2020. *The Tragedy of Heterosexuality*. New York: New York University Press.

Wardlow, Holly, and Jennifer Hirsch. 2006. "Introduction." In *Modern Loves: The Anthropology of Romantic Courtship and Companionate Marriage*, edited by Jennifer S. Hirsch and Holly Wardlow, 1–31. Ann Arbor: University of Michigan Press.

Ware, Helen. 1979. "Polygyny: Women's Views in a Transitional Society, Nigeria 1975." *Journal of Marriage and the Family* 41 (1): 185–195.

White, Douglas R. 1988. "Rethinking Polygyny: Co-Wives, Codes, and Cultural Systems." *Current Anthropology* 29 (4): 529–572.

White, Douglas R., and Michael L. Burton. 1988. "Causes of Polygyny: Ecology, Economy, Kinship, and Warfare." *American Anthropologist* 90 (4): 871–887.

Whitehouse, Bruce. 2012a. *Migrants and Strangers in an African City: Exile, Dignity, Belonging*. Bloomington: Indiana University Press.

———. 2012b. "Centripetal Forces: Reconciling Cosmopolitan Lives and Local Loyalty in a Malian Transnational Social Field." In *West African Migrations: Transnational and Global Pathways in a New Century*, edited by Olufemi Vaughan and Mojubaolu Olufunke Okome, 145–165. New York: Palgrave McMillan.

———. 2016. "Sadio's Choice: Love, Materialism, and Consensual Marriage in Bamako, Mali." *Africa Today* 62 (3): 28–46.

———. 2017. "The Trouble with Monogamy: Companionate Marriage and Gendered Suspicions in Bamako, Mali." *Mande Studies* 19: 131–149.

———. 2018. "The Exaggerated Demise of Polygyny: Transformations in Marriage and Gender Relations in Contemporary West Africa." In *International Handbook of Gender and Demographic Processes*, edited by Nancy E. Riley and Jan Brunson, 299–313. New York: Springer.

———. 2021. "Mali: Collapse and Instability." In *The Oxford Handbook of the African Sahel*, edited by Leonardo Villalon, 127–146. New York: Oxford University Press.

WILDAF. 2018. "Lutter contre les mariages précoces par l'autonomisation des filles au Mali: Rapport définitif de l'étude de base." www.girlsnotbrides.org/wp-content/uploads/2018 /04/Repport-MALI.pdf.

Willey, Angela. 2016. *Undoing Monogamy: The Politics of Science and the Possibilities of Biology*. Durham: Duke University Press.

Wilson, Monica. 1950. "Nyakyusa Kinship." In *African Systems of Kinship and Marriage*, edited by A, R, Radcliffe-Brown and Daryll Forde, 111–139. New York: Columbia University Press.

Wing, Susanna. 2012. "Women's Rights and Family Law Reform in Francophone Africa." In *Governing Africa's Changing Societies: Dynamics of Reform*, edited by Ellen Lust-Okar and Stephen N. Ndegwa, 145–176. Boulder: Lynne Rienner Publishers.

Wittrup, Inge. 1990. "Me and My Husband's Wife: An Analysis of Polygyny among Mandinka in the Gambia." *Folk* 32: 117–142.

Wyrod, Robert. 2016. *AIDS and Masculinity in the African City: Privilege, Inequality, and Modern Manhood*. Berkeley: University of California Press.

Yamani, Maha A. Z. 2008. *Polygamy and Law in Contemporary Saudi Arabia*. Reading: Garnet Publishing.

Zimmerman, Sarah J. 2020. *Militarizing Marriage: West African Soldiers' Conjugal Traditions in Modern French Empire*. Athens: Ohio University Press.

INDEX

Afropolitanism, 20, 177, 182
agency: definition of, 13; women's, 6, 31, 83, 106–107, 170–175
Albania, 151
Arabic language, 19, 20, 25, 131
Austen, Jane, 29, 186n4, 186n7

Ba Konaré, Adame, 84, 106, 145, 188n24
Bamako, demographic growth of, 13–16, 185n7
birth rates, 12, 14, 114, 124–126, 128, 170, 172
bridewealth, 12, 32, 34, 46, 128, 139–140, 192n3; efforts to restrict, 32, 39, 144, 153, 186n6
Burkina Faso, 152

caste and caste groups, 18, 22, 39, 187n11, 187n16
CEDAW (United Nations Convention on the Elimination of All Forms of Discrimination against Women), 153, 179, 194n13
childbearing, 28, 53–54, 103, 173
Code des Personnes et de la Famille (2009 Malian bill), 132, 154–157, 159
Code des Personnes et de la Famille (2011 Malian law), 134, 157–159
Code du Mariage et de la Tutelle (1962 Malian law), 138, 141–143, 144, 153–154, 191n6, 194n9; monogamous option of, 142–143, 145, 147–150
colonial rule, 9, 19, 39, 113, 121, 133, 171, 185n10, 193n1; and marriage, 137–138, 141, 142, 145, 194n11
corruption, 17, 28, 132, 150–151, 176
couples, problematic nature of, 41–42, 49, 58, 100, 110, 149, 162, 187n21
co-wives: relations among, 2, 57–59, 68, 72, 77–79, 92, 101, 190nn7–8, 190n14; relations among children of, 71–73, 82, 189n1; residential separation of, 79–83, 176
cultural relativism, 6–7, 23, 24, 50; definition of, 5, 6, 7, 107, 128–129; limits and utility of, 177–179
culture: definitions of, 84, 104–105; dynamism of, 24, 106; factor underlying polygamy, 84–87. See also Afropolitanism; cultural relativism; Mande

demography, 12, 14, 53, 175, 195n6; and polygamy, 110–129, 167, 170, 172, 192n4. See also birth rates; differential marriage age; marriage: age at first; marriage squeeze; sex ratio
Diakité, Fatoumata Siré, 8, 22, 156, 157
differential marriage age, 31–32, 37, 124, 125, 128, 169–170
divorce, 12, 33, 39, 40, 43, 44, 54, 146; and remarriage/polygamy, 47–49, 62, 146

economic conditions, 9, 16–18, 113–114; marriage and, 32, 33, 40–41, 45, 46, 50–52, 100, 144, 178–179
education, 16, 17, 19, 37, 171–173; access to formal, 16, 171; female agency and, 37, 172; literacy and, 16, 172; marriage and, 173
egalitarianism, 6, 24, 50, 137, 138, 158, 160, 171
ethnocentrism, 5–6; polygamy and, 7

feminism, 11, 91, 105, 133, 166; African, 5, 191n13; Muslim, 89
France: colonial policies of (see colonial rule); neocolonialism and, 133, 135; polygamy in, 4
French language, 3, 19, 20, 22, 94, 135, 178

gender equality, lack of public support for, 159–160
gender ideology, 20, 91–93, 107, 108, 122, 128, 129
gender roles, 20, 31, 33, 42, 182; female, 43–46, 54; male, 45–46. See also munu (forbearance of suffering)
griots. See caste and caste groups
Guinea, 152, 188n24

Haïdara, Chérif Ousmane Madani (Muslim cleric), 98
holism, 11, 22
household: composition of, 1, 15; economic structure of, 10–11; men's duties to, 32, 106, 143; polygamy and, 52–54, 71–83, 89–90, 100, 166; women's duties to, 33, 44–46, 48–49, 94, 100. See also labor, household

ABOUT THE AUTHOR

BRUCE WHITEHOUSE is an associate professor of anthropology at Lehigh University, where he also is affiliated with the Africana and Global Studies programs. He is the author of *Migrants and Strangers in an African City: Exile, Dignity, Belonging*.